Trademark 2.0

Defining Your Value in a Web 2.0 World

Trademark 2.0

Defining Your Value in a Web 2.0 World

R. Todd Stephens, Ph.D.

> **If you don't like change, you are going to like irrelevance even less**
> **– General Eric Shinseki**

Forward

I am change. I work for you, with you, and along side of you. I am your partner and competitor. I am an opportunity and a threat. I am a Lion and you are the Gazelle. I will not come at you straight ahead and announce my arrival with an executive memo. I will leap over you or go around you. If you stand in my way, I will run over you. I will replace you either through advanced technology, outsource you with more productive resources, or eliminate your job when I destroy your business model.

I am change. While you cut my coffee, eliminate my training, and reduce travel in the name of cost transformations, I am buying iPhones, reading Business 2.0 and seeing the world on my own dime. I can read Peter Drucker and know 99% that you learned during the 1980's. While you attempt to polish the last grain of efficiency from Enterprise 1.0, I have moved to Enterprise 2.0. You stand in fear of 2.0 while I and millions of people like me are embracing it. I can destroy your business by simply posting a bad experience on a weblog. At the same time, I can make your business by buying into your brand and helping define the experience.

I am change. While you try to make your organization more efficient, I will replace you. You love control and hierarchal structures which focus communication from the top down. I will communicate from the ground up. You have 5 direct reports that are bound to listen to you. I have millions of people that will listen to me and what I have to say. You focus on the physical and I focus on the meta-physical. I am agile, flexible, and I can emerge and disappear in a matter of seconds. I can be inside any organization in six tenths of a second and creating value in moments.

You grew up with my grandparents; tradition. You embraced my parents; re-engineering. Now it is my time, change is here and it's already later then you think. I will not seek you out but our confrontation is inevitable. My children, yet to be named, will create a tear in the fabric of value and the basic definition of what is means to be human. Are you ready for Web 2.0?

Good Luck,

R. Todd Stephens, Ph.D.

Contents

It is not the strongest of the species that survive, nor the most intelligent, but the one most responsive to change.
- Charles Darwin

Introduction

Globalization has taken on a whole new definition and meaning since 1999 when only a few organizations sent work overseas during the Y2k crises. Today, just about every organization is trying to stay competitive by sending operations, development, and design to countries such as India, China, or Russia. For the information worker the facts can be unnerving to say the least. While the percent of jobs lost due to outsourcing remains in the single digits, no one can deny the trend of exponential growth will continue. With research firms continuously publishing reports on how organizations can leverage technology from these countries, there will be no shortage of fear in the coming years.

Hardly an information technology book or magazine can be picked up that does not mention the focus to achieve enterprise effectiveness or share information in a manner that allows the organization to react in an effective manner across the entire supply chain. The result of these efforts to lower the costs and gain a competitive advantage within the supply chain has lead to a much more diverse community of individual suppliers. This transformation from hierarchal controlling structures to distributed flat organizations has created what Dan Pink calls the *Free Agent Nation*. The reality is that free agents may not come from next door but rather the next country. Employees need to adapt by creating unique value propositions that are captured with their Trademark.

This book will discuss several dimensions of building a personal Trademark. Unlike other books on this subject, this book will focus on the "How" an individual can move from local labor to global talent in the new world defined as Enterprise 2.0. Enterprise 2.0 commonly refers to organizations that operate under an open communication model where interaction and communication is encouraged from the top down. Enterprises are accomplishing this feat by not only addressing the technology requirements of Web 2.0 but the social and organizational changes required to sustain a competitive advantage.

The domain of the book is the creation, development, and ongoing utilization of a personal Trademark. Wikipedia defines a Trademark as follows:

> A trademark is a distinctive sign of some kind which is used by a business to uniquely identify itself and its products and services to consumers, and to distinguish the business and its products or services from those of other businesses. A trademark is a type of industrial property which is distinct from other forms of intellectual property. Conventionally, a trademark comprises a name, word, phrase, logo, symbol, design, image, or a combination of these elements. There is also a range of non-conventional trademarks comprising marks which do not fall into these standard categories.

The choice of the Trademark over the conventional term branding is by design. Information workers think of themselves as members of a trade. A trade is a long term progression where skills, competencies, and experiences come together to create subject matter expertise. The new world of business is built around ambiguity, collaboration, networks, distributed leadership, loosely coupled processes, and a dispersed workforce. For many in the industry, the transformation has been overnight and the majority of us are not prepared to handle a world without hierarchal structures. The Trademark is a physical representation of who you are as opposed to the concepts of branding which are more metaphysical. Much of this book will focus on the physical creation of informational elements that define a brand or brand position. Generally speaking, information workers are more receptive to the hard elements of a Trademark versus the emotional elements of a brand. Historically, trademarks have been associated with professions like the pharmacist's mortar and pestle, the anvil for the blacksmith, the red and white pole for a barber or the wooden Indian statue for tobacco stores. These symbols represented something about the profession and those that practiced it.

In the 2.0 environment, these physical trademarks have been replaced by more meta-physical ones such as logo, slogans, and reputation. Still, like every organization, we must learn to build both the physical and meta-physical trademarks in order to compete in the next 25 years. This book is designed to give the information worker an overview of personal branding and provide a process for the creation of their physical Trademark in a 2.0 world.

1

If you have knowledge, let others light their candles at it.
- Margaret Fuller

The Information Worker

There has been a lot written about outsourcing and the impact of globalization on our economy. Some authors have even named this natural progression of value creation as the China effect, the Wal-Mart effect, and even the Starbucks effect. The essence of this progression is that organizations are utilizing the dramatic advancements in technology to streamline their business and create competitive advantages. Wal-Mart developed a highly efficient supply chain and literally destroyed the business models of Montgomery Ward, Sears, and J.C. Penny. Many people believe that Wal-Mart was the first retailer to challenge this business model but actually J.C. Penny started the down fall of Sears and Montgomery Ward; Wal-Mart simply finished them off. Change is progress and for most of us, creates uncertainty. Individuals that embrace change will succeed and flourish in the long run. Without change nothing would grow or blossom. No matter what business, position, or role you are in, you can't sit still and watch as others pass you by.

Charles Darwin's theory of evolutionary selection holds that variation within species occurs randomly and that the survival or extinction of each organism is determined by that organism's ability to adapt to its environment. Organizations and individuals ability to compete in the new world will be based on their ability to adapt and prosper.

This book will discuss several dimensions of building a personal Trademark. Unlike other books on this subject, this book will focus on the "How" an individual can move from local labor to global talent in the new world defined as Enterprise 2.0. Enterprise 2.0 commonly refers to organizations that operate under an open communication model where interaction and communication is encouraged from the top down. Enterprises are accomplishing this feat by not only addressing the technology requirements of Web 2.0 but the social and organizational changes required to sustain a competitive advantage. Wikipedia (2006) defines a trademark as follows:

> A trademark is a distinctive sign of some kind which is used by a business to uniquely identify itself and its products and services to consumers, and to distinguish the business and its products or services from those of other businesses. A trademark is a type of industrial property which is distinct from other forms of intellectual property. Conventionally, a trademark comprises a name, word, phrase, logo, symbol, design, image, or a combination of these elements. There is also a range of non-conventional trademarks comprising marks which do not fall into these standard categories.

The choice of the trademark over the conventional term branding is by design. Information workers think of themselves as members of a trade. A trade is a long term process where skills, competencies, and experiences come together to create subject matter expertise. The new world of business is built around ambiguity, collaboration, networks, distributed leadership, loosely coupled processes, and a dispersed workforce. For many in the industry, the transformation has been overnight and the majority of us are not prepared to handle a world without hierarchal structures. The trademark is a physical representation of who you are as opposed to the concepts of branding which are more metaphysical. Much of this book will focus on the physical creation of informational elements that define your brand or brand position.

Generally speaking, information workers are more receptive to the hard elements of a trademark versus the emotional elements of a brand which has roots in sales and marketing. Historically, trademarks have been associated with professions like the pharmacist's mortar and pestle, the anvil for the blacksmith, the red and white pole for a barber or the wooden Indian statue for tobacco stores. These symbols represented something about the profession and those that practiced it. In addition, these symbols drew attention as people walked by a place of business.

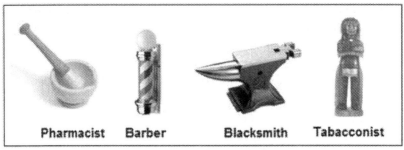

Pharmacist   Barber   Blacksmith   Tabacconist

Figure 1.1: Traditional Trademark Symbols

In the 2.0 environment, these physical trademarks have been replaced by more meta-physical ones such as logos, slogans, and reputation. Still, like every organization, we must learn to build both the physical and meta-physical trademarks in order to compete in the next 25 years. This book is designed to give the information worker an overview of personal branding and provide a process for the creation of their physical Trademark in a 2.0 world.

While most of us would easily recognize the corporate trademarks of Coca-Cola, Wal-Mart, or IBM, many of the Web 2.0 organizations are only beginning to define who they are. Web 2.0 organizations are still trying to find their place and create value for their customers. Much like the Web 1.0 and the Dot Com companies, organizations have emerged with new business models. Over time they will converge just as past innovations in industries like automobile and telecommunications. The winners will be able to sustain their business models with profits within 5-10 years.

Organizations that fail to deliver profit or value for an extended customer base will die a slow and painful death. The majority of these organizations create value around the concepts of social engineering. The concepts around Web 2.0 and social software will be covered in Chapter 3.

Corporate Transition
Not too long ago, travel agencies were about a numerous as Chinese restaurants; just about one on every corner. In the late 1990's, the electronic commerce environment invaded the field of travel. "It's inevitable that the business of travel agencies changed," says Alastair Morrison, professor of restaurant, hotel, institutional and tourism management at Purdue. The Internet is a way to bypass travel agents and provide products and services directly to the end user. Travel agents had to go back to their old way of doing business, becoming travel counselors instead of agents. The amount of information available online increases exponentially as more organizations enter into the market. Organizations like Travelocity and Expedia understand the concept of locality and have integrated this concept into their service offering. Travelocity now offers air, lodging, car rental, and local attractions via the vacation planner. What these online services did was to cut the value-add of the middleman and provide better service to the end customer. However, they too may be undercut by Web 2.0 organizations, like kayak.com, which utilize the concepts of "mashups" to pull from 20-30 different sources. This allows the end user to see all of the rates advertised on the web and not just the special deals negotiated by the intermediaries.

The internet has also changed the auto industry to the benefit of the consumer. What impact has the Internet had on the monolithic, slow-footed automotive industry? Equate it to the huge meteor that slammed into the Earth and wiped out the dinosaurs; it's a global impact event. The ability of the consumer to instantly compare prices, features and interact within a social context with other customers has removed the veil of secrecy that once protected profits. Issues and problems are communicated around the world and auto makers are forced to respond with light speed. As profit margins shrink, American automakers are finding it difficult to compete on price and looking toward others sources of income such as financing and service. Today, if you pay cash for an automobile then the retailer will only make a profit of $46.00. In fact, if you were to take an aerial photograph of a car dealership and label each area of the property that contributes to the bottom line of the organization. The number one profit center would be the finance office not the showroom. The showroom ranks near the bottom which is a dramatic turn around from 10-15 years ago.

How about Dell who basically destroyed the HP, Compaq, and Gateway business models by focusing on supply chain efficiencies? Low cost and direct selling to the end user changed the basic business model for personal computers. Imagine that a single Dell computer will come into contact with over 400 external vendors; from design to delivery. That kind of integration requires velocity, process efficiencies, and a focus on cutting costs. While much is written about Dell's supply chain, their corporate culture creates a competitive advantage by enabling agility. According to a study conducted at MIT, Dell's culture fosters an unwavering focus on immediate goals and personal accountability which in turn allow the business to change directions at a moments notice. Once again, the ability to adapt is the secret for long term success for both business and the individual information worker.

Historical Transformation of Work Itself
Perhaps the best place to discuss the future of the information worker is to look to the past and see what lessons we can learn. One topic that has a fair share of reference is the ages of civilization. These ages define how we work and prosper. Clearly at some point in time, we survived as hunters and gathers. Eventually, we figured out that as farmers, we could produce enough food for our family and still have additional products to sell. The age of agriculture not only brought us food, but also land ownership, communities, concepts of trade, and many other facets of our economy that are still widely used today. Unfortunately, the rise of agriculture also created cities, states, and government bodies which eventually brought us the tax code. In fact at some

point in time, 95% of us were classified as farmers. Today, that number has dropped to below 2%. The significance of this number is that we can feed the world with only 2% of our labor resources (starvation is a political and logistical problem, not a production problem). What caused this enormous improvement in productivity? Standardization, automation, machinery, biological advancements, and economies of scale are some of the primary reasons. The beginning of the end of the age of agriculture started with the industrial revolution. We can thank people like James Watt, Henry Ford, Edwards Deming, and Eli Whitney for taking us off the farm and into the factory. At one point, 75% of us worked on the factory floor. Today that number sits at around 11.7%. Why? Again, containerization, automation, robotics, information management, and a litany of other advancements account for the increase in productivity.

In his book, Re-Imagine, Tom Peters (2006) reflects on a conversation a co-worker had with a dock worker. In 1970, when a ship pulled into the London Harbor, it took 108 men and five days to unload that ship. Today, that same ship pulls in to the harbor and it takes 5 people and one day. Taken on face value, that would be a 98% gain in efficiency. Imagine, the corporate office today with 10,000 people running around moving information from point A to point B. We don't build physical structures nor grow peas; we move information. We can take information in the form of raw data and assemble concepts and structures to create information. Information can be described as a collection of facts or elements of data that are related in some form or fashion. Information is data with meaning and understanding. For data to be transformed to information it must be related to other data components. Patterns and relationships in the data must be discovered, assimilated, related, and discussed so that the data is made informative. Knowledge is simply information placed into context. A 98% gain in efficiency for knowledge workers would reduce the workforce from 10,000 to 200. Hard to imagine? Well, I am sure there are several dockworkers that had that same thought 30 years ago. The 20th century saw almost all its leading businesses disappear or fall behind in productivity, while entire new industries have risen to the fore.

The age of information arrived with the development of the computer and information management systems. Today, 70% of us work in the information field and many of us are wondering about the next age. Take a look at the following chart and you will see these ages in action starting back in 1860.

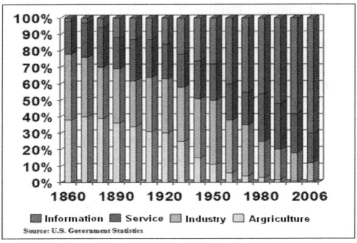

Figure 1.2: Natural Progression of Work

There are several points to make about Figure 1.2. First, as described in the previous paragraphs, is an enormous reduction in labor of the industry and agriculture jobs as well as the steady increase in information jobs. Second, notice that the service jobs remain a constant 18-22% for the past 150 years. Does that sound odd that the service sector has remained constant for 150 years? If I were to ask you what you want your son or daughter to grow and become, most people would say a doctor, lawyer, dentist, or teacher. These are all jobs in the service sector. When was the last time you heard someone say I hope my son grows up to be a farmer or work on an assembly line? Will there come a day when we push our daughters away from information workers type jobs? The National Science Board, an independent body that advises Congress and oversees the National Science Foundation, recently warned of a "troubling decline" in the number of U.S. citizens studying to become scientists and engineers, even as the number of jobs requiring science and engineering training grows.

If you assume that information jobs will continue to grow, from which sector will these jobs be taken from? While agriculture doesn't have much to give and service should remain steady, this only leaves the industry category. Perhaps we can continue to improve productivity but only up to a certain point and that's not very likely to provide us much more than a 5-10% growth opportunity. Have we reached the tipping point of the information age? Is there a fifth age that doesn't show up on the radar? These questions will be addressed in this book but for now let's keep moving with the information worker.

Information Worker
Information worker is a label used to broadly describe those of us that work with information technology. Information workers were initially those inside the organization responsible for the production, analysis and distribution of information: the writers, editors, financial analysts, planners and facilitators who were the first adopters of technology such as the word processor, the spreadsheet, email and presentation software. As information technology spread across the enterprise and applications became less structured and more user-friendly, the tools and practices of information work came to be adopted by more and more roles within the organization. Today, information pervades every aspect of the modern organization, from executive decision-makers to customer-service representatives, skilled professionals like doctors and engineers, and those who work in the call center or the retail bank branch. Advances in technology over the last two decades have transformed the world of work and commerce, driving wave after wave of economic growth and opportunity worldwide, dramatically changing many industries and opening new competitive opportunities for organizations small and large. Companies like eBay, Amazon, Wal-Mart, Dell, Jet Blue and Etrade have transformed the playing field in all industries, from

retailing to manufacturing to transportation and financial services (Microsoft, 2006).

The driving force in the growth of information workers is the innovations that have occurred over the past 10-20 years. Specifically, the advancements in hardware, software, and the Internet have given organizations a whole new business model in order to derive value.

Examples of an Information Worker include:
- A travel agent that utilizes the Internet to look for deals and exotic experiences for the high traveler.
- An application developers utilizing .Net to develop an internal ordering application for Business-to-Business transactions.
- A Pharmacist reviewing online Diabetes information before a one-on-one session with a patient.
- A Creative Memories consult utilizing the Internet to order supplies and read about best practices for hosting parties.
- A magazine publisher checking on the author's background of a recently submitted article.

Each of these examples, demonstrate that data, information, and knowledge is not only accessible 24 hours a day but also an imperative to ones ability to actually perform the task at hand. The proliferation of advanced technologies like wide area networks, wireless local networks (Wi-Fi), laptop computers, and mobile telephones have enabled the enormous growth in the information worker environment. Globally, over a billion people connect to the internet and while the United States still holds onto 63% of that traffic, the percentage is shrinking. Within the corporation, information workers are now the primary points of value creation. Empowering information workers means more than just giving them more software and more training. It means making it easier for them to bring their unique talents, experience and judgment to bear in situations where they can make an impact on the business.

Long Tail of Performance

Chris Anderson (2004) wrote an interesting article on a concept referred to as the "Long Tail". The long tail is basically the products and services that have lost their "sale" ability within a geographical area. One of the my favorite books on personal marketing was published in 1997 titled "The Persona Principle: How to Succeed in Business with Image Marketing" by Derek Armstrong and Kam wai Yu (1997). You would be hard pressed to locate this book in any book store and even Amazon has it ranked #1,140,052.

Online retailers can carry a much larger inventory than physical stores which allow them to generate more sales along the long tail of popularity. For example, Barnes and Noble carry 120,000 titles while Amazon.com boasts 2.3 million titles. The obvious reason is that shelf space inside Wal-Mart, Blockbuster, and Books-A-Million is limited and these organizations only have so much real estate to display their products to the customer. This physical constraint forces organizations to focus their marketing and promotion on the top selling items. Online organizations do not carry shelf costs and therefore an additional item is simply an update to the online catalog. The advancements in technologies such as search, social software, and product comparison sites allow for more fragmented channels and niche products. Interestingly, 57% of the sales at Amazon.com come from titles not available at your local book store. This phenomenon seems to be true from books to application software. But, is it true for the relationship between the value delivered and the ability of the information worker?

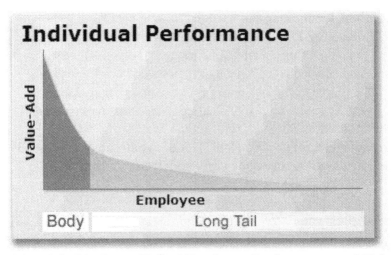

Figure 1.3: The Long Tail of Employee Performance and Value-Add

Assuming Figure 1.3 is accurate then very few employees create the majority of the value within an enterprise. Bill Gates once commented that if you took the 20 smartest people from Microsoft, you would be left with an insignificant company.

Clearly, individuals have different values since the open market dictates the salary of the employee, the rate of the consultant, or the price to the solution. Microsoft's Chief Scientist; Nathan Myhrvold was reported to have said "The top software developers are more productive than average software developers not by a factor of 10X or 100X, or even 1,000X, but 10,000X". Geoffrey Colvin (2006) reviewed the driving forces of the top CEO prospects. The keys components included creativity, irreverence, boundless energy, and relentless determination. After 500 years, the scarcest resource is no longer capital; It's Talent! For the first time in history, he says, talent has supplanted financial capital as the most fiercely sought-after resource in business. Even though business schools are cranking out record numbers of MBAs every year and new regions are joining the world economy with scores of eager participants, there aren't enough good leaders to go around. The crème de la crème still rise to the top and the best companies battle for them, leaving everyone else to flounder with what they've got (Hopfinger, 2006).

To the benefit of us all, the hyper demand for technology professionals and information workers allowed for the less skilled to enter into the game as well. The Y2k and Internet boom took this demand to an even higher level than ever before. This was the perfect storm for the generation of high wages, job security, education opportunities and the Dot Com crash. Highly skilled employees left the corporate environment and like the early settlers headed west. Only in our case, they headed to the consultant companies and startup organizations. As the high performers left, those with higher priorities watched as those positions were back filled with less skilled and knowledgeable resources. Or perhaps, one can simply say that the less experienced people were promoted into positions that should have been reserved for the cream of the crop. The leadership which had little experience now controlled million dollar budgets and organizations were willing to bet the entire business. The phenomenon wasn't just small start up companies in Silicon Valley but major Fortune 100 companies like AT&T who bet their business on purchasing Cable companies. Bottom line, talent matters, today more than ever.

Three Forces of Change
Over the past few years, three specific trends have forced organizations to rethink how they create value and more importantly define the value-add of the information worker. "globalization, standardization, and automation will have profound impacts on the services industry," said Sophie Mayo, director for Worldwide Services at IDC. The most significant examples include the globalization of services delivery, the standardization phenomenon in the software industry, and new technologies that drive the automation of services in both the consumption and internal delivery processes. These three forces will have a dramatic impact to our employability in the near future.

Globalization

Globalization and the worries of the middle class seem to have collided as more and more information workers concern themselves with lower standards of living. Globalization has taken on a whole new definition and meaning since 1999 when only a few organizations sent work overseas during the Y2k crises. Today, just about every organization is trying to stay competitive by sending operations, development, and design to countries such as India, China, or Russia. For the information worker, the facts can be unnerving to say the least. While the percent of jobs lost due to outsourcing remains in the single digits, no one can deny the trend of exponential growth will continue. With research firms continuously publishing reports on how organizations can leverage resources from these countries, there will be no shortage of fear in the coming years.

Hardly an information technology book or magazine can be picked up that does not mention the focus to achieve enterprise effectiveness or share information in a manner that allows the organization to react in an effective manner across the entire supply chain. The result of these efforts to lower the costs and gain a competitive advantage within the supply chain has lead to a much more diverse community of individual suppliers.

In 2004, I attended an Academic conference where the opening speaker touched on the impact of globalization. He indicated that the erosion of jobs within the Information Technology community could be fixed by simply increasing the supply and quality of students within computer science or any related field. Fueling this perception are article after article telling us the same thing.

"The economic rise of Asia's giants is the most important story of our age. It heralds the end, in the not too distant future, of as much as five centuries of domination by the Europeans and their colonial offshoots" Martin Wolf (Financial Times)

"There is no job that is America's God-given right anymore." - Carly Fiorina (HP)

22

"Currently, India is becoming the back office of the world. Everest estimates companies all over the globe are sending as much as $5 billion in work to Indian outsourcing service providers. But all the headlines about the Indian success story are obscuring a development that can have just as much impact. I predict China will be the next big wave in offshore outsourcing." – Todd Furnis

"Income Confers No Immunity as Jobs Migrate" – USA Today

"The world has arrived at a rare strategic inflection point where nearly half its population—living in China, India and Russia—have been integrated into the global market economy, many of them highly educated workers, who can do just about any job in the world. We're talking about three billion people." – Craig Barrett (Intel)

Ok, you get the idea that plenty of people believe that we are entering into a new world of work where the globalization of labor, capital, and innovation will take center stage for years to come. However if we step back a few feet, we can see another perspective where history paints a different picture. Globalization is clearly in the early stages of hitting the white collar world and especially the upper and middle layers of the organization. Despite what is reported in the media, globalization is not the predominant reason we have job erosion. Globalization is only the tip of the iceberg; the vast majority of reasons for job erosion revolve around the fact that we have been very good at what we do. Automation, reuse, standardization, communications, and universal access to knowledge are the real reason we need less and less information workers. Perhaps the erosion of jobs is the wrong analogy to use since it implies that jobs are flowing out but nothing flow in. The reality is that you have to be willing to destroy jobs in order to create jobs on a large scale. History supports this notion where during the automation of the manufacturing, we lost 44 million jobs. However, we created 75 million new jobs in the information worker space. Compare this to other countries where government controls didn't allow jobs to be eliminated and they only added 4 million new jobs during this same time period (Peters, 2004). Today, a significant share of the value of many products is created at the stage of marketing, sales, research and development (RD), and service, rather than at the stage of material production. Daniel Gross (2002) of Stern Business commented that information has replaced physical assets as the driver of value, which leads one to believe that the management of those information-based assets is critical to the future growth of business. It seems that change and value creation are correlated either positively or negatively.

Standardization

How does standardization impact our roles as information workers? Clearly, if we all agree to the same language or semantics then the cost of doing business will be lowered. The number of resources needed to translate those semantics into your corporate language will diminish. In addition, standards create a more open organization where the value chain pieces can be outsourced easily to the lowest cost vendor. What difference does it make if you are running a web service internally developed or on a leased basis per transaction. If the transaction cost is lower then businesses should take a hard look at the value-add of keeping the effort in house.

Apple IIe   Commadore 64   TRS-80

Figure 1.4: Early Personal Computers

Think about the PC market and the evolution over the past 10 years. Without getting too deep in the technical aspects of the hardware, early PC computers (Figure 1.4) used a wide variety of motherboards, chips, storage, and peripherals. This was costly for the consumer in that you paid for that uniqueness. I can clearly remember paying $3,000.00 for a computer in the 1980's that had a tenth of the computing power of today's $500.00 machines. Overtime, the PC market standardized on the various hardware components and winners in this space were the ones that had the lowest supply chain costs, such as Dell and Gateway. You see this same evolution of standardization with motorcycles in Asia where the key contributor of value comes from the design, not the individual components.

Think about the electric plug that is used in the United States. Imagine the confusion if every state had a different type of outlet. Like many foreign counties where not only are the plugs different, voltages differ as well. On my first trip to Australia, my wife and I endured a 24 hour flight from Atlanta, Georgia to Sydney. We had just had our second child and my wife needed a medical type device which most women know more about than I do. As soon as we got to the hotel, she plugged the device into wall outlet and bam! The machine started to smoke and clearly one of us was in trouble for not purchasing a voltage converter. While all plugs have one goal, the lack of standards creates problems that require planning in order not to get caught in the same situation as we did.

It is not uncommon for an information worker to access the financial accounting system in order to extract this month's general ledger transactions. Then, these transactions are imported into Excel where using the "Pivot Table" function summarizes the transactions in order to calculate summary metrics. These metrics are then written up in a monthly summery and posted to a presentation. If critical standards existed, all of this movement of data would be automated. It may be hard to imagine a day when this type of information work will be eliminated but people said the same thing about business intelligence. Our organization implemented a collaborative solution for project management several years ago. The system basically automated much of the consolidation, summarization, and presentation of project data. This allowed the project managers to stay focused on the project details without getting bogged down with the communication and reporting aspects. This was especially critical in the financial reporting area where automation freed up an average of eight hours a week per manager.

As with most technology innovations, time creates few winners. In the 1870s the railroad industry boomed to the point of over investment and speculation, and subsequently came to a halt as it weathered bankruptcies and stock market losses. A new wave of investment then followed, driven by engineering advances and economic recovery, which made railroads a driving force in American business for decades. Similarly, the early twentieth century saw a host of car manufacturers that evolved into a few survivors–but these survivors turned the car industry into an icon of economic progress. In the same way that the railroad, automobile, electricity connections and the airplane developed huge new industries and capitalist conglomerates, the evolution of standardization was the same. While it seems normal that the driver sits on the left (or right in some countries), the gas pedal is on the right, and gear shift is located on the floor, this was not always the case. Standardization is inevitable due to consumer demand and natural progression. While the "Sea of Sameness" seems like a direct link to a commodity world, the reality is that standardization enables automation which drives costs down.

Electronic Data Interchange (EDI) is the computer-to-computer exchange of structured information, by agreed message standards, from one computer application to another by electronic means and with a minimum of human intervention. In common usage, EDI is understood to mean specific interchange methods agreed upon by national or international standards bodies for the transfer of business transaction data, with one typical application being the automated purchase of goods and services (Wikipedia, 2006). The advent of Electronic Data Exchange (EDI) had a dramatic effect on shrinking the supply chain and enabling organizations to communicate in the 1980's and early 1990's. Reducing costs are not the only reason for implementing EDI. EDI reduces the number of errors, improves cycle time, and integrates supply chains. Emerging over the past few years is a new standard called Extensible Markup Language (XML). On the surface, the introduction of XML seems like just another technology invention. The reality is that EDI focused on a data exchange while XML presides over not only data exchange but service and semantic exchange as well. Industry after industry is jumping into the standards race in order to the first to declare and take advantage. Eventually, the market will decide which standards to adopt. Several organizations like OASIS, WC3, and IETF are working on these standards and will eventually be able to define 80% of the business models needed for the business. In other words, the business processes around the world will get more and more standardized in the future. Much of the work in Business Process Modeling (BPM) is doing just that. Competitive advantage will be reduced to the ability to create value, velocity, and efficiency with the remaining 20%. Brett Champlin has done some great research in the world of Business Process Reengineering which is about managing the business processes not just replacing them. Replacing them is one of the options but it's about managing change in the business and about managing your business in a process oriented way. Process Reengineering was very focused on alleviating pain, trying to fundamentally change certain processes rather than certain management. Business Process Management has a much broader scope which focuses on standardizing the standardization of business processing.

Automation
The final trend is by no means the weakest of the three. Automation of activities continues at an unprecedented rate. Have you taken note of the progression that tax software has made over the past 10 years? The tax code is more than 60,000 pages in length and by some estimates four times longer than the Bible. Yet, tax preparation software has automated the task so much that many tax preparers have been put out of business. Not too long ago, the do-it-yourself tax preparer ran down to the local computer

store to purchase a copy of the software and load on a 486 system. Once complete, the individual printed two copies of the forms with the 9 pin dot-matrix printer. Eventually, EDI type transactions were made available and there was no longer a need to waste the paper. At the same time the application made great strides in usability and automation. Later, the requirement of driving to the computer store to purchase the software was eliminated and one could buy the application online. Today, you don't even have to download anything. The entire application can be purchased over the web and runs as a web service. The tax software margins may have been squeezed but think about the impact on the computer retail store, printer, paper, post office, etc. These groups lost more than a small reduction in profits. The point of this is that automation creates value, service, and jobs while at the same time destroying them.

The above mentioned automation doesn't really tell the story of how Web 2.0 applications are now emerging, especially when Tim Berners-Lee wanted a more open sharable web in the first place. The reality is that we needed a baby step first which is referred to as the Internet (Web 1.0). While this is small baby step was arguably worth trillions, it was a needed step in order to lay the foundation for the next phase.

The amount of telecommunication hardware that was put in place for the overinvestment of the dot com craze opened the door to enormous amounts of capacity. In addition, the cost of this hardware continues to drop exponentially. For example, in 1985 a Gigabyte of storage cost $10,000 but today that same amount of storage can be purchased for $0.50. When you think of the business models of Flickr and YouTube, you have to wonder how you could generate a profit with petabytes of storage required. The key was the dramatic drop in storage costs, the distributed abilities with low cost servers, and the high speed communications networks. With these three elements in place, mass amounts of services could be moved outside the enterprise and delivered to the individual for little or no costs.

The desktop has also undergone some tremendous changes in the last 10 years. The speed and lower costs allow every information worker to have a laptop and desktop. With increased memory and speed, application processing can be moved back to the desktop in form of active java-scripting or better known as Ajax. According to Jesse James Garrett of Adaptive Path, Ajax is a combination of technologies which incorporate standards-based presentation using XHTML and CSS, dynamic display and interaction using the Document Object Model, data interchange and manipulation using XML and XSLT, asynchronous data retrieval using XMLHttpRequest and JavaScript binding everything together. This allows the application to react to end user behavior versus waiting for a back end data call to retrieve data from the server. This functionality will dramatically alter how applications have been built and value defined.

Chapter Summary
Chapter one focused on defining the trademark which is a physical representation of who you are. Who you are sounds like a simple question but answering it can be a challenge even for the best of us. Regardless of industry, your trademark is the defining element of your career. Throughout history, the creation of value has been transformed from manual labor to the present day information worker where results are determined by your mental capacity and human imagination. The role and responsibilities of the information worker will change based on the three major influences of today: globalization, standardization, and automation. Globalization is the result of ubiquitous computing, dramatic drops in computing costs, and low cost resources available around the world. Standardization describes the consolidation of knowledge, technology, and communication mediums. Automation describes the advancement of technology as seen over the past 10-15 years. The future of the information worker remains a chapter unwritten. Recently, I had the opportunity to attend a conference where one of the speakers defined performance as an equation of delivery, diversification, and differentiation. It's hard to imagine a better definition for a trademark.

2

You do not merely want to be considered just the best of the best. You want to be considered the only ones who do what you do.
- Jerry Garcia.

High Performance

Much has been written about high performance and the impact to the organization. Many authors discuss the collaborative environment and new tools that allow the information Worker to access corporate information anytime and anywhere. Other authors focus on the performance rules of accountability, metrics, and objectives. Both of these views of high performance are accurate and should be reviewed by the reader.

The average yearly increase in U.S. workers' productivity has doubled from 1.5 percent during the period 1987-1996 to 3 percent from 1997 to 2006, according to U.S. Labor Department figures. Information workers must define their own path to productivity and based on these metrics are doing a great job. The key ingredient is multi-tasking with technology. According to an Oregon State University study, knowledge workers spend the majority of their working hours processing and manipulating information. The information they manipulate may be encoded in many different formats: documents, databases, software code, web pages, email messages, phone conversations or collaborative workspaces. At the center of productivity is the concept that almost all knowledge workers organize their work into discrete and describable units, such as projects, tasks or to-do items. Years ago, the organization was expected to define what value and performance meant but not today. The old go to work from 9 to 5 is being replaced by a 24 hours a day information flow. For many information workers, the transformation from being told what value is to defining that value is unnerving.

The most important aspect of high performance is to take ownership and responsibility for the work. Technology and business processes change almost daily and the ability of a single person to keep tract of all of the changes is near impossible. Today, managers may not be isolated into a single business unit or organizational structure where they can control knowledge dispersion. In fact, you may be the one and only person with the specialized knowledge required to integrate the technology or process the business requested. The responsibility and decision making authority will be delegated to you since you are the subject matter expert. Embrace the confusion, chaos, and uncertainties; as you move up the corporate ladder. Taking responsibility also means jumping on the opportunities that present themselves to you. I can't count the number of times I have seen a golden opportunity pass someone by that wasn't looking. Be careful not to blame others for your vision or lack of. Oprah Winfrey once commented that "Luck is a matter of preparation meeting opportunity". When you take responsibility for your work, the doors will open up and the whole organization will know your brand.

As the owner of the work, you will also be the person that sets the standards for performance for your team as well as yourself. Most middle management has been removed from the corporate structure which means managers are actually just information workers with additional responsibilities. These responsibilities include setting the objectives and plans for the group. Be careful; set the objectives too low and your reputation as an easy rider will be pervasive. In that same vain, set the bar to high and nobody will be able to meet the objectives. People need stretch commitments in order to push themselves out of their comfort zone.

High Performance Components

In the old economy, a competitive edge could be gained through acquisition of capital and physical assets at a lower cost, and this is how many low wage economies managed to increase their market share and squeeze the supply-chain profits. However, today's economy is driven by different economic factors, such as knowledge, innovation, technology and human capital. Organizing and managing people in such a way as to increase skills at both the higher and lower levels of the organization will bring about competitive advantage. Recruiting people who share the organization's values and have core competencies is essential in this process, but so are ongoing training and development schemes. Strong leadership is critical within an organization to create vision; high performance workplaces also strive to create a distinct and clearly defined workplace culture with core goals and values that are understood by all members of staff. These goals should also be supported by reward schemes for employees, it has been shown that workers with an economic stake in the organization perform better and are consistently more productive (Lawler, 2005).

The World Bank estimates that the U.S. has 60 percent of the wealth in the form of human capital, and 40 percent in the form of land and natural resources. George McClure co-chaired an effort that looked at the ability of organizations to maximize employee value and the paradox of human asset depreciation. Businesses are familiar with the concept of depreciation of physical assets, and create sinking funds to cover costs of renovation or replacement. Taxing authorities provide tables of accepted depreciation rates for buildings, vehicles, computers, and other assets. The concept of depreciation of a knowledge base, while real enough (and painfully evident to the holder) has not yet been legitimized by appropriate tax deductions. The point is that you and I lose value everyday because of the change in technology or the business environment. The rate of depreciation could be staggering when viewed at the corporate level. We have a responsibility to continuously build knowledge and skills in order to stay employed and create value.

Organizations that focus on human capital will have a clearly defined method of evaluating employees with various backgrounds. One of the issues with evaluating information workers is that most jobs are a function of ability as well as skills. While there are many different methods or categories of evaluation, here are some that we have used in the past:

- Breadth of Technology
- Breadth of Management
- Delivery
- Relationships
- Reducing Costs
- Generating Revenue
- Firefighting
- Intangibles

Breadth of Technology
The breadth of technology focuses on the utilization of technical skills by the information worker. These skills may include specific core technology such as Oracle, SQL, Visual Basic, or Visio. More general technology skills may focus on disaster recovery, security, storage, and network. Other technology skills may include more of the information worker type technologies such as office automation, collaboration software, forms processing, or search tools.

The information worker should be able to distinguish between technical skills versus competency and management skills. Generally speaking, technical skills are more focused on products, standards or processes definitions. For example, a database administrator will have technical skills associated with:

- The specific database application (Oracle)
- The database language skills (SQL)
- The principles of database design
- The techniques of data modeling
- The understanding of system performance tuning (Unix)

- The principles of data quality, metadata, and data access
- The capability to perform data backup and recovery

Skills are tightly associated with the specific technology implemented by the organization. For any role, there are numerous technical skills that come into play. The key for the individual is to recognize what those skills are and focus on continuous development. In addition, the information worker should also concentrate on the key competencies that are critical to the success of their role. If or when an information worker believes they have reached the point of diminishing returns of skill enhancement then they should look for ways to build on related skills.

Other than education and experience, how else can you build on your technical skills? One of the best ways is certifications. Employers view certifications as a method to increase skill levels within the technology organization or as a hiring requirement. Many technology professionals leverage them to advance their careers. On the other end of the spectrum, some people view certifications as yet another revenue stream for product vendors without significant merit attached. Certificates offer a great way of testing the basic proficiency in a specific technology domain. Thus, in conjunction with training, they provide a very useful tool for people and organizations interested in acquiring and developing technical knowledge (Tekiela, 2004).

Breadth of Management
Management skills are essential in today's competitive environment. Unlike technology skills which are more specific, management skills span a much wider spectrum. Management skills include time management, collaboration, presentation, communication, delegation, interpersonal, and project planning. While most information workers will utilize these skills in various situations, some will have greater responsibility than others. Despite the calls for flattening the organization, every group needs people to help with the overall management of the business process.

Suppose the organization is about to launch an enterprise effort on Service-Oriented Architecture and needs management skills to ensure the project is delivered on time and on budget. The management skills needed might include:

- The ability to multitask on various efforts
- The knowledge of project management techniques (Project management software experience could be considered a technical skill)
- The techniques to verbal and written communications
- The knowledge of leadership essentials
- The ability to manage people

While some of these skills can be associated with technical skills, information workers that excel at management may or may not have the technical skills. Many leaders understand that management needs a basic understanding of the technology but 80% of their time will be focused on the skills of management.

The best way to improve ones management skills is to exercise them with your growing responsibility. As you advance or grow the business, your management skills will improve or bad things will happen, such a demotion or losing market share. Even if, you don't have a staff of people, you still need to manage yourself in today's environment.

Delivery
The ability to deliver projects or programs is essential for the information worker. Delivery requires both technical and managerial skills in order to be successful. Larry Bossidy and Ram Charan (2005) wrote an excellent book on the discipline of execution where they indicate that execution is the greatest unaddressed issue in the business world today. Many corporate executives will agree and one of the most important aspects of getting things done is finding the right people that can execute the corporate strategy. Employees that succeed in the delivery role

have the ability to focus on the details as well as provide leadership.

The successful delivery of the project is largely dependent on your skills and experience. These skills include both the technical and managerial skills as well as the competencies. The critical element in delivery is actually delivering on the projects as requested by executive management. Delivery is about making things happen with no excuses. The corporation is full of people that want to slow progress down and apply the rules of process to every situation. Most corporations are looked at as slow moving monoliths that make everyone feel important and part of the team. People use the term agility to describe people that can operate in a non-structured environment and adapt to the circumstances of the situation. While others want to slow down, agile workers want to accomplish and are driven by the impossible. Integrating groups, sharing information, communicating, and getting people focused are keys for delivery minded people.

People who can deliver tend to move up the organization faster than those that might have better technical or even managerial skills. We all know people that seem to get the most difficult projects. These people charge a premium for their ability to focus, assess the situation, and leadership skills. Technical skills allow you to get things done while management skills provide the oversight. At the end of the day, the question remains: did you deliver value.

Relationships
With the age of outsourcing upon us, information workers must be able to manage vendor relationships. Key skills for vendor management include contract negotiation, service level agreements, communications, and program oversight. Several years ago, the trend was to simplify and reduce the number of vendors but seemingly this has changed. Today, vendor competition is needed to ensure the checks and balances. Managing vendor relationships is no longer as easy as appointing a technology employee to be the company's official representative.

Outsourcing, the trend toward longer and more complex deals, and an increase in the number of vendors of all sizes have prompted companies to rethink the skills and experience required to manage these contracts on a daily basis. For many companies, the technology and business units must join forces (Collett, 2005). Relationships in the business environment may come in many flavors including:

- Software Companies
- Operations
- Executive Leadership
- Business Units
- Customers
- Suppliers

Relationship managers have the ultimate responsibility for collaborating with each major vendor or service provider regarding value-chain performance. Outsourcing relationships present opportunities for building stronger organizational capabilities, but their true value comes when the relationship grows, blossoms, and provides sustained value. Without constructive working relationships, the value of outsourcing usually falls short of its potential (Jones, 2004).

Every information worker will have some type of relationship to manage. All of us have customers and suppliers in our daily work. For example, most folks reading this text know that my area of specialty is enterprise metadata which is a form of knowledge management. Like knowledge management, someone must produce the content and ensure a high degree of quality. At the same time, knowledge must be used in order to gain the reuse and value-add needed. Hence, knowledge management has both suppliers and customers in order to operate efficiently.

Reducing Costs
Historically, information workers as well as technology have been deployed to make the business run more efficiently. Automating

tasks lowers the overall cost of doing business. Information workers can be evaluated on the basis of their contribution to reducing costs for the business. This may include deploying new technology which carries a lower maintenance cost or reduces the required resources. For the business, a key source of competitive advantage will be business agility and flexibility through cost structure optimization. To achieve this, executives are challenged not only to develop a more comprehensive and enterprise wide approaches to business transformation, but also to finance a series of cost optimization initiatives that will achieve the overall transformation goals of the organization.

The implementation of many technological advances over the past decade has enabled the businesses to reduce administrative costs, overhead, and complexity; to cope with growing workloads; to enhance communication across departments; and to provide easy access to information and data in support of decision-making. While technology has enabled the business to increase overall productivity, the funding of continuously improving technologies and expanding services, and the growth and maintenance of the information technology infrastructure, represent major challenges for the business. The reality is that technology of today is outdated tomorrow. Enterprise cost reduction improves short-term cash flow through staff reductions, benefit plan restructuring, tax refunds, real estate portfolio financing, inventory reductions and other quick win improvements. Long-term savings are driven by organizational restructuring, supply chain improvements, tax structure arbitrage, implementation of shared services and process/technology integration (Deloitte, 2004).

Information workers need to have the financial skills in order to ensure projects stay on track and deliver the total cost of ownership reductions required. Rewarding employees who deliver cost cutting initiatives is critical since many times those efforts include automating jobs and reducing staff. In any economy, cutting staffing is an emotional and demoralizing job.

Generating Revenue

Depending on the business, the ability to generate revenue is an ideal position for the information worker. As the prior paragraph discussed, historically we have focused our attention on the reduction of complexity and cost. Today, businesses are moving their competitive advantages into revenue generation. David Thompson (2006) put it this way "Business operations have evolved to where IT must now broaden its focus to help the company attract, retain, and grow customer relationships and increase customer satisfaction". As the information age matures, the vast majority of value-add comes from the services and solutions which are driven by information workers. Each and every information worker should be able to communicate how they contribute to the generation of revenue for the company.

One of the most prolific revenue generation strategies over the past decade has been the Customer Relationship Management (CRM) effort. CRM is both a technical and business solution comprising of methodologies, strategies, software, and other web-based capabilities that help an enterprise organize and manage customer relationships. The end result of a CRM effort is to identify existing profitable customer segments and determine what will establish a profit-based profile for moving forward. Then develop the business requirements to support sustained, and structurally bonded, relationships. Additionally, business want to find cost effective alternatives for non-buyers or low-margin customers: Not all customer relationships are profitable and very few companies can afford to pay to deliver an equal level of services. Control costs and save your best resources for premium accounts while working to bring low performers into an acceptable profit portfolio (Harris, 2003).

For the information worker, who has traditionally worked on cost cutting initiatives, a revenue generating project can seem like a rebirth. As with cutting costs, solid financial, business, and technical skills are needed.

Firefighting

While very few people will admit that we spend way too much time fighting fires, the truth is that many of us do just that. Information workers have the skills to be able to handle situations that are not structured and need to be handled in a timely manner. Invariably in technical companies, there are more problems and opportunities than time or people to deal with them. There are more things that the organization should work on than it can, realistically, work on. At best, this leads to situations where minor problems get ignored. But too often, it leads to a syndrome called "firefighting" (Bohn & Jaikumar, 2000). Information workers that can perform under these circumstances can be extremely valuable.

In the firefighting syndrome, engineers, managers, and other knowledge workers rush from task to task, not completing one before another interrupts them. Things that are merely "important" but not "urgent", such as long-range development, are continually interrupted by the latest fire. Although the most urgent tasks do receive attention, productivity suffers. Some jobs get "overtaken by events" and never completed. And although a task may appear to be completed, it may need to be redone later, perhaps in another form, because it was not truly solved the first time. Management is a constant juggling act, of deciding where to allocate overworked people, and which incipient crisis to ignore for now (Bohn & Jaikumar, 2004).

Interesting that Robert Hayes (1981) reported that American managers seem to enjoy working in crisis mode while Japanese managers consider it evidence of failure. While there might be a cultural aspect to firefighting, many managers in corporate America thrive in this type of environment. Is firefighting a result of too much work and not enough people to properly work the project? Clearly, the flattening of the organization has an impact on the strategy, planning, and execution of any large scale program. Others lean toward the fact that technology changes almost daily and the needs of the business must be addressed; planned or unplanned.

Information workers who are skilled in situational assessment, organization, and have a sense of urgency find success here. Unfortunately, the organization begins to execute operationally in an emergency mode if firefighting is not held in check. Eventually, firefighting consumes people and resources to the point where human capital diminishes.

Intangibles
Intangibles of performance are the million points of light that you contribute each and every day. For example, your organization may have a patent program where you can contribute to the intellectual property of the enterprise. The intellectual property may turn into a revenue stream in the future or create a whole new business line. Are you easy to work with or a pain in the butt? What about customer comments that reflect your customer service focus and belief? For example, we once received this comment from a customer of our online ordering product and the service delivered by a developer.

"As I said earlier, I was very frustrated with the whole process the first time I talked to John. John was very patient. If John was getting aggravated with my calling him several times, he did not let it show in his voice. John not only helped me with my order but he also helped me to regain my sense of humor and lowered my frustration level immensely".

We get these types of emails all of the time but imagine the impact during the annual review when we bring out our customer appreciation portfolio. The intangibles are very closely associated with competencies which help you become a more valuable employee. Characteristics like working with others, passion and commitment, willingness to take on assignments, or simply providing good customer service, can make a big difference in your performance.

High Performance Summary
Each of these evaluation components indicates the breath of knowledge and experience required. Very few knowledge workers

can simply focus one a single component and expect to be successful over the long term. Each of us needs to evaluate our own personal renewal plan and ensure there are no gaps. Many scholars are predicting two scenarios for the information worker. The first is a talent shortage where organizations will be unable to fill open positions with senior people. At a time when there are more jobs for skilled workers than there are skilled workers, it makes good sense to upgrade skills in the existing workforce where possible, rather than compete in a wage spiral for the few available unattached workers. This situation may grow worse with the impending retirement of the Baby Boomer generation. The second is scenario is that we will have too many people for too few jobs. With globalization and the enormous quantity of educated information workers coming out of Asia, you will need to find ways to differentiate your talent like never before.

Thomas Friedman (2006) noted the quality of information workers from Asia is enormous. In the words of the CEO of InfoSys "The playing field is being leveled." Knowledge work can originate almost anywhere in the world today, and people in countries like India are increasingly differentiating themselves in terms of education, skills, ambition and diligence to the point that they will be competing for just about any kind of job where the work can be done or supported electronically. And not just low-level coding assignments, mind you: many jobs already being sourced globally involve
high-end research (Mindrum, 2007).

Social, political, economic and demographic trends are transforming the landscape of global commerce, but businesses are still challenged to achieve success according to traditional measures: profitability, market share, customer satisfaction and innovation. Over the past 50 years, information technology (IT) has played a critical role both in creating the conditions for change and in helping organizations adapt to it. As we move toward a world that is more fluid, less centralized and less certain about old assumptions and old models, IT is evolving in ways that will empower organizations, teams and individuals to realize their potentials in a new world of work. Certainly much of the change in the world is driven by technological innovation: more powerful software and computing systems, the Internet and pervasive wireless connectivity. The proliferating use of information has been instrumental in achieving better outcomes for businesses and higher productivity for workers. However, in celebrating the success of these advances, we should not forget that the ability to adapt and innovate is fundamentally a human talent. Empowering people to work more efficiently and effectively in the "digital workstyle" of the new world of work should be at the center of any organization's strategy as it addresses the coming era of rapid change and increasing global integration (Microsoft, 2006).

Personal Branding Overview
Regardless of which scenario plays out, you will need the ability to stand above the norm. Tom Peters published on the topic in his 1997 Fast Company Article called "A Brand Called You".

"Regardless of age, regardless of position, regardless of the business we happen to be in, all of us need to understand the importance of branding. We are CEOs of our own companies: Me Inc. To be in business today, our most important job is to be head marketer for the brand called You. It's that simple -- and that hard. And that inescapable."

The essence of Mr. Peters message is that you are in charge of your brand and that all of us can own some part of the market. Everyone can learn, and educate themselves to become, at some level, an expert. The vast majority of knowledge is available on the Internet and if you look hard enough you can find information pertaining to your specific situation. Mr. Peters didn't just stop at his magazine article, he went on to publish several books on the subject as well as travel the world giving speeches on this very topic. Almost 10 years after the article, the message is still being spread daily. Many books have been written on the subject and the importance branding in the new world of work.

- Peters, T. (2003). *Re-Imagine*. DK Adult.

- Peters, T. (1999). *The Brand You 50*. Knopf.
- Setty, R. (2005). *Life Beyond Code*. Select Books.
- Montoya, P. (2003). *A Brand Called You*. Peter Montoya Pub.
- Montoya, P. (2002). *The Personal Branding Phenomenon*. Peter Montoya Pub
- Pink, D. (2002). *Free Agent Nation*. Warner Business Books.

What is personal branding? Here are a few definitions from the experts:

"Personal branding is a revolution in the way we manage our careers or businesses. It's a way of clarifying and communicating what makes you different and special and using those qualities to separate from yourself from your peers so that you can greatly expand your success. Personal branding is the strategy behind the world's most successful people. People like Oprah, Madonna, Richard Branson and Bill Gates. It is the difference between an ordinary career or business and an exceptional one."
- W. Arruda

"Personal Branding is the art of attracting and keeping more clients by actively shaping public perception. You can control the way you're perceived by the community you serve. Oprah, Tiger, Madonna – they realized early that that talent alone would not take them to the top of their fields."
- P. Montoya

"Brand You is that special, personal connection you have with the customer. Your brand helps the customer remember the value of your service. A solid brand shows that you are responsible and committed for the long term. Whether you are an individual consultant, an IT executive, or a staff techno guru that personal "brand" will help boost your value and career. "
- R. Reilly

"A personal representation that represents a skill set, a big idea, a belief system, and value-equation that other people find of interest. Personal branding is everything you that differentiates and market yourself, such as your messages, self-presentation, and marketing tactics".
- C. Kupta

All of these opinions come to the same conclusion that in a world of sameness, you need to stand out even if that point of light is faint. You and only you are responsible for transforming that faint light into something bigger and that can only be done by a focused effort over a period of time. Kellaway (2007) wrote an interesting article for the Financial Times. In the article, she describes her emotions over the past ten years of branding ones self.

"We are not cans of baked beans. We are complicated human beings and therefore not suited to crass branding activity. So I didn't start that day to create the Brand Called Me. Nor on any of the 3,500 days that followed. However, a lot of other people did: in the past decade personal branding has become a big thing.

I still think it's ghastly, but now, belatedly, I have decided that I am a can of baked beans after all. There are some differences in terms of size (I'm bigger) and colour (I'm less orange) and uniformity (my quality is more mixed). But like beans, humans can be branded. We each have a name, an image, a reputation and something to sell. Which means it is sensible to think about how these things could be managed better.

This realisation has come slowly through the steady drip, drip of proof. Every day I am exposed to the marketing activity of Brand Someone Else. A man I've never met has just sent me an e-mail saying "Lucy, watch me on Bloomberg TV today!" Readers endlessly direct me to their personal websites. Even quite normal people boost their brands by routinely forwarding any complimentary e-mails to their bosses."

Credibility

Credibility is the believability of ones history, actions, capability, or communications. In the information worker world, all we have is the credibility of our experience and knowledge. But how do we get other people to believe in our vision or capability? How can we convince other people they should hire us or hand us a high profile project? In the business world, one source is expertise in the field. When the Surgeon General tells us that we should stop smoking, we tend to believe him over other people. If Steve Jobs says that the iPhone will take over the market we tend to believe him based on his past success with computers and the iPod. When Tim Berners-Lee says that Web 2.0 is the next evolution of the Internet, you can bet that that we will see it in our life time. Information Technology has also provided us with examples of thought leaders that are well aware of personal branding. Bill Gates, Steve Jobs and Larry Ellison are great examples who not only are well known but redefined the world of work. While many people belittle their contributions and even attribute their success to more luck and timing than skill, very few can deny the impact they have made on the world today. These gentlemen, along with many others, transformed our economy from being industrial focused to information and knowledge focused.

In 1984, Robert Levering, Michael Katz and Milton Mosokowitz authored a book called "The Computer Entrepreneurs". Take a look at the following list of technology leaders of the early 1980's; can you remember any of them?

- Daniel Bricklin: VisiCalc
- Joel Berez: The Zork Trilogy
- Jack Tramiel: Commodore 64
- Chuck Peddle: Victor 9000
- Gary Kildall: Pascal and C-Basic
- Go Sugiura: Grenn and Amber Monochrome Monitors
- Jeffrey Wilkins: Compuserve
- Terry Johnson: PC Hard-Drives
- Dennis Hayes: Hayes Modems

- Reid Anderson: Verbatim

The most interesting aspect of reading this book is that of the hundred or so thought leaders included, less than 10% remain today. Credibility comes and goes depending on the evolution of the technology.

Personal Trademark Framework
The Personal Trademark Framework is a result of an extensive research effort by the author. Most of the current references of branding fail to deliver a roadmap or game plan that you can follow and ultimately measure yourself against. You see plenty of antidotes and questions and discussions on "Why" you should embrace personal branding but very little on the "How". The framework presented in Figure 2.1 provides a high level overview which will be discussed in the subsequent chapters. The first obvious conflict is the use of the word trademark versus brand. The distinction made by the author is that trademarks are the physical representations of an entity while a brand is an emotional component. Plus, branding brings on images of having a hot poker placed on your skin to mark ownership which is not the most pleasant of experiences. Trademarks are different in that they represent the brand. Coca-Cola, whom the author worked for in the early nineties, owns the color red and the trademark wave. When a customer sees the familiar bottle, the symbolic wave, and the scripted "Coca-Cola", the customer experiences the brand of coke. Everything that the company represents from the taste to the nostalgia comes back to the consumer. That's why trademarks are so valuable to the branding perspective. How about Disney where the emotional attachment to the company revolves around customer service and the customer experience? Our photographs represent these emotions by associating physical components like Cinderella's Castle, the parade, characters signing autograph books, hotels, and the fudge shop located right on Main Street. It's the physical components that we associate to the emotional aspects of brands.

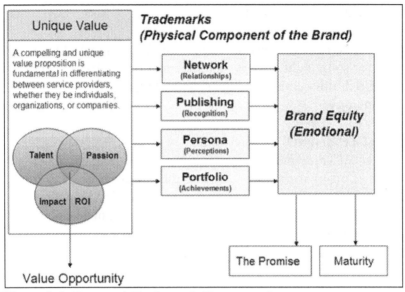

Figure 2.1: Personal Trademark Framework

The framework contains four basic elements of value for the reader to consider: unique value opportunity, trademark portfolio, brand development, and utility valuation.

Unique Value Opportunity
Unique value is a compelling and unique value proposition that fundamentally differentiates you from everyone else. The term unique indicates that you are one of the relative few people that work in your business, area, or space. What is it that really sets you apart? Here is where relativity comes into play. Initially walking through the framework, the domain of your competition will become critical. In much of the same vein as supply and demand, value is subject to the number of people doing what you do. For example, suppose you are the world's greatest grill master. I doubt you will make much money off of it unless you have a TV show like Emeril Lagasse. Truth be told, Rachel Ray worked tirelessly for years without regard or recognition before becoming one of Food Network's brightest stars. While talent and value are important, passion is what will ensure your long term commitment.

The combination of your talent, passion, and value should create a unique value opportunity.

Trademarks
As mentioned in the previous section, trademarks are the physical elements of your brand. The trademarks can be separated into four main categories.

1. Networking: Use the Harvey McKay meta-model and create an active metadata implementation to manage your personal relationships. (See Chapter 6)

2. Publishing: You don't have to be a world class writer to publish (clearly!). Check out you local professional organization, they would kill for your ideas and innovative thoughts. You need to be recognized, so find a medium and speak your mind. (See Chapter 7)

3. Persona: Define who you are and how that gets represented in all of your physical trademarks including blogging, web site, resume, CV, and press releases. The persona helps define and support the perceptions of you. Perceptions of value are real, the only question that remains is are those perceptions established by a default association or defined by you? (See Chapter 8)

4. Portfolio: Your portfolio of degrees, awards, honors, certifications and patents define your achievements. These efforts establish your long term commitment to excellence. (See Chapter 9)

Each of these trademark components, paint a picture of value. They are the physical elements of your personal brand and I would argue your most valuable asset.

Brand Equity
Located to the left of the trademark elements is a box labeled brand equity. Brand equity is the value of the defined brand in financial terms. Most definitions include the physical assets (trademarks)

with the meta-physical (brand) in their valuation equation. Brand equity is created by executing an overall brand strategy. Ultimately, the value of the brand will be defined by the future earning of the individual or their business. Based on that value and inventory of trademarks, the brand equity can create a barrier to entry for other individuals looking into the same space. One example of a competitive advantage is when an author or inventor establishes himself by being one of the first people in the space. This can be accomplished by publications such as a book or Academic publication. Tim Berners-Lee will always be known as the inventor of the Web. This universal knowledge and fame will keep anyone else from ever claiming that title. John Zachman was the first person to publish an article on enterprise architecture and his framework is the de-facto standard. For anyone wanting to become known within this space will need to define a niche association (See Chapter 5).

The Promise

The promise of personal branding varies from individual to individual. However, the basic question remains the same; what's in it for me? Over the past few years, I have seen people dabble into the personal branding space but were disappointed by the lack of reward. They seemed to have this impression that if they could get published once that they would be on air with Oprah. The reality is that a single publication may work for some people, the vast majority of us require a life time of effort. Take a look at the following individuals who have hit it big time with their first publication.

- Search of Excellence (Tom Peters)
- Information Architecture (Louis Rosenfeld and Peter Morville)
- Free Agent Nation (Dan Pink)
- Swim with the Sharks (Harvey McKay)
- What They Don't Teach You At Harvard Business School (Mark McCormack)
- Good to Great (Jim Collins)

- Getting Things Done : The Art of Stress-Free Productivity (David Allan)

It isn't that these people didn't publish more books or articles, but the success of these publications established them as an expert with their unique value opportunity. Keep in mind, that there are 3,000 books published every day and so few success stories. The trouble with the success of these books is that it is a romantic notion that you can write a single book and boom; you're famous. We don't see the countless hours they spent working on their concepts or breakthroughs. The Nobel Prize reflects more accurately the achievements of those that stake the claim of world class expert. The prize is awarded for a lifetime of achievement not a single body of work (See Chapter 10).

Maturity Model
Most of us in the information worker field have personalities or skills developed during the information age. Thus, we like to have models to measure ourselves against as we progress up the maturity ladder. The purpose of the Trademark Maturity Model is to provide guidance for improving your personal brand and its ability to manage the plan, develop, and deliver the essence of you. The model will provide a practical structure, proven methods, establish priorities for improvement, and guide you to a Brand Called You (See Chapter 4).

Summary
High performance is an elusive concept that few people really understand in a world were the measurement of success is subjective. We have identified several factors that you should take into account in your current job including: breadth of technology, breadth of management, delivery, relationships, reducing costs, generating revenue, firefighting, and intangibles. The personal trademark framework establishes a standard for measuring yourself against the best that you can be. In order to create your unique value in an age where being one in million means there are 6,000 people just like you, you need to create something of a story or experience. Think of building a home; a pile of bricks, wood,

nails, and glass doesn't resemble a home. The key is to have a solid design, appropriate materials, and a plan for production. This framework is the same thing, only instead of building houses, we are building careers.

3

If you are going to be naked, you had better be buff.
- Don Tapscott

Everything 2.0

Have you read or seen much on the next evolution of the web called Web 2.0? Web 2.0 is a collection of technologies and frameworks that enable collaboration from a social perspective. We can see this transformation from Web 1.0 to the more collaborative Web 2.0 all around us. Products like Microsoft's SharePoint, IBM's Connections/Quickr, SocialText and many others are transforming the corporate landscape for knowledge. Outside the corporation, the success of Wikipedia, Folksonomies, RSS, and weblogs are undeniably changing every aspect of our lives.

If I were to ask you what Microsoft's fastest growing product is, which product would you choose? In 2003, *The Register* reported that SharePoint was the fastest growing product with over 30 million licenses. Collaborative products are not new and the Lotus Notes folks will sing in unison "been there, done that". Yet, 30 million licenses are nothing to sneeze at. The impact to traditional applications is enormous in the sense of how work is organized and value delivered.

Web 1.0

Web 1.0 focused on a read only web interface while web 2.0 focuses on the read-write capabilities where value emerges from the contribution of a large volume of users. The Internet as well as the Intranet initially focused on the command and control of information. Information was controlled by a relative small number of resources but distributed to a large number which spawned the massive growth of the web itself. Like television, the web allowed for the broadcasting of information to a large number of users. Unlike television, consumers now have the ability create, edit, and spread the message.

Inside the organization, the Intranet has changed the way organizations structure and operate their business. Specifically, the Intranet has centralized communications and corporate information as well as built a sense of community across organizational boundaries (McNay, 2000). Typical organizations will have office-based employees in various locations, telecommuting, and off-shoring staff. The traditional day by day communication landscape has changed from personal to electronic. The migration to electronic communications emerged as standards, technology and infrastructure matured. This allowed more information sharing and community building to occur without a requirement of physical location. Over the past several years Intranets have emerged as the key delivery mechanism for application and business information. Intranets may be thought of as providing the infrastructure for intra-organizational electronic commerce (Chellappa & Gupta, 2002). This allows organizations to utilize the technology to achieve its organizational goals and objectives. Web 1.0 allowed the organization to govern the information flow and focus on achieving the business goals. Unfortunately, most technologies fail to deliver competitive advantages over an extended period of time. Investments in information technology, while profoundly important, are less and less likely to deliver a competitive edge to an individual company (Carr, 2003). This is especially true in the world of the Web 1.0 since much of the knowledge and information is disseminated all over the world as quickly as it gets published. Organizations are beginning to see that the command and control model is no longer effective at developing a high performance work force which opens the door for the next evolution in technologies as described by the Web 2.0 framework.

Web 2.0

While Web 2.0 has been debated by researchers as to who and when the concepts emerged, little argument exists that the technology has arrived. Unlike Web 1.0, this new technology encourages user participation and derives its greatest value when large communities contribute content. User generated metadata, information, and designs enable a much richer environment where the value is generated by the volume of employees. Sometimes referred to as sharing, collaboration, aggregate knowledge, or community driven content, social software creates the foundation of collective intelligence (Weiss, 2005). Much of the Web 2.0 technology is difficult to nail down an exact definition, the basic truth is that Web 2.0 emphasizes employee interaction, community, and openness (Millard & Ross, 2006). Along with these characteristics, Smith and Valdes (2005) added simple and lightweight technologies and decentralized processing to the mix. O'Reilly (2005) defined Web 2.0 as a platform, spanning all connected devices; Web 2.0 applications are those that make the most of the intrinsic advantages of that platform: delivering software as a continually-updated service that gets better the more people use it, consuming and remixing data from multiple sources, including individual users, while providing their own data and services in a form that allows remixing by others, creating network effects through an "architecture of participation, and going beyond the page metaphor of Web 1.0 to deliver rich user experiences. While Web 2.0 has many and often confusing definitions most include the concepts of weblogs, wikis, Really Simple Syndication (RSS), social tagging, mashups, and user defined content.

Weblogs or Blogs
Weblogs or blogs have become so ubiquitous that many people use the term synonymous for a "personal web site" (Blood, 2004). Unlike traditional Hypertext Markup Language (HTML) web pages, blogs offer the ability for the non-programmer to communicate on a regular basis. Traditional HTML style pages required knowledge of style, coding, and design in order to publish content that was basically read only from the consumer's point of

view. Weblogs remove much of the constraints by providing a standard user interface that does not require customization. Weblogs originally emerged as a repository for linking but soon evolved to the ability to publish content and allow readers to become content providers. The essence of a blog can be defined by the format which includes small chunks of content referred to as posts, date stamped, reverse chronological order, and content expanded to include links, text and images (Baoill, 2004). The biggest advancement made with Weblogs is the permanence of the content which has a unique Universal Resource Locator (URL). This allows the content to be posted and along with the comments to define a permanent record of information. This is critical in that having a collaborative record that can be indexed by search engines will increase the utility and spread the information to a larger audience. With the advent of software like Wordpress and Typepad, along with blog service companies like blogger.com, the weblog is fast becoming the communication medium of the new web.

Wikis

A Wiki is a web site that promotes the collaborative creation of content. Wiki pages can be edited by anyone at anytime. Informational content can be created and easily organized within the wiki environment and then reorganized as required (O'Neill, 2005). Wikis are currently in high demand in a large variety of fields, due to their simplicity and flexibility nature. Documentation, reporting, project management, online glossaries, and dictionaries, discussion groups, or general information applications are just a few a examples of where the end user can provide value (Reinhold, 2006). The major difference between a wiki and blog is that the wiki user can alter the original content while the blog user can only add information in the form of comments. While stating that anyone can alter content, some large scale wiki environments have extensive role definitions which define who can perform functions of update, restore, delete, and creation. Wikipedia, like many wiki type projects, have readers, editors, administrators, patrollers, policy makers, subject matter experts, content maintainers, software developers, and system operators (Riehle, 2006). All of which create an environment open to sharing information and knowledge to a large group of users.

Wikis are making inroads inside the corporation where they are eliminated many barriers to communication. Companies like Disney, AT&T, Nokia, Kodak, Intel, Ebay, Emory, Motorola, Novell are integrating wiki based technology into the daily activities of doing business. With the constant focus on cost cutting, wiki technology allows the end user to update information without the need of technology resources. The ease of use, rollback, editing, and common usability framework are all key in the mass adoption of this technology.

RSS Technologies
Originally developed by Netscape, RSS was intended to publish news type information based upon a subscription framework (Lerner, 2004). Many Internet users have experienced the frustration of searching Internet sites for hours at a time to find relevant information. RSS is an XML based content-syndication protocol that allows web sites to share information as well as aggregate information based upon the users needs (Cold, 2006). In the simplest form, RSS shares the metadata about the content without actually delivering the entire information source. An author might publish the title, description, publish date, and copyrights to anyone that subscribes to the feed. The end user is required to have an application called an aggregator in order to receive the information. Upcoming releases in Microsoft Office, Internet Exployer, and Mozilla have RSS readers built in. By having the RSS aggregator application, end users are not required to visit each site in order to obtain information. From an end user perspective, the RSS technology changes the communication method from a search and discover to a notification model. Users can locate content that is pertinent to their job and subscribe to the communication in order to stay informed. Traditional email pushed messages to the end user while RSS is pulled. While this seems like a small change, the implications are enormous.

Social Tagging

Social tagging describes the collaborative activity of marking shared online content with keywords or tags as a way to organize content for future navigation, filtering, or search (Gibson, Teasley, & Yew, 2006). Traditional information architecture utilized a central taxonomy or classification scheme in order to place information into specific pre-defined buckets or categories. The assumption was that trained librarians understood more about information content and context than the average user. While this might have been true for the local library with the utilization of the Dewey Decimal system, the enormous amount of content on the Internet makes this type of system un-manageable. Tagging offers a number of benefits to the end user community. Perhaps the most important feature to the individual is the ability to bookmark the information in a way that is easier for them to recall at a later date. The benefit of this ability on a personal basis is obvious but what about the impact to the community at large. The idea of social tagging is allowing multiple users to tag content in a way that makes sense to them, by combining these tags, users create an environment where the opinions of the majority define the appropriateness of the tags themselves. The act of creating a collection of popular tags is referred to as a folksonomy which is defined as a folk taxonomy of important and emerging content within the user community (Ahn, Davis, Fake, Fox, Furnas, Golder, Marlow, Naaman, & Schachter, 2006). The vocabulary problem is defined by the fact that different users define content in different ways. The disagreement can lead to missed information or inefficient user interactions (Boyd, Davis, Marlow, & Naaman, 2006). One of the best examples of social tagging is Flickr which allows users to upload images and "tag" them with appropriate metadata keywords. Other users, who view your images, can also tag them with their concept of appropriate keywords. After a critical mass has been reached, the resulting tag collection will identify images correctly and without bias.

User Contributed Content

One of the basic themes of Web 2.0 is user contributed information. The value derived from the contributed content comes not from a subject matter expert, but rather from individuals whose small contributions add up. One example of user contributed content is the product review systems like Amazon.com and reputation systems used with ebay.com. A common practice of online merchants is to enable their customers to review or to express opinions on the products they have purchased (Hu & Liu, 2004). Online reviews are a major source of information for consumers and demonstrated enormous implications for a wide range of management activities, such as brand building, customer acquisition and retention, product development, and quality assurance (Hu, Pavlou, & Zhang, 2006). A person's reputation is a valuable piece of information that can be used when deciding whether or not to interact or do business with. A reputation system is a bi-directional medium where buyers post feedback on sellers and vice versa. For example, eBay buyers voluntarily comment on the quality of service, their satisfaction with the items traded, and promptness of shipping. Sellers comment about the prompt payment from buyers, or respond to comments left by the buyer (Christodorescu, Ganapathy, Giffin, Kruger, Rubin, & Wang, 2005). Reputation systems may be categorized in three basic types: ranking, rating, and collaborative. Ranking systems use quantifiable measures of users' behavior to generate a rating. Rating systems use explicit evaluations given by users in order to define a measure of interest or trust. Finally, collaborative filtering systems determine the level of relationship between the two individuals before placing a weight on the information. For example, if a user has reviewed similar items in the past then the relevancy of a new rating will be higher (Davis, Farnham, & Jensen, 2002).

Mashups: Integrating Information
The final Web 2.0 technology describe the efforts around information integration or sometimes referred to as "mashups". These applications can be combined to deliver additional value that the individual parts could not on their own. One example is HousingMaps.com that combines the Google mapping application with a real estate listing service on Craiglists.com (Jhingran, 2006). Chicagocrime.org overlays local crime statistics onto Google Maps

so end users can see what crimes were committed recently. Another site synchronizes Yahoo! Inc.'s real-time traffic data with Google Maps. Much of the work with web services will enable greater extensions of mashups and combine many different businesses and business models. Organizations, like Amazon and Microsoft are embracing the mash-up movement by offering developers easier access to their data and services. Moreover, they're programming their services so that more computing tasks, such as displaying maps onscreen, get done on the users' Personal Computers rather than on their far-flung servers (Hof, 2005)

Web 2.0 Implications Overview

To really get the impact of the new 2.0 environment, we need to back up and take a look at this transformation from a different perspective, other than the technology view. We all have questions about this new medium and the corresponding technology. Here are a few of mine along with some insight into the possible answers.

Free Information

What happens when all information is free, freely available, to anyone, at anytime and from anywhere? With telecommunications, mobile devices, and ubiquitous networks, technology is making this a reality from San Francisco, CA to London, England. But, this is more than a technology advancement. Organization like Sun, Microsoft, IBM, Boeing, McDonalds, Wells Fargo and many others are publishing blogs that are exposing their business strategy to anyone that wants to read it. Wikipedia now boasts 2.4 million entries and the vast majority are annoyingly accurate. Considering that the average dictionary or encyclopedia only has 60,000 entries, Wikipedia extends knowledge far beyond where possible just a few years ago. Google, the search engine, is the first stop most of us go when we want to know something about someone or a product. They index over five billion information sources and handle over 91 million searches per day. Most of what you can read in books, magazine or from the research firms is freely available if you are willing to spend the time searching and evaluating. Seth Godin (1999) gives away one of his books, *The Boot Strappers Bible* while Tom Peters provides his presentation slides for every keynote he gives. A new Web 2.0 site, Slideshare.net, was developed so people can share presentations and slideshows. You can upload your PowerPoint, OpenOffice, Keynote or PDF presentations, tag them, embed them into your blog or website, browse others' presentations, and comment on individual slides. What's more, the transcripts of your presentation will be indexed by internet search engines and show up in search results. Today, we see that the information is not the container of value but the knowledge that goes along with it. These field experts understand this and have no issue giving you their complete play book. They understand, the devil is in the details and in the execution. Massachusetts Institute of Technology (MIT) has made all or most of their course material freely available on the Internet. While a few of these are limited to chronological reading lists and discussion topics, a majority provide homework problems, exams and lecture notes. Some courses include interactive web demonstrations in Java or Metlab, complete textbooks written by MIT professors and streaming video lectures.

What happens when all information is free? Innovation and opportunity emerge, not just from new technology but from the application of the old. All information can be delivered with just a click of the mouse. It's ironic that information replaced gold as the most valuable resource and now, it's practically free.

Presence and Communications
What happens when all physical things have presence and communications capabilities? Let's start with you, the information worker. You carry your cell phone where ever you go. That pager never leaves your side and the phrase "Crackberry" hits way too close to home. The truth is that we now have the technology to stay in constant contact with anyone in the world. Text messaging, Instant Messaging, and other technologies have also reduced the latency of communications to the point of instantaneous. All of this communication capability comes at a price with information overload. Information overload is basically having too much

information to make a decision or stay informed about a specific topic.

In an oversimplification, the vast majority of data captured revolves around the consumer transaction. This transaction begins with the initial order and travels all the way through delivery. In many cases, the transaction continues with customer support services. Radio Frequency Identification (RFID) tags may very well change this. RFID tags can do many things from sensing temperature changes to tracking products. Imagine a world where inventory can be automatically done by simply walking down the isle of the supermarket. Groceries are automatically scanned and you can check out without even needing to stop at the register. RFID technology will add state information which will require enormous amounts data and storage. Our ability to store the data will be pale compared to the need for managing the volume of information. Performing business intelligence on the transaction data will need to be expanded to include the state data that will be collected. One can only dream of the value and utility that could be created with advanced business intelligence.

Global Positioning Systems (GPS) provide any vehicle the ability to communicate with satellites which orbit the earth twice a day at an elevation of 11,000 miles, emitting a continuous signal containing the satellite's time and position. The user devices then analyze the signals from three or more satellites to determine the device's precise location. Early systems provided accuracy to within about 70 feet. Further enhancements can bring that number down to within one centimeter, even while the receiver is moving. Sears Holdings Corp. of Hoffman Estates, Ill., for example, recently implemented a new system to optimize routes for its 11,000 field service technicians. Called the Sears Smart Toolbox, Sears and Environmental Systems Research Institute, Inc. (ESRI) of Redlands, Calif, co-developed the applications. Each service vehicle contains a GPS, satellite and cellular communications system, as well as a wireless LAN access point. It also contains a ruggedized laptop from Itronix, a part of General Dynamics Corp. of Falls Church, Va. (Robb, 2006).

When everything has communication and presence capabilities, you will see instantaneous access to information. We will have access to state information which defines where something is in correlation to a business process. Imagine your refrigerator that is designed to track the inventory of what's inside and in the pantry. The system will be able to display expiration dates and the nutritional information of every item in the house. The system would be able to create menus for the week based on the inventory and create a shopping list. Systems will be far more agile and have the ability to adapt to the environment with little or no control from a human. This adaptation will result in integrating the various systems of the home to build an entire home eco-system that adapts to your lifestyle.

Frictionless Commerce
What happens when all organizational barriers and friction have been removed via technology? Organizational barriers are forms of control or governance that seemed appropriate in the past but now add little value to business. Wal-Mart's program for eliminating the "stupidest thing we do" program was about identifying this friction and removing it. The barriers can be difficult to spot because they are part of the culture or a part of the business process itself.

One of the best examples of removing barriers is Progressive Insurance. It would be a mistake to say that Progressive is in the insurance business. While they may sell insurance, they clearly are in the business of speed. In eight minutes you can get a quote from the online system. They freely publish the rates of their competitors in order to keep you from having to jump around from site to site. Better stated, they have removed the need for you to look around. Their biggest claim to fame has to be the speed at which they deliver the claims check after an accident. In many cases, the Progressive claims adjustor will arrive on the scene and have a final check in your hands in less than 20 minutes. With over three million inventory parts moved each day, Dell has focused on removing every element of friction out of their supply chain and ordering system. Throughout the product lifecycle, a dell computer will come into contact with over 400 suppliers. They are determined to remove barriers and ensure that they run as smoothly as possible by reducing the friction in every business process.

How about inside the corporation? Over the past three years, our organization has developed an online ordering system. The Approved Product Listing (APL) provides an online shopping experience for the corporate community for ordering standard products. Prior to the development of the system, orders required a form to be completed by the end user and faxed around the organization for approvals. The form itself was complicated, confusing, and the source of an enormous amount of friction. The entire customer experience was a hassle from just trying to locate the form to actually fulfilling the order. Many people simply used their corporate credit card and bought online or from a local retailer. The APL changed this by offering a better product and service to the end user. Instead of faxing a complicated form, the APL shopping experience includes shopping cart functionality, account management, search integration, procurement processing, and order notifications which most people are familiar with. The essence of the APL is to take the enterprise IT architecture standards to a higher level of maturity where the basic processes are standardized and automated to insulate the end user from the complexities of the architecture environment. By utilizing a familiar framework like online shopping, the APL facilitates a greater adoption of the architecture standards while creating a satisfying customer experience. The value of this application is the fundamental removal of friction from the business processes. Orders that took 6-10 weeks, can now be completed in two. Three employees can do the work of 15, thus reducing the cost to the business. The collaborative environment that is constructed around the APL is an ecosystem that brings together the product experts with the internal consumer. This feedback loop ensures that the standard products meet the needs of the business.

Is it possible to create a frictionless environment? Removing barriers and friction isn't just about automation but also the development of a system around the business process. When we automated the ordering processes, we had a clearer vision of the entire ordering environment. The elimination of one barrier exposed three others in the accounting system, procurement process, and the architecture standards environment. The system could be expanded to include automatic price adjustments or bundling pricing by the vendors. Bulk purchases could be handled by combining orders which lowered the cost of doing business. Implementing a single system for ordering products allowed the company to have tighter security on the network. Until the friction was removed, no one understood the entire environment or the impact to the bottom line.

Consumption Value
What happens when the consumption of products increase the value? Suppose I go online and order a brand new F-150 pickup truck. Everyone in Georgia has a pickup truck; it's a state law. The price, including all of the additions, is around $30,000. I drive that truck one mile down the road, now what is the value of that truck? My guess would be around $25,000. That first mile is a killer from a value perspective.

In most cases when we consume products and service the value decreases along side. Not any more; organizations are beginning to figure this out. Take Ebay as an example, every transaction increases the ranking and rating of the buyer and seller. This will enable them to transact more in the future. Amazon has added book reviews, comments, tagging, wish lists, discussions and many other social opportunities for those that have read the book. The consumer is increasing the value of the product based on the consumption experience. The new web allows them to communicate that message to anyone at anytime.

Netflix is another example, with over a billion reviews, they have one of the ultimate databases for movie information in the industry. Recommendation systems such as those used by Netflix,

Amazon, and other Web retailers are based on the principle that if two people enjoy the same product, they're likely to have other favorites in common too. Based upon this information, they developed an algorithm that will suggest movies that you haven't seen. This algorithm is so valuable that they are offering you a million dollars if you can improve it slightly. The company is putting out a call to researchers who specialize in machine learning, the type of artificial intelligence used to build systems that recommend music, books, and movies. The entrant who can increase the accuracy of the Netflix recommendation system, which is called Cinematch, by 10 percent by 2011 will win the prize (Greene, 2006). When the consumer can adjust the product value or sales then standardized products are a thing of the past. We have all been interested in what others have to say about books or movies. We want to see the critic's comments or what movies have been nominated for an academy award. This support has influenced our purchasing behavior for a very long time. The web simply expands this concept to everyone one in the world, not just the paid reviewers.

Would the Ford Pinto ever make it in this new environment? How long would it have taken the public to post comments and recommendations about products that fail to meet even the most basic of standards? Making products and services that meet the basic needs of the consumer is simply the price of entry in today's environment. Cars had a limited life span of 100,000 miles, washing machines lasted 5 years, and that eight track tape player was all you ever needed. Today, nothing is constant, everything changes, and whatever assumptions we have made in the past are no longer valid. The good news for the consumer is that they play a heavy role in the products success or failure.

Eight Days a Week
What happens when work can be done anywhere, by anyone, at anytime? There can't be a better example of this other than McDonalds outsourcing the drive thru to India. The idea is simple enough; instead of using minimum wage workers here in the United States, you will be speaking to a call center in India. The

interesting point of this story is that unlike most outsourcing ventures, this isn't a cost saving venture. This is a revenue generation activity. How? The idea is simple, from the drive through perspective McDonalds is in the business of speed and a 5 second improvement can add up over time. Jean Abelson (2006) put it this way when she reviewed Wendy's effort. "I had absolutely no idea I was talking to someone in New Hampshire," Moncada said in a phone interview later that day. "Our order was ready at the window. It was really quick." It took a total of 66 seconds. The Burbank store is one of several Wendy's restaurants around the country that have been testing the concept, and franchisees plan to expand to at least 200 stores by next spring because the initial tests are so promising. Other fast-food companies, including Burger King, Panda Express, and McDonald's, have also started routing drive-through calls to remote locations to get faster and more accurate orders and let in-store employees concentrate on making food, keeping the store clean, and ringing up sales. The trend is transforming the fast-food industry in ways that are usually invisible to customers but can yield big results for the restaurants, which count on the drive-through business for about two-thirds of all sales. Every second counts in the race to deliver food faster, and no chain takes that challenge more seriously than Wendy's, which held the top spot as the industry's speediest server for seven straight years until Checkers took first place this year, according to "The Best in Drive-thru 2006" report released last month by QSR magazine. Checker s' average order was delivered in 125.5 seconds, measured from the time the customer reaches the speaker until the bag of food is passed through the window.

Advanced technology and Feature Sets are No Longer enough
Imagine a world where delivering the most advanced product with the greatest number of features actually losses the war for customer's attention. This is exactly what happened to the feature rich Diamond Rio MP3 player. The Rio hit the world with a simple design, advanced features and a collection of technology advancements that forced the recording industry to file suit to protect their interest. Yet, today 75% of the market is owned by

Apple's IPod which has far fewer features, cost more, and operates on top of a proprietary music format which cannot be accessed by other devices. On the surface, this seems to fly into the face of Web 2.0 openness. What happened to the traditional framework where value dictated the winners and losers?

Describing the competitive market where the Apple IPod competed head to head with the RIO is leaving out a few details. Specifically, the emergence of ITunes and the ITunes Music store altered the entire music ecosystem. The advanced functionally was transformed to the computer application which eliminated the need for that kind of feature set to be housed within the device. Add the ability to buy any song for $0.99 and you have a complete transformation worth billions. What Apple delivered is the "music experience" for the end user. This transformation from the traditional buying CD's and loading the songs on the computer then trying to manage the music was Apple's greatest accomplishment.

The IPod story is an Enterprise 2.0 success story based on collaborative designs, viral marketing, and the implementation of the experience over technology and features. Businesses, organizations, and individuals are all changing the way in which value is delivered. Enterprise 2.0 is about you, your collaborative ability to contribute to the vast amount of knowledge in the world today. We are starting to see power shift from the few that controlled the flow of information to you; Times Person of the Year for 2006. The business implications of this new media are unclear. No one is really sure where the rich user interfaces, self-service, the long tail, agility, transparency, and the emergent components of trust are going to take us.

How did this happen?
The message is clear, we need a complete re-invention of every aspect of who we are and what we do. The 2.0 label is not really a numeric sequence, but rather a designation of a transformation. Take a look around at the different areas that are jumping on the 2.0 moniker: metadata 2.0, library 2.0, enterprise 2.0, employment

2.0, shareholder 2.0, customer 2.0 and many others. How did we get here and what conclusions can we draw from this opportunity?

Enterprise 0.0
In chapter one, we discussed the natural progression of work. This section continues that discussion with a focus on the enterprise. In 20th century, large organizations began to form. Perhaps, Henry Ford can be labeled as the leader for change for this area. Organizations could gain return on investment by creating repeatable processes, not unlike an assembly line. Large organizations were bound by hierarchal structures that created boundaries, friction and structure of ownership. A hierarchical organization is an organization structured in a way such that every entity in the organization, except one, is subordinate to another. This is the dominant mode of organization among large organizations; most corporations, governments, and organized religions are hierarchical organizations. Hierarchies denote a singular/group of power at the top, a number of assistants underneath and hundreds of servants beneath them. Hierarchy originally meant "rule by priests", and it is from the organization of hierarchical churches such as the Roman Catholic and Eastern Orthodox churches that the name of this concept arises. In these organizations, the pope or patriarch was the highest visible part of the hierarchy, with God as the nominal top of the hierarchy (Wikipedia, 2006). The industrial revolution had a profound impact on how large organizations operated. Executives assumed you needed a large degree of control in order to build a standard product. This control came in the form of time and motion studies, time management systems, and decision support. Employees were considered interchangeable due to the basic skills required with manual labor. This control created a sense of hierarchy where those at the top had the knowledge and those at the bottom were regulated to second class. This model worked well since value came from stable and consistent delivery of the product. However organizations were seeing the vast majority of manual labor was being automated and value was emerging from the innovation and customer experience. This customer experience was not gained from the top of the organization but rather the bottom.

Enterprise 1.0
Something started to change in the later part of the 20th century.
Organizations, work, and people started to alter their behavior in so
many ways. Organizations started to shrink due to outsourcing
non-strategic functions like human resources and information
technology operations. This made sense because we started to see
the shift from cost centers to business value. This is not a trivial
shift in mind set, this is a fundamental change in how business gets
done. Prior to the 1990's, you never heard the concepts of return
on investment, business value, or bottom line contribution. Cost
centers, like information technology, were the price of doing
business. That started to change and the focus of technology
moved away from "paving the cow paths" to the generation of
competitive advantage. Globalization produced lower production
costs but not an equivalent increase in integration costs. Hence,
work started to move to the lowest cost provider, for information
technology, this meant operations to EDS, Integration to IBM, and
software support to Accenture. Enterprise 1.0 did see a fair share
of web and technology advancements including Customer
Relationship Management (CRM), Service Oriented Architecture
(SOA), Enterprise Resource Planning (ERP), and Enterprise
Application Integration (EAI). The web brought us enormous
amounts of information and access to products and services. The
web essentially destroyed business models like the travel agency
and new car dealerships.

Within the enterprise, we moved away from localized
documentation where the messages were kept locked inside the
minds of management. The advent of the Intranet brought forth
the concepts of a connected enterprise versus disconnected
collections of business functions. The intranet is a protected
environment that allows the organization to publish information for
consumption across the enterprise. This allowed information to be
distributed much more efficient than utilizing email of other forms
of one on one communications. Unfortunately, this was still a one
way communication medium where the information was controlled
and edited by a communication group.

Enterprise 2.0

It seems like we hardly had the opportunity to perfect 1.0 when 2.0 emerged and once again, technology is in the middle of it all. What would Enterprise 2.0 look like? Well, look no further than Time Magazines "Person of the Year" (2006): You. "It's a story about community and collaboration on a scale never seen before. It's about the cosmic compendium of knowledge Wikipedia and the million-channel people's network YouTube and the online metropolis MySpace. It's about the many wresting power from the few and helping one another for nothing and how that will not only change the world, but also change the way the world changes." Enterprise 2.0 is about you, your collaborative ability to contribute to the vast amount of knowledge in the world today. We are starting to see power shift from the few that commanded and controlled the flow of information to the many. The business implications of this new media are unclear. No one is really sure where the rich user interfaces, self-service, the long tail, agility, transparency, and the emergent components of trust are going to take us. Examples of organizations that are starting to get this stuff include Goldcorp.

The Goldcorp had purchased a mine with a history of low productivity and the company spent five years trying to increase the production. The mine was located in the Red lake district which had a history of producing gold; since the 19020's the area had produced over 24 million ounces. Rob McEwen knew there was gold on the property but the question remained where, how much, and the resources required in order to extract it. After spending a week at the Massachusetts Institute of Technology (MIT), he started to put several ideas together: Gold, Open Source, and the collaborative nature of the Enterprise 2.0. He would port 50 years of information including maps, reports, and geological reference information. However, the challenge would not go unrewarded; he added a $500,000 prize to be divided among the finalists. The results were an increase of $2.5 billion dollars of gold. The contributions included new software, applied mathematics, physics, and many other solutions. Goldcorp isn't the only company jumping on the band wagon; Staples runs a contest every year to find the next great office product and they are willing to offer $25,000 for the best of the best. Since the inception of Invention Quest, Staples has received more than 22,000 entries and ideas. The 2005 contest drew the largest number of submissions to date. From the nearly 14,000 submissions, ten inventors were chosen to present their ideas at the Invention Quest Finals in New York City.

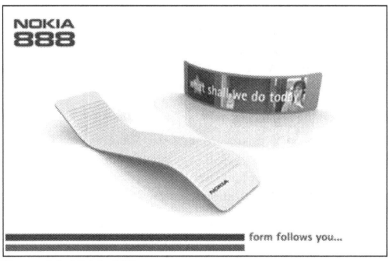

Figure 4.1: Nokia 888

You're not going to see this in stores any time soon. But if you'd like to get an idea of what Nokia thinks the future of communications will look like, take a look at the Nokia 888 communicator (Figure 4.1), a concept design that recently won Nokia's Benelux design contest. The bracelet-like 888 is envisioned to use a liquid battery, feature speech recognition, a flexible touch screen, and a touch sensitive body cover. A video showing off the device's potential features shows off close to a dozen functions, including an alarm clock, PDA, GPS, phone, push email receiver, digital wallet and, of course, jewelry. And, other than the "liquid battery," we can actually see this in the not-too-distant future (Perton, 2005).

What does this transformation mean to organizations and individuals? Clearly, the new technologies make it easier to collect and share information at all levels of the organization. The ability of organizations to spin or manipulate customer's opinions will be limited. The current term used to describe this type of environment is openness. An open organization freely shares information up and down the food chain. Individuals are encouraged promote their experience, skills and knowledge. We will work networks internal and external of the corporate hierarchy in order to deliver value. Open organizations don't limit people but encourage interaction and innovation. The command and control that defined Enterprise 0.0 will be completely removed and the adaptive organization emerges. Organizations that operate in an open environment do so by trusting each other. Those that abuse that trust will be exposed and dealt with socially, if not within the management structure. As power shifted to the customer, power will also shift to the employee. Information will flow just as the transaction flowed with Enterprise 1.0. We are entering into a new world that we are only beginning to understand and embrace.

Personal Implications
Do you worry about globalization? How about India? The data and information is mounting against us.

- In 2007, The number 1 language of the Internet will be…
- In 2050, the number 1 economy will be…
  Wait, an update: 2030 by a 2006 World Bank Article
- 80% of Wal-Mart's Suppliers are…
- Every 24 Minutes a Factory Opens in…
- 65,000 vs. 6,000,000 Students USA vs…
- The combined GDP of China and India will exceed the seven current wealthiest nations
- China is run by Engineers and Technologists while the United States is run by Lawyers
- United States Education Ranks 18th of 24 and Georgia Ranks 48th of 50; Up from 50th in 2004

- The 25% of the population in China with the highest IQ is greater than the total population in the United States
- In India, it's the top 28%
- China will soon become the number one English speaking country in the world

Asia will be a force in the coming years and very few of us are prepared to handle the increased level of performance. The diminishing demand for technology professionals (Labor) has an inverse relation with the increasing demand for Information Technology Talent. Labor, especially local labor, is a commodity that can easily be automated or moved over seas. With the advancements in technology, a call center employee can be sitting in Destin, FL or India and still provide great service. For the information worker, we have seen change and disruption as more and more jobs are moved to the lowest cost provider. While this change may seem sudden, the truth is that it is simply an evolution.

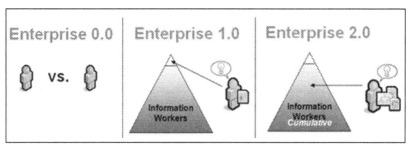

Figure 4.2: Competing in a New Environment.

When I started in Information Technology, I only had to compete with my co-workers; we worked in night operations on alternate days. The only exception was two to three times a month we would work as a team to processes month end reports and billing. This wasn't a bad job considering I was attending school during the day. Still, the point is that in order for me to move ahead, all I needed was to be a little bit better than the next person. I was protected by organizational boundaries and limited information flow in the industry. Keep in mind this was 1984 so technology jobs were not all that hot. This was the final calling card of what might be labeled Enterprise 0.0. As described earlier in this text, this was a command and control business model where organizations performed every task required in order to deliver value to the customer. I really saw this when I went to work for Lummus Industries who manufactured Cotton Gins. They did everything from design, construction, sales, and engineering. Everything was an in-house activity. The integration costs were fairly low while production costs were high. While no one can state a specific date, Enterprise 1.0 emerged with the advent of the Internet. As information flowed and technology advanced, competition grew. I no longer just competed with the local labor. I had to compete with everyone around the world. People started to move around and Information Technology was no longer something hidden in the back office. Now, you had to be the best of the best. Managers could evaluate your skills along with anyone else through standardized tests or technology degrees. To be the best was to build your trademarks as this book has stressed. Those that published what they knew did so through articles, books, and conferences. They started consulting organizations and established themselves as the experts. All of us could read what they thought and learn from their best practices. The only way for them to stay at the top was to continue to push the envelope of trademark development. As someone that made it to the top of my field, I can tell you that you can never stop learning from those ahead of you. That all changes in Enterprise 2.0, you no longer know who is ahead of you or behind.

In Enterprise 2.0, we now compete not with the five people in front of us but the cumulative knowledge of everyone in the field. Let me say this again, in the old days I knew who the competition was, where they were and what they knew. Think of it as a landscape. In the physical world, I know the environment where I live, I know the people within my network, I have a really good idea of the weather, and I know what to expect most days. In 2.0 world, there is no landscape and nothing that would indicate the formation of one. We have no idea of who we are competing with nor how many. That's the issue with a world built upon the architecture of participation, you simply don't know, what you don't know.

The key component of Enterprise 2.0 is participation; we must all get involved and add to the body of knowledge. We must define who we are and what makes us special. "Good Enough" is no longer the definition of success. This road to transformation will be blocked by everyone up and down the food chain. Managers, who have made a career of controlling information, will feel out of control in this new world. However, managing the human imagination will be the corner stone of value delivery in this next environment. How will this manifestation occur? For each of us the drive will be different; some will be forced while others will choose.

In 2004, our organization started to look into collaborative solutions and the value that could be generated. The collaborative architecture environment included team workspaces, work flow, information access, integrated communications, Intranet platforms, presence, web conferencing, and many more. These technologies brought an entire new perspective to a traditional culture of command and control. Control is the key here. Corporations enjoy control because it is a great predictor of outcomes. The tighter the control, the more predictable the outcome will be. Collaborative applications eliminate the control and this can be unsettling for some. We have been taught that without control chaos will emerge. Look around the web world and see where these assumptions have been wrong.

When Amazon allowed customer reviews, the prevailing opinion was that sales would drop with the negative comments, sales didn't drop they rose. When Ebay allowed seller and buyer feedback, the world said that the business model would crumble. When Google went to a value add business model versus an advertisement one, we all wondered what the end result would be. When Wikipedia started, everyone said that the quality of the information couldn't compete with published papers and encyclopedias. In the end, the errors in Wikipedia are less than 2 per 1,000 as revealed in a recent study as compared to the traditional encyclopedia. The point is that today, the architecture of participation seems far-fetched but in reality, we are simply in the early stages of the next revolution.

Summary

There is no mistaking that the architecture of participation is upon us and making inroads into the corporation. As we have automated and standardized on the vast majority of business processes, we tend to spend the majority of our time on the "out of scope" effort. The vast majority of employees don't do business processing anymore, due to the years of optimizing supply chains, outsourcing, automation, and striping the costs and inefficiencies out of the back office (Tapscott & Williams, 2007). Hence the result of the transformation from Enterprise 0.0 to Enterprise 2.0. We must collaborate in order to continually raise the bar in productivity and value generation. The implications are clear; we must transform and reinvent every aspect of our environment including the business, the organization, and the individual.

4

You miss 100%   of the shots you never take.
- Wayne Gretzky

Performance Maturity Model

In 1986, the Software Engineering Institute (SEI) was asked by the United States Air Force to create a systematic method of evaluating software contractors. In conjunction with the MITRE Corporation, the study group produced a questionnaire that enabled the Air Force to judge a software provider as either successful or unsuccessful in its capabilities. The questions were divided in a number of groups (key process areas) and then assigned to specific levels within the model. The resulting model was called the Capability Maturity Model (CMM).   The levels describe the path a software provider must follow in order to move to the higher levels of maturity. These paths are actually a collection of key practices that must be mastered before moving to the next level (Baskerville & Pries-Heje, 1999). Maturity implies a potential for growth in capability and indicates both the richness of an organization's software process and the consistency with which it is applied in projects throughout the organization. In addition, productivity and quality resulting from an organization's software process can be improved over time through consistent gains in the discipline achieved by using its software process (Chrissis, Curtis, Paulk & Weber, 1993). The CMM provides five levels of maturity: initial level, repeatable level, defined level, managed level, and optimized level.

The People Capability Maturity Model (CMM) takes the standard fives levels of maturity and cross references them with four process areas: developing competencies, building workgroups, managing performance, and shaping the workforce. The Process Maturity Framework was designed to apply practices that contribute directly to the business performance of an organization, that is, to the organization's capability for providing high-quality products and services. Since the capability of an organization's work force is critical to its performance, the practices for managing and developing them are excellent candidates for improvement using the Process Maturity Framework. Thus, the People CMM has been designed to increase the capability of the work force just as the Software CMM is designed to increase the capability of the organization's software development processes (Curtis, Hefley, & Miller, 2003). The issue with the People CMM and other derivatives is that these models look at the impact of high performance from the organizational point of view and not the individual. The purpose of the maturity model presented in this chapter is to provide you with a framework by which you can measure your progress in the development of your brand. The model is set in context within a corporation but could easily be adapted for independent consultants. The framework The Seven Stage Model for high performance is presented in Figure 4.1.

Figure 4.1: Seven Stage Model of High Performance.

The model provides the seven stages an individual needs to ascend in order to claim world class classification. Each of the stages builds upon the prior and rarely can one actually skip a stage. The progression from local labor to world class designation is a journey that requires risk, vision, and perseverance. Many people will fail because they quit too soon and lose faith in their vision. They do not have the courage to stick with the plan when others attack their actions. We should all work hard to accomplish the impossible; as the old saying goes, nothing is impossible.

If you were to ask any executive if their people were world class, what answer would you expect to receive? The automatic response would an astounding, "Yes". Yet, that simply cannot be true across the entire organization. Every organization will have a portfolio of employees at various levels of performance. Several research studies indicate the actual number of high performance employees is fairly low. This is not a bad thing; take, for example, the Men's Olympic Basketball Team. Cleary, everyone one of them are the cream of the crop. However, these experts lack the teamwork and collaborative effort required to be Olympic champions. Organizations need diversity within the ranks in order to produce an effective team capable of beating the world's best. To be considered world class, you must compete on the world's stage. This means you must develop your trademark program as if your career depended on it; it does.

Figure 4.2 presents a "Bell Curve" view of the high performance classification. Clearly, the actual performance of any organization won't be a perfect bell curve but rather a left or right skewed curve. I am going to use the bell shaped curve simply for communications rather than an academic proof.

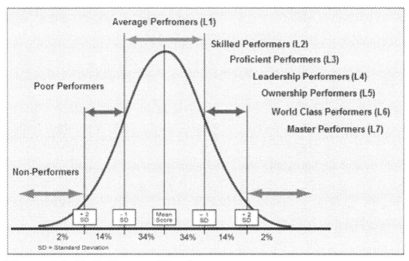

Figure 4.2: Bell Curve of Performance

The first thing that you should notice is that the Seven Stage Model doesn't spend much time on poor performers or non-performers, even though they make up 16-20% of the information worker population. In many cases, non-performers are simply in the wrong job or haven't received the correct training. Executives spend too much of their precious time addressing poorly performing employees. They lament that they squander 90 percent of their hours dealing with the bottom 10 percent of their work force. When they are not either disciplining them or somehow trying to compensate for them, they find themselves creating new systems and procedures to counterbalance poor performance. My assumption is that if you have purchased this book then you are not a poor performer. Your motivation is to take your current success to the next level.

Level 1: Local Labor as an Information Worker
Historically, when an individual started in a trade they came in as an apprentice. Here a young person would learn the skills of the trade from the ground up. By pairing an apprentice with a master craftsman, the knowledge and experience could be passed from one generation to another. Most apprentice type programs were in place before the ability to transfer information electronically. Still,

working in a controlled environment where lessons can be learned and experienced is critical for developing talent.

For the technologist, the apprentice path usually started in operations. From there, they could extend their knowledge and move up the value chain. I myself started as a night operator at a small mortgage company where they used the IBM System 34 and 36. One of my good friends and I worked split shifts during the night. The only exception was the nights we worked together for end of the month processing. While operational jobs have changed in the past several years, this job taught me the basic skills needed to move into a programming position and beyond.

For the information worker, we classify the level 1 skill set as "Average". Unlike agriculture and industry jobs, the concepts of average are very difficult to measure. Each role or responsibility is so diverse that tracking and measuring performance is a challenge. Applying industrial-age measures such as speed and throughput to knowledge-age work means that companies focus on familiar but arguably less-valid aspects of knowledge workers' output. In knowledge work, what you "see" is someone using a keyboard, talking on the telephone, peering at BlackBerry devices, engaging in conversation, using whiteboards or watching a computer screen. What you don't see are the intangible, mental aspects of knowledge work, thinking, reflecting, listening, analyzing, collaborating, responding, brainstorming, coordinating, seeking, learning, synthesizing, reading and processing, all of which are applied in unpredictable ways to companies' designs, plans, services, products, decisions, innovations and actions. Failing to acknowledge the intangible aspects of knowledge work, companies focus instead on the more-familiar aspects of speed, cost and throughput; ignoring the more-difficult issue of measuring intangible benefits (Logan & Stokes, 2004).

For the individual information worker, the term average is used quit frequently. What is average and how do managers calculate this performance variable? From the mathematical perspective, average would be the performance of everyone on in the pool divided by the number of individuals. Some might view the average as actually the medium where every individual is lined up and we choose the middle person as the benchmark. The result of being average would be that half of the population would be higher performing while the other half would produce less value. One might think that being in the middle would be a good thing but socially speaking, telling someone they are average is taken as an insult. Most organizations have a five tier review system where the middle ranking is considered average. In addition, these organizations will force fit employees into a standard grading system. In this case, being average would place you somewhere in the top 70-80 percentile. It's a good thing this average doesn't resemble online dating where 75% of singles claim "Above Average" looks. Worse yet, we could use the public education system definition of average which is a "C" but where 90% of our young folks make A's and B's. Clearly, the concept of average in the information worker area is difficult to establish. That being said, we all know weak performers when we come across them in a project. In some cases, the individual has a skill or competencies gap that hasn't been addressed. In other cases, the individual lacks the focus or commitment to delivery as expected. For what ever reason, these folks are labeled "Average".

Average is what I am calling local labor and a commodity collection of skills. Local labor has skills that are easily transferable to another person, location, or company. Local labor in the sense that the individual utilizes the essence of locality to remain employed. Why does a company hire a data steward that lives 5 miles from the office? Clearly, because they can be counted on to physically show up to work and work extended hours. While you might be able to find a more experienced individual living in south Florida, issues around travel and family create an environment where they may not be able to be onsite 100% of the time. With the advent of online meeting software and conference calling, this is becoming less and less of an issue. There was a time where my skills competed with other local labor. As consulting companies emerged, my skills were compared to those living in the Southeast. Today with globalization, I compete with everyone around the world. Just suppose you give me the assumption of being the in the top five Metadata experts in the world. The problem with being number five in the world is that one through four are only six tenths of a second away from any organization. Of course, availability and price will come into play but the fact remains the best in the world can be in your company in the blink of an eye. They are the best based on many of the characteristics described in this book. The good news is that I can watch their every move and read every publication in order to stay competitive. All of which will change in the Web 2.0 world as described in Chapter 3.

Over the past 10 years or so, information workers have focused their attention on similarity based skills versus differentiation skills. The reason for this is obvious, with a set of common skills (even advanced common skills), Individuals can move from one job to another or from one role to another. You don't have to worry about getting trapped into an isolated job with no chance for advancement. The problem with generic skills is that if they enable the movement for the individual then they enable the movement to an outsourcer. Common skills, jobs, and functions can and will be performed by other organizations. Information workers are assets and as assets, we have a defined cost and value. If the company can decrease the cost without losing value then they are compelled to change the environment. Most of us don't like to think of companies as entities that are only out for profit and not serve the greater good of the community. That, of course, depends on how you define community. In the global community, hiring information workers around the world does help and create prosperity. Unfortunately, the cost of that global prosperity is local pain and wage pressure.

The reality is that what worked in the past won't work in the future. What techniques you utilized to advance your career in the past will not be enough in the future. You must change the game entirely. My father told me once that if you can change the rules of the game then you can win. That's where we are today, the game has changed and we must change with it.

Level 2: Skilled Professional
Level 1 is not a short coming but a transition phase as an information worker passes to becoming skilled at their trade. Enhancing ones skill requires patience and persistence. While it is true that good enough often is, being better will enhance your capabilities and set a path toward the future. In order to enhance your skills at anything requires that you get involved and try new things. Most innovations won't work and may even seem silly upon later reflection, but the failure is with those that don't try. You must expect failure and embrace the lessons that emerge. Paul Saffo commented that Silicon Valley of today is built less atop the spires of earlier triumphs than upon the rubble of earlier debacles. William Marston wrote "Every success I know has been reached because the person was able to analyze defeat and actually profit by it in the next undertaking". Additionally, Thomas Watson Sr. (IBM) said that "The way to accelerate your success is to double your failure rate". We are talking about moving beyond the 80 percentile and now is the time for action.

A skilled information worker is someone that understands the basic functionality of a system or has received training in that technology. Many texts refer to this knowledge as "Tools of the Trade". The bottom line is that the information worker has a solid foundation of skills which can be built upon to advance productivity.

Suppose an information worker claims to be skilled with Microsoft's Excel. Based on our definition one would expect the individual to be able to perform the following tasks:

- Insert a Mathematical Function
- Format a Chart from a Series of Data Points
- Format the Font of a Character String
- Insert Conditional Formatting
- Hide and Unhide Cells
- Create an Auto-Filter for a Column

These technical skills would be required from any employer needing Excel experience and can only be learned over time with extensive training. A skilled employee should be able to take on a task with little guidance from a manger. The biggest difference between a skilled employee and one of average skills is the amount of guidance required. The success of a skilled information worker is generally based upon speed and required supervision. Here is where the competencies come into play.

One of the challenges in defining competency is that the term has been used by different people at different points in time within disciplines such as human resource management, organizational theory, behavioral science, industrial psychology, and education. Chuck Allen (2001) defined a competency as a specific, identifiable, definable, and measurable knowledge, skill, ability and/or other deployment-related characteristic (e.g. attitude, behavior, physical ability) which a human resource may possess and which is necessary for, or material to, the performance of an activity within a specific business context. Characteristics of an individual that are observable, measurable, and predictive of high performance within a given role or job. Examples of competencies include accountability, innovation, teamwork, communication, customer service, and vendor management.

Skilled professionals have a solid understanding of the technology, business and environment. These capabilities come together to create an understanding of how your area of interest can deliver value to the organization as a whole. Skilled professionals can be given a task and run with it. The expected results will be predictable and efficient.

Level 3: Proficient Talent
Now, we are going to take a deep dive into semantics and the details of performance. In order to move to the third level, the information worker must extend their level of competencies, integrate innovation, and add the element of professionalism.

John Seely Brown (2000) described knowledge as having two dimensions, the explicit and tacit. The explicit dimension deals with the "Know-what" which corresponds to the level 2 in our model. The tacit information deals with the "know-how" which is manifested in work practice skills. The level 3 designation brings into the equation a valuation of success. While level 2 only concerned itself with the ability of the information worker to perform the task and how fast, level 3 focuses on the quality of the solution.

The developmental psychologist Jerome Bruner made a brilliant observation years ago when he said we can teach people about a subject matter like physics-its concepts, conceptual frameworks, its facts-and provide them with explicit knowledge of the field, but being a physicist involves a lot more than getting all the answers right at the end of each chapter. To be a physicist, we must also learn the practices of the field, the tacit knowledge in the community of physicists that has to do with things like what constitutes an "interesting" question, what proof may be "good enough" or even "elegant," the rich interplay between facts and theory-formation, and so on. Learning to be a physicist (as opposed to learning about physics) requires cutting a column down the middle of the diagram, looking at the deep interplay between the tacit and explicit. That's where deep expertise lies. Acquiring this expertise requires learning the explicit knowledge of a field, the practices of its community, and the interplay between the two. And learning all this requires immersion in a community of practice, enculturation in its ways of seeing, interpreting, and acting (Brown, 2005)

Returning to the Excel example, an employee with a high degree of talent would know a lot more than just the formulas in Excel. Once you have the basic functions of Excel down, you should be able to perform any task assigned. However, take a look at Figure 4.3 and notice the enormous difference between the products built by someone that is skilled vs. proficient.

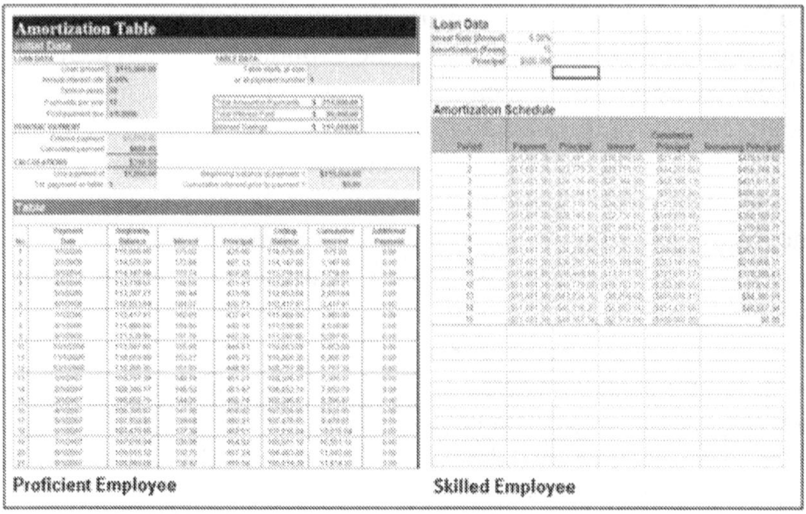

Figure 4.3: Skilled Employee vs. Proficient Employee

Both of these solutions will calculate the payment amount and provide an amortization schedule but the quality of the solution on the left is far more usable, efficient and creates an experience for the end user. In many ways, the proficient information worker has the ability to make complex algorithms look easy. The ability to hide the complexity from the user and embed that into the system must be learned and experienced over a period of time.

Proficient people perform, as do artists or actors. When someone is proficient, we are drawn to them in admiration. Does it matter how difficult the task or skill is? Several Christmases ago I was shopping at Macy's in downtown Atlanta. After purchasing my wife a dress, I headed up to gift wrapping. While this young lady wrapped my present, I stood in amazement. It wasn't just the fact that she knew how to wrap a present but the efficiency, speed, and limited waste of movements. Every move was crisp and elegant to the point that I never took my eyes off the box. While this person had the skills needed for the, she was also one of the best examples of proficiency.

Level 4: Connoisseur of Talent (Leadership)

The next two levels of high performance are going to shake the very foundation of your beliefs. In fact, you may very well jump off that chair and scream that you have hundreds of examples where the following is simply not true. Be that as it may, let's proceed into the key ingredient of level 4: ownership. In my education sessions, I usually open with a remark on how talented the available Metadata consultant pool is within the industry. However, at some point this talent will leave and you will be held responsible for the long term success and failure of the program. The responsibility for the environment will be transferred to an employee eventually. Notice the progression; we have moved from ability, speed of delivery, to quality of the solution. The next step must be ownership and the responsibility of the solution.

Leadership has got to be the most talked about subject in business. With all these best practices, you wonder why we are all not leadership experts. I won't spend a whole lot of time on the subject except to say that there are plenty of great managers but very few great leaders. Leadership is essentially the process of building and maintaining a sense of vision, culture and interpersonal relationships, whereas management is the co-ordination, support and monitoring of organizational activities. For the information worker, accountability is one of the main differences between level 3 and 4. Accountability focuses on the bottom line results, honoring commitments, communicating, delegating, and creating value for others. Creating a vision, laying out a strategy, building a roadmap, and then executing is the responsibility of the leader.

Suppose for example, you have responsibility for building an online ordering system. You bring in the best designers and developers available and in fact, they create an award winning application. However after the first 2 months, only a few orders come through the system? Who is to be held responsible for the failure of the application? Who didn't take into account the politics of the organization and the resistance to change? More importantly, who will lead the effort to correct the situation and focus on delivering value over the long term? Why does accountability provide a broader view or a higher performance classification? What additional skills are required to take ownership of your area of interest? Without the accountability, you can never fully claim ownership and responsibility. Even if your director is a "hands off" manager, they will still have claim. As the owner, you are responsible for allocating resources, making decisions, and defining what success is or is not.

Keep in mind that failure is not the opposite of success and success is not the opposite of failure. Suppose you have own an application then what are your measurements of failure? I would include down time, mean time to repair, and capacity issues. If these metrics get out of hand then your application has failed to meet the business needs of the organization. However, these metrics are not metrics of success. Most of us can recall implementations that had great up-time and plenty of capacity but could never be classified as a success. Here is where most technologists fail to see the bigger picture. Metrics of success include customer satisfaction, usage, customer retention, data quality, etc. These metrics have little to do with the infrastructure but everything to do with mass adoption. Those with accountability for the program understand this and ensure that business value is delivered.

Level 5: Business Responsibility
Level 5 and 6 are fairly closely related. Harold Green, former president of ITT, once commented "Leadership is the very heart and soul of business. No one really manages a business by shuffling the numbers or rearranging organizational charts or tallying the latest business school formulas. To my mind, the quality of leadership is the single most important ingredient in business." The next step in the natural progression of talent is to treat what you do as a business. Can you take your unique talent on the open market? Are corporations willing to pay for your experience and talent? If you can't imagine that situation then you might need to begin to worry about your future. As organizations

continue to reduce costs, all non value-add jobs will be eliminated or automated.

You are a business; regardless of your current situation you are the business. You generate income, you have expenses, you pay taxes, and you have a brand image. That sounds a lot like a business to me. Yet, many of us don't really look at ourselves that way. Up until now, we have been talking about getting things done or execution. Now, we turn our attention on value-creation that can generate income and create a competitive advantage. Michael Porter (1998) created a value chain matrix where at the most basic level, the value chain is based on assessment of the processes of a firm. It shows the firm as a system, made up of subsystems of inputs, transformation processes and outputs. Porter developed the concept of the value chain to aid analysis of a firm's operations, while more specifically it has two uses. First, it is used to better understand the activities of the firm and how it might develop a competitive advantage. Second, it is used to position the firm in the chain of upstream and downstream suppliers and buyers called the channel or value system.

As you are faced with slower growth and stronger competition, competitive advantage becomes crucial to the maintenance of superior performance. Competitive advantage grows fundamentally out of the value you create for your customers. In competitive terms, value is the amount buyers are willing to pay for what a firm provides them. Porter uses the concept of a value chain to disaggregate buyers, suppliers and a firm into the discrete but interrelated activities from which value stems. Such a process is necessary in order to understand the behavior of costs and the sources of differentiation. Taking your unique value and applying the value chain will help you understand the role you play within a much larger organization.

Level 6: World Class Designation
One would think that if you accomplished all that has been presented in the first five levels that you would be considered world class but unfortunately that simply isn't true. World class

91

means that you compete at the highest level across the industry. While there are programming contests, normal information worker activities are not held in competition. The key component of world class designation is to be recognized by your industry or peers for your contributions.

When you think of world class who do you think of? In the sporting world, we have athletic contests to determine the world's best and many times the difference between the best and everyone else is less than a second. In the world of business, there seems to be three paths to this designation: innovation, publishing, and execution. Take a look at the following list and see if you agree with me on the designated world class expert.

- Internet – Tim Berners-Lee
- Enterprise Architecture – John Zachman
- Information Technology Commodity – Nicholas Carr
- Business Management – Peter Drucker
- Customer Experience - B. Joseph Pine II and James H. Gilmore
- Data Modeling – Steve Hoberman or Graeme Simsion
- Metadata – David Marco or Adrienne Tannenbaum
- Information Architecture – Loius Rosenfeld and Peter Morville
- Data Warehouse – Bill Inmon
- Time Management – David Allen
- Re-Engineering – Michael Hammer
- Business Processing Management – Brett Champlin
- Marketing – Sergio Zyman
- Semantics – Dave McComb

What made these people world class? Clearly, all of them have taken a variety of paths to both success and failure. They have over came obstacles to become the world foremost authority on their subject area. The following takes a look at three key characteristics of a level six expert.

Innovation

When you think of the Internet who do you think of? Most people will quickly bring up the name of Tim Berners-Lee. Others will suggest Marc Anderson (Browser Fame) or Ted Nelson (Linking Documents) as individuals who helped pushed this technology forward. Today we look toward Amazon's Jeffrey P. Bezos or Google's Larry Page and Sergey Brin as the innovators of the new technology. What's these people and many others like them did is created value where there was none before. Innovation is everywhere and is the primary driver of business value.

For myself, metadata was a crowed field by the time I arrived in 2000. Yet, no one seemed to take the next logical extension of metadata to all assets of the corporation. Hence, the creation of "Enterprise Metadata" was inevitable but I was one of the first people to put these concepts together and go public. One of the lessons, I picked up from my dissertation work was that the expansion of the body of knowledge comes in small increments not in large scale innovations. The key to your long term growth and development is innovation and the execution. Without innovation, you will become a cost commodity where the only thing that differentiates you from everyone else is price. Innovation does not need to be isolated to some grand new technology; innovations can be found in any process, product, service, or strategy. As of 2006, I have been awarded four patents with six more in patent pending status. Successful people innovate, while they may not file patents, they define the future for themselves and those that follow in their footsteps.

Execution

People that can execute strategies and programs will emerge as a world class expert. Up until now, most of the improvements are internal to the organization. People who can execute on a world class level will get recognized in company write-ups or professional publications. Too many leaders fool themselves into thinking their companies are well run. They're like the parents in Garrison Keillor's fictional Lake Wobegon, all of whom think their children are above average. Then the top performers at Lake

Wobegon High School arrive at the University of Minnesota or Colgate or Princeton and find out they're average or even below average. Similarly, when corporate leaders start understanding how the GE's and Emerson Electrics of this world are run—how superbly they get things done—they discover how far they have to go before they become world class in execution. Bossidy and Charan (2005) have written an excellent book on execution. They indicate "Execution is the great unaddressed issue in the business world today. Its absence is the single biggest obstacle to success and the cause of most of the disappointments that are mistakenly attributed to other causes". Execution can create the recognition you need to become world class.

Publishing
Being the first (innovation) or being the most impacting (execution) doesn't come close to the value of being published. Return to the prior list of experts and notice the degree to which they are all published. If we were to actually have a technical contest between experts in the field and the practitioners then my money would be on those that perform the task on a daily basis. In other words, being published doesn't guarantee that you are the best in the world; it only creates the perception that you are. Getting published is taking your ideas and concepts to the world's stage and opening yourself to the criticism of everyone. However, that's how your ideas get better and you truly expand the body of knowledge. Going public with your ideas and experiences is gut wrenching. Based on my experience, you will need very thick skin. Review Chapter 7 for more specifics on getting published.

If you take a look at these three components you should also take notice of the trademarks created during the process including: patents, awards, and publications. These will build your brand and take you to the world class level. What about Web 2.0 publishing capabilities? Have you ever heard of a gentleman named Robert Scoble? Robert was employed by Microsoft and operates one of the best known technology blogs called the "Scobleizer". Robert was able to alter the perception of Microsoft as a monopolistic bully by providing honest feedback and insight concerning

Microsoft products. The new technology allows anyone to rise to status of expert. We see example after example, where the human voice can be raised above the noise that is the Web 2.0 environment.

Level 7: Master Classification of Being the World's Best
Our definition of world class is top 1% of the field. Unfortunately, some fields like development or Six Sigma the population of practitioners is very large and a top 1% designation will make you one in a million. The final level of our model is top 10 in the field. The secret ingredient to becoming a top 10 is time.

There are plenty examples of one hit wonders in the field of technology. People that come up with an idea or concept that is so revolutionary that they are instantly taken to the front of the line is very rare. One example is Nicholas Carr's book "Does IT Matter". This book, which started with his Harvard Business Review (May, 2003) article, must be the most villain-ized book for the IT professional. Unfortunately, it captures the general feeling for senior managers of large organizations, especially for those managers that have not taken a deep dive into the fundamentals of competitive advantage. Competitive advantage is the process of developing products, services, processes, and capabilities that give an organization a superior advantage over other organizations.

Most master information workers earn their title over time. Before diving into the concept of time, allow to demonstrate the value of time with an analogy. Suppose for a moment, I challenged you that you only had one day to get wealthy; what would you do? The obvious answer is to take a sum of money and play the lottery where the odds are one chance in 175,711,536 per dollar invested. What if I told you, you had 2 weeks to become wealthy? While you could play two weeks of the lottery, a better chance would be to head to Las Vegas and play your favorite game for a week. Based on your talent and luck, you may very well accomplish the wealthy task. Still, the odds are not very good depending on your game of chance. What if you had ten years to get wealthy? The most obvious choice to become an entrepreneur which would produce odds of about 1 in 10 or maybe 1 in 100. Still, these odds are far greater than playing the lottery and hitting the Vegas strip. One more question, what would you do if you had 40-50 years to get wealthy? The answer, which will thrill all financial analysts, is to simply save 15% of your earnings and over time wealth creation is easy.

This analogy provides a great bench mark on how one becomes the world's best. Think of the Nobel Prize; the award generally goes to those that dedicate their life to a cause. Every year, since 1901, the Nobel Prizes have been given for achievements in physics, chemistry, physiology or medicine, literature and for peace. The Nobel Prize is an international award administered by the Nobel Foundation in Stockholm, Sweden.

Summary
Looking back to the natural progression of this model one thing is clear; the amount of effort grows exponentially at each stage. While many people may never reach the stage of their dreams, win industry awards, or even a Nobel Prize, we all can strive to be world class. In many ways, that's why this book exists. I want to demonstrate how the process works and over time you can become the world best at the field of you are choosing. This chapter laid the foundation for maturity models in the world of high performance. The Seven Stage Maturity Model defined a natural progression through a variety stages for delivering unquestionable value. Each of these levels were broken out and described in detail. The goal was to show the reader that moving to the next level is possible and that there is no rest for the weary. You need to keep pushing when others have stopped. This is the only way to be the world's best.

5

Uncertainty is the only thing to be sure of.
– Anthony Muh

Unique Value Opportunity

The prior chapters focused on convincing you that the journey you are about to take is worth the pain. This book is not meant to provide you short cuts because the reality is that there are no short cuts. Everyone focuses on Tiger Woods winning majors and the enormous endorsement deals. Not many focus on the countless hours he spends practicing shots (450 a day), 8 miles of running and three hours in the gym.. Vijay Singh's worth ethic is legendary; whether it's his physical workouts or the eight hours a day he spends hitting practice balls on the driving range. Hershel Walker used to do 1,000 sit-ups and push-ups every day; same story for Annika Sorenstam with 700 to 1,000 sit-ups per day. If you want to become the worlds best then you are going to have to put in the time. To be successful in any sport, you must train with intensity. To be the best, you must train better that all of the rest. There are no shortcuts or magic pills that will take you to the top of the mountain. While natural talent helps, specific focus on your area of specialty is crucial in today's environment.

Each of the following chapters will start with a theme that speaks to the basic philosophy of the content. For the unique value opportunity that word is action. Action is a word I just love. The world is full of dreamers but very few people that act upon those visions. Here are a few supporting quotes from people who were action focused.

"There are risks and costs to action. But they are far less than the long range risks of comfortable inaction" - John F. Kennedy

"To become successful you must be a person of action. Merely to know is not sufficient. It is necessary both to know and do" – Napoleon Hill

"I think there is something, more important than believing: Action! The world is full of dreamers, there aren't enough who will move ahead and begin to take concrete steps to actualize their vision" – W. Clement Stone

"Apply yourself. Get all the education you can, but then, by God, do something. Don't just stand there, make it happen" - Lee Iacocca

"The great composer does not set to work because he is inspired, but becomes inspired because he is working. Beethoven, Wagner, Bach, and Mozart settled down day after day to the job in hand. They didn't waste time waiting for inspiration." – Ernest Newman

People of action get things done. They perform work with energy and drive; value the art of planning, but will take quick, decisive action when an opportunity presents itself. Action oriented people take risks; you should be willing to take risks, push the envelope, or try something new. The essence of this first stage is to take the steps required to understand where your opportunities exist.

Talent, Passion, and Value-Add
At the end of the day, your unique value opportunity will be defined by addressing three fundamental questions:
- What are you really good at?

- What are you passionate about?
- What do you do that creates value?

Take a look at Figure 5.4 where we can utilize circles to represent these questions and how they might overlap.

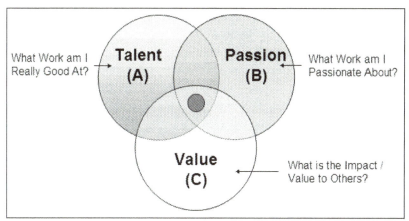

Figure 5.4: Circle of High Performance

Within this model, we can identify seven possible areas where we can classify our unique value opportunity. These areas include: A, B, C, AB, AC, BC, and ABC. "A" represents the area located in the upper left hand side of the image. This area indicates that you are very talented in your area but you're not very passionate about it nor does it create much value. "B" represents the upper right hand side where you are very passionate about the topic but you still need to develop skills and a market for your services. "C" represents the area that has great market potential but your skills are weak and you really don't have a passion for the topic to begin with. For the vast majority of information workers that classify their value creation in one of these three areas understand that they have gaps that need to be addressed. Individuals here recognize their weaknesses and begin to layout a game plan to addresses the obvious gaps. Where people get into trouble is when they have a combination of two components but fail to acknowledge the gap with the missing one.

"AB" represents something that you are very good at and have a deep passion for it but the market isn't really there or is saturated by other information workers interesting in the same topic. You see this when people are looking to taking their hobbies and converting them into a small business. The key to turning a hobby into a business is to understand the demand components and business model. My brother is really passionate about fishing and by any standard; he is very good at it. The problem is that there really isn't much of a market for that here in Georgia. Fishing and even hunting are just part of growing up. Access to lakes, streams, or farm ponds is not an issue. While wanting to turn his passion into a business as a guide, my brother understands that the demand simply isn't there for long term viability.

"AC" represents an opportunity that you are really good at and has tremendous market value. This is what makes a great Hollywood script. Our hero, who has expert skills as a warrior, has retired and living in the Okefenokee Swamp. His country needs him to serve a greater cause and we see him struggle with the fact that he doesn't have the fire within. While this is great for Hollywood, we cannot have a unique value opportunity without passion. You must be committed to the craft and willing to do whatever it takes in order to succeed.

"BC" represents an area that has the market value and we have the passion. We simply need to develop the skills required to be world class. Of the three dual combinations, this one is the easiest to move to the center. Movement here is controlled by your dedication while the other two have outsides obstacles that are much harder to overcome.

Clearly, the very best opportunity is the "bulls eye" located where the three circles intersect. This is Nirvana and you need to take advantage while you have the opportunity. The bad news is that economic, personal, and professional forces are continuously pushing you out of the middle. Catastrophic events in your personal life can alter your passion and commitment. Think about people going through a divorce or losing a grandparent; these events can change how you look at your job, your life, and your commitment to excellence. New entrants or business models can change the basic skills required to be considered an expert. When 9/11 occurred, the demand for disaster recovery and security skills jumped exponentially while E-Commerce skills plummeted. Overnight, the business value was altered and the opportunity was either lost or gained depending on where you were at the time. The greatest of these forces is time. Time is like a stream; no matter solid that stream bed is the water will eventually wear it down.

The next section will take a deep dive into the three main components of the framework with the sole purpose to help you identify your unique value opportunity.

Talent Analysis
The first step in the process is to determine what you are actually good at. A landmark McKinsey & Company (1997) study exposed the "war for talent" as a strategic business challenge and a critical driver of corporate performance. According to the year long study, a study involving 77 companies and almost 6,000 managers and executives, the most important corporate resource over the next 20 years will be talent: smart, sophisticated businesspeople who are technologically literate, globally astute, and operationally agile. And even as the demand for talent goes up, the supply of it will be going down.

A more recent, study performed by IBM, covered 300 Chief Human Resources Officers (CHROs) found that despite Australian organizations leading the world in HR process benchmarks, they must stem voluntary turnover at the senior and middle management levels to maintain competitiveness. Global findings of the Global Human Capital Study (2005) include:

1. Companies in mature markets are more exposed to an aging workforce, hampering competitiveness, compared to emerging and growth markets. The mature marketplaces of Australia, North America, Europe and Japan have built their workforces on the

'baby-boomer' generation, one of the largest demographic booms in history and are more exposed to the aging workforce than companies in developing nations. CHROs in mature market companies reported they were less able to implement staffing flexibility.

2. Few companies hold their executives or HR staff accountable for improving and retaining human capital. Employee performance measurements are often not built into senior leader compensation plans. Only a third of the respondents' leadership teams were rewarded on the growth of key staff and less than a third were evaluated on the retention of them. Almost two-thirds of companies surveyed reported that the rewards of their HR employees were not tied with overall HR performance.

3. Money spent on employee training is poorly accounted for. The study showed that very few companies are measuring the effectiveness of training. Less than half of the companies surveyed measured the business impact of employee programs and less than a third measured the return on investment for such programs. These figures highlight that training budgets are not being evaluated for the contribution they make to the business and could be failing to contribute towards company competitiveness.

4. Buying' talent from outside the company potentially risks alienating the existing workforce and increasing the loss of talented employees. Companies with a higher percentage of middle management brought in from the outside, rather than promoting 'home grown' talent, suffered from a five percent higher turnover as well as generally lower morale. This means that companies that bring in middle managers from the outside must be careful to manage the expectations of talented individuals within the companies regarding their potential for advancement.

Based on Malcolm Gladwell's (2005), *The Talent Myth,* being the best and brightest may not be as valuable as you might imagine. Gladwell suggests that companies that rely solely on recruiting very "talented" people, and promote a culture that rewards perceived "talent", and sometimes self nominated or elected "talent" at that, without any rational measure of performance, are more likely to fail. It's a great read, and a nice antidote to the business cult that attributed success to the "individual super star" style of upper management (Moffat, 2002). Gladwell pointed out the most successful organization in hiring talent was Enron. Of course, it's all in how you define talent and at Enron that classification was untested MBA's. Our model for talent analysis will focus on four key areas: skills, competencies, disciplines, and leadership essentials.

Skills (Foundation of Talent)

Earlier in this text, we discussed skills and the basic difference between competencies. Skills are the essence of your ability to accomplish tasks. Information worker skills cover a wide range of areas and your goal is to identify which of these skills increase your efforts of creating a unique value opportunity. Skills fall into four main categories: basic literary skills, technical skills, interpersonal skills, and conceptually integrated skills.

Basic Literary Skills

Depending on your level of information work, basic literary skills may or may not be of a concern. Many organizations are creating training programs for just the basic skills of grammar, mathematics, safety, reading, and writing. In addition, call centers in India are focusing on training workers in telephone etiquette and how to sound "American".

John McCormack (1990) wrote a very enjoyable book titled *Self Made in America*. While the book is very hard to find today, I vividly remember a story he told about creating a ledger of your skills. The company he was working for went belly up, and at 25, McCormack lost his fortune and found himself $250,000 in debt. Depressed and downtrodden, he began spending his days at the beach where he met a man named Abe a man McCormack says changed his life. Over the next nine weeks, the two men met almost every day at the beach. Abe, a German immigrant, told McCormack that if he wanted to learn to succeed in business, he should study under other foreigners who came to America with nothing and went on to become successful entrepreneurs. Over the next several years, McCormack worked under three self-made men; all immigrants who were unable to speak English when they arrived in the United States. One of the first exercises that Abe made John do was to perform some internal inventory of his skills. After an hour or so of thinking and unable to identify any skills at all, Abe helped him understand that he had skills that most immigrants don't have, yet went on to be hugely successful. These skills included the ability to find his way around in a large city, to speak the language fluently, to be able to make change, and a high school education. Basics skills are often overlooked by information workers but they give each and every one of us a step forward over the majority of the people in this world.

Technical Skills
Technical skills are critical in today's knowledge intense environment. Due to the rapid changes in technology and the implementation of office automation, technical skills must be rebuilt frequently. By the nature of the work, information workers create an environment where experts are defined by their contributions. With a focus on results, technology cultivates those who specialize within certain domains. Information Technology professionals master hardware systems, programming languages, applications and procedures. These rules require complete conformity but deliver excellence. The technically skilled, curious and expert bunch strives to maintain a technical edge: clean design, efficient programming, clean interfaces, good documentation, timely delivery, test runs and optimization. The following list provides a short inventory of possible skills to choose from:

- Windows Operating System
- SQL Server
- Microsoft Exchange
- Visual Studio and .NET
- Access, Excel and Office Automation
- Programming Languages

- Web Development and Design
- XML Training and Web Services Courses
- Oracle Database
- Security and Disaster Recovery
- Network Training and PC Support
- TCP/IP, Cisco, and Telecom
- UNIX, Linux and Open Source
- Software Engineering
- Systems Analysis
- Project Management

For every information worker, the specific technical skills required will vary. The list provided here is simply to be used as a guide.

Interpersonal Skills
Interpersonal skills include communications, human resources, management, performance appraisals, leadership and negotiations. Most middle managers tend to utilize their interpersonal skills more than their technical ones. One of the newest skills is working in collaborative environments where technology has replaced the face-to-face methods of years ago. These new skills must be learned and advanced especially with the threat of the Bird Flu and Terrorist attacks.

It's a whole new world of work! Organizational change, diversity and electronic communications have changed the face of the workplace. Today more than ever, success depends upon the combined cooperation, commitment and action of people—both face-to-face and across electronic and cyber channels. That's why your interpersonal skills are so critical to your own effectiveness as an information worker.

Conceptual Integrated Skills
Skills in strategic and operational planning, organizational design, and policy skills are what we mean when we describe conceptual integrated skills. Adapting to complex and changing environments is often the work of executive management. Still, information

workers need to understanding of these skills and utilize the benefits provided when one knows how to execute them.

Competencies
A primary point of contrast is between individual competencies, knowledge, skills, and abilities that individuals in the organization possess, and organizational competencies; those things that characterize collective action at the organizational level. In terms of individual competencies, the literature identifies a wide range of factors that are generally important for staff and management success in organizations and provides ample guidance for how to analyze specific jobs and positions to determine which skills and abilities are most relevant to a particular job, e.g. job-task analysis. However, determining which competencies have true strategic value to an organization requires a different perspective (Bolton & Olson, 2002). Competencies are those interpersonal characteristics that you are either born with or have learned over a period of time. Competencies represent many of the attributes, behaviors, areas of knowledge, skills, and abilities required for successful job performance. The following list is an example of competencies you may have already developed in your own career.

Individual Competencies
- Building Effective Teams
- Customer Focus
- Integrity and Trust
- Interpersonal Skill
- Listening
- Managing Relationships
- Managing Vision and Purpose
- Motivating Others
- Negotiating
- Personal Learning and Development
- Valuing Diversity

Operating Competencies
- Developing Others

- Directing Others
- Managing and Measuring Work
- Managing Through Processes and Systems
- Organizing
- Planning
- Priority Setting
- Time Management
- Timely Decision Making

Leadership Essentials
Similar to the competencies, leadership essentials focus on more of the strategic side of talent. Leadership is crucial at the higher levels of the maturity model. Peter Drucker defined leadership as "The only definition of a leader is someone who has followers." To gain followers requires influence but doesn't exclude the lack of integrity in achieving this. Indeed, it can be argued that several of the world's greatest leaders have lacked integrity and have adopted values that would not be shared by many people today. John Maxwell (2004), in his book *The 21 Irrefutable Laws of Leadership*, defines of leadership as "leadership is influence - nothing more, nothing less." This moves beyond the position defining the leader, to looking at the ability of the leader to influence others - both those who would consider themselves followers, and those outside that circle. Indirectly, it also builds in leadership character, since without maintaining integrity and trustworthiness, the capability to influence will disappear. Warren Bennis defines leadership as a focus on the individual capabilities of the leader: Leadership is a function of knowing yourself, having a vision that is well communicated, building trust among colleagues, and taking effective action to realize your own leadership potential. Each of these definitions hit at the heart of leadership; leaders must lead. Leadership is a process by which a person influences others to accomplish an objective and directs the organization in a way that makes it more cohesive and coherent. Leaders carry out this process by applying their leadership attributes, such as beliefs, values, ethics, character, knowledge, and skills. The following lists contain a solid foundation of the

leadership essentials required by information workers moving to the highest levels of performance.

Strategic Competencies
- Creativity
- Dealing with Ambiguity
- Decision Quality and Problem Solving
- Functional/Technical Skills
- Intellectual Acumen
- Learning on the Fly
- Strategic Agility and Innovation Management
- Technical Learning

Leadership Competencies
- Assessing Talent
- Conflict Management
- Managerial Courage
- Comfort Around Authority
- Organizational Agility
- Presentation Skills
- Written Communications
- Results Focused
- Action Oriented
- Execution

Disciplines
The final area for talent analysis is disciplines. A discipline is the area of specialty where you will be focusing your efforts to build your brand. Disciplines are specific areas of study or a branch of knowledge that one focuses their attention. Ideally, you will have several disciplines that when pulled together create a unique view. Disciplines may include subjects like science, engineering, aerospace, bioscience, professional or administrative. They allow you to demonstrate an understanding of the development, resources, and essential questions within the discipline itself.

Passion Analysis

As in the previous section, passion analysis is about identifying what you are passionate about and how valuable that passion is. What is it that you would work 8-10 hours a day at your current job then go home and devote another three hours? Unfortunately, passion is like many emotions it's hard to measure it but you know it when you see it. I routinely run into people that people that claim a passion for metadata but that passion is only a popularity passion. When people have passion they raise their game to a whole new level and they have the ability to see things that others do not. The problem with passion is that most people will claim some level but in most cases the fire isn't really lit. The emotion of passion can be confusing and at times lead you astray. Think about sports teams that come and go; fair weather fans is the term that comes to mind. People seem to get passionate about areas when others get excited about it. Personally, I am big fan of the Dallas Cowboys. Since the days of Tony Dorsett, Drew Pearson, and Rodger Staubach, I have been a true blue fan. During the 1-15 season, not many people pulled for the boys. That changed during the Troy Aikman and Emmit Smith years. Today, we are back in the average category and once again the fair weather fans have moved to other teams.

Over the past six or seven years, we have seen another type of passion develop where we get focused when life gives us no other options. We have seen this in the globalization and outsourcing phenomena. In the early 2000's, I often wondered why people were not investing in advancing their knowledge and education. The general answer was "Why should I"; demand is so high. Of course, that all changed and many were caught off guard. Once unemployed, these people caught fire and developed a passion for their professional development. For many people, this was too little too late. This type of passion is not unusual in our world. The founder of Mother's Against Drunk Driving (MADD) got mad when her son was killed by a drunk driver. John Walsh got passionate about crime when his son was kidnapped. In many cases, the problem with desperation passion is that when the storm passes, so does the passion.

The final type of passion is the one that we need to focus on is one that has a core and is based on ones vision of the future. The art of creating and maintaining passion in business, as in all human endeavors, is dependent upon nurturing an environment in which systems, attitude and culture continuously engender and promote positive feelings akin to love for the company, as well as its products, services, employees, customers and other stakeholders (Lazof, 2004). Tom Peters, the author of the best-selling business book, "In Search of Excellence," noted that "Nothing good or great can be done in the absence of enthusiasm." You can know everything about your industry - buyer perception, package appeal, pricing, promotion and the environmental impact of the product. The kind of passion that I am talking about is the passion that drives people to leave a comfortable job to start their own business; the kind of passion that won't take no for an answer. The kind of passion that these people showed when faced with the word "No":

Lee Iacocca wanted convertibles but the engineers said no, the salesmen said no, the dealers said no, the plants said no. Lee said "Yes, if you have to take a can opener and pull the tops off each car, we are having convertibles".

Mark Twain said the man with a new idea is considered a crank until the idea succeeds.

Beethoven wrote the "Heroic Symphony", which broke every rule of the classics; the orchestra said no we can't play it.

Stravinsky premiered the "Right of Spring", the critics declared him insane.

Marcel Duchamp painted "Nude Descending a Staircase"; everyone declared it the worst picture ever painted until it was recognized as a turning point in art history.

Freud described the unconscise world, while the concise world said no.

James Joyce changed the literature world forever by writing in the stream of concise technique and everybody declared him deranged

Passion overcomes the risk of failure as well as push beyond your fears. So back to the task at hand, what area do you have a passion? Perhaps, a better way of asking this is what area are you willing to develop a passion? Are you interested in SOA, High Performance, Library Science, Call Centers, or Collaborative Solutions? What you will find is that a topic map will emerge where one topic in influenced by multiple others; this insight will emerge once you begin to dwell in the details.

You probably already have a good idea of your area of interest that will ultimately become your source of your unique value opportunity. The question that needs to be asked is that are too broad or too narrow. For example, if you say that you want to be the expert at Customer Relationship Management (CRM) then I might argue that that subject is too broad and you need to narrow it down. However, if you were to say you want to be the very best at the Dublin Core standard then that might be too narrow since the subject is so well established.

Value Analysis
So far we have documented an inventory of skills as well as your domains of interest. Now, we need to add the concept of value. Many authors use the word viability to define the long term sustainability of your unique value opportunity. How do you know if your unique value opportunity has value? One method is to determine if anyone else is doing this activity, especially if that person is a consultant. For example, in the metadata space there is a collection of individuals who earn a living consulting within this space. In fact, I can deconstruct my topic map and identify subject matter experts in every area. This would indicate that value is to be found within the neighborhood.

Another method is to apply some of the ROI models available. Industry has developed a myriad of models to address this situation. Most existing models for measuring knowledge assets and intellectual capital are motivated by research and practice in domains of accounting, economics among others. Many of them emphasize that non-financial measures which complement the financial measures. A key difference between the various models is in terms of the priority given to the measurement of human and social capital. Let's walk through the process of defining value from the strategic, economic, financial, and overall business impact.

Strategic Value
Your strategy must be appropriate for the available resources, environmental circumstances, and core objectives. The process involves matching your strategic advantages to the business environment that your unique value will face if implemented. One objective of an overall strategy is to put you into a position to carry out your mission effectively and efficiently. A good strategy should integrate your goals, policies, and action sequences (tactics) into a cohesive whole, and must be based on business realities. Strategy must connect with vision, purpose and likely future trends. Based on the inventory of skills completed in the prior section, we now need to understand how they fit into the overall strategic plan of personal development.

Economic Value
Economic value focuses on your ability to execute the strategic value defined in the prior step. Here you will see we tend to focus on the various options, critical success factors, and delivery options. The goal is to begin to layout out an understanding of how we would execute our area of interest. Economic valuation helps you to understand how difficult your journey will be in the future. You want to understand the different options and critical success factors that may come into play when developing your action plan.

Financial Value

Can you make money at this? Yes, there are plenty of reasons that we can define as a "Higher Calling" but the bottom line in business is can you make a profit. Economic viability is defined by your areas ability to generate revenue for yourself or the customer. There are plenty of resources out there for you to review that will go into exhausting details of financial calculations.

Business Impact

The final area of value opportunity is to define the business impact. Does your idea have a impact on the business? Not just a small impact, but are you offering something that will fundamentally change the way people see their environment? In many cases you will need to be able to answer the following questions:

- What is it and why should I care?
- What good happens if we implement your innovation?
- What bad happens if we don't implement your innovation?

Organizations live by their business model; the execution of a core set of business processes. You must be able, in clear and concise statements, define how you will improve or enhance their current strategy.

SWAT Analysis

In business we use a technique called SWOT (Strengths, Weaknesses, Opportunities, and Threats) to analyze the position within a particular market or to evaluate an opportunity. Knowing your strengths, weaknesses, opportunities and threats is a competitive advantage because you perform the research needed to define your roadmap or game plan. SWOT tells a company whether they should or should not participate in a given market. SWOT (pronounced SWAT) analyzes the internal (strengths and weaknesses) and external environment (opportunities and threats) in terms of a strategic plan, market, or opportunity. It's not difficult to use and it can provide a company with the insight needed to be competitive in the marketplace. SWOT can even be adapted and used by an individual to evaluate the internal and external environment at different stages in life or to evaluate career decisions. An individual will better know themselves in terms of strengths and weaknesses when the analysis is complete. Ultimately it is an aid to the understanding of one's self so they are ready for the next opportunity or threat that comes their way (Shade, 2005).

Strengths
In looking at your strengths, think about them in relation to others within your area, including those who you consider to be world class. Be careful not to confuse a strength as a necessity. A necessity or requirement is the price of entry. If you are considering Data Modeling then understanding ERWIN and Barker Notation is not a strength but a requirement just to be considered in the market.

- What advantages do you have over everyone else?
- What do you do better than anyone else?
- What do people in your market see as your strengths?
- What skills, essentials, and competencies do you bring to the table?
- What knowledge areas do you combine that generates insight?

Weaknesses
Weaknesses are much more difficult since it forces us to think of our problems. The importance of focusing on your weaknesses is to help you understand where other competitors could come in a seize your market share.

- What could you improve?
- What should you avoid?
- What keeps you from starting a business within your area?
- What are people in your market likely to see as weaknesses?

Again, consider this from an internal and external basis: Do other people see perceive weaknesses that you do not see? Are your competitors doing anything better than you? It is best to be realistic now, and face any unpleasant truths as soon as possible.

Opportunities:
One of the most interesting comments I get is people asking how and where metadata can be implemented beyond the traditional data space. What's amazing is that I see opportunities everywhere. My belief is that as your skills improve you too will begin to see opportunities everywhere.

- Where are the good opportunities facing you?
- What are the interesting trends you are aware of?
- Useful opportunities can come from such things as:

Opportunities may be ideas where you can expand or create markets. Think of things that you are currently not engaged or actively tracking.

Threats:
What obstacles or threats do you see over the next few years that might impact your area? Is there a new technology coming down that could redefine how you provide value?

Unique Value Opportunity
My unique value opportunity was developed over the past seven years of working in the Collaboration and Metadata space. The following areas or disciplines were used to establish the foundation of value.

- Metadata
- Enterprise Architecture
- IT Governance
- Data and Information Architecture
- Information Architecture
- Collaboration

115

- Reuse

When taken together these disciplines are combined into what I call "Enterprise Metadata" or "Metadata 2.0". The meta-discipline creates my unique value opportunity. Metadata 2.0 is taking the repository to the collaborative stage beyond the traditional unidirectional communication medium. Does this mean that all metadata is open for update by anyone in the organization? Maybe one day, but I would start by allowing people to test drive the collaboration components first. Take the typical repository and think about what collaborative type functions you could add on top of the controlled metadata. How about these:

- Discussions or Weblogs around Data Domains (i.e. Customer, Product, Order)
- RSS Feeds for notifications of changes to the environment
- Collaborative Lists for Data Steward Contact Information
- Wiki Based Data Definitions
- Self-Publishing Documentation
- Virtual Communities of Practice
- Online Meetings for Content Discussions

Each of these components keeps the traditional command and control model in place. Eventually, that too will break down and you will need to open up the repository to not only universal access but universal update. Metadata 2.0 describes how Web 2.0 advancements could and should be implemented into the knowledge environment. Success is moving away from the structured and un-structured to a conversation of value. Like Web 2.0, Metadata 2.0 is characterized by open communication, decentralized authorship, freedom to share information, and a market for the conversation itself. The purpose of describing how I'm transforming metadata is to show how you can alter any subject into a collaborative subject. Hence, we are creating a unique value opportunity.

If your area is unique enough, try to review the best of the best in another closely related subject. Why should you review the work of others? Clearly, you want to learn from the best of the best; how and why did they emerge as the voice or establish their expertise. Understanding their journey can reveal much about the path you will need to take and more importantly, what you will find when you ultimately get there.

One technique that I use, that might help guide you as a place to start, is to identify those individuals that are in my space or a closely related space. Within the metadata space, here are a few people that I keep close tabs on.

Metadata
- Adrienne Tannenbaum (Database Design Solutions)
- David Marco (EWSolutions)
- Stu Carty (Gavilan Research Associates)
- Robert S. Seiner (KIK Consulting and TDAN)

Related Topic Experts
- Sid Adelman (Sid Adelman & Associates)
- Peter Aikin (VCU and DataBlue Print)
- Davida Berger (DebTech)
- Joseph A. Busch (Taxonomy Stratagies)
- Joe Celko
- Ron Daniel (Taxonomy Stratagies)
- Larry English (Information Impact International)
- Marcie Barkin Goodwin (Axis Software Design)
- Michael Gorman (Whitemarsh Information Systems)
- Steve Hoberman (Mars)
- Claudia Imhoff (Intelligent Solutions)
- Bill Inmon (Corporate Information Factory)
- Ralph Kimball (Kimball Group)
- Dave McComb (Semantic Arts)
- Danette McGilvray (Granite Falls Consulting)
- Peter Morville (Semantic Studios)

- Louis Rosenfeld
- Len Silverston (Universal Data Models)
- Graeme Simsion (University of Melbourne)
- Tony Shaw (Wilshire Conferences)
- Bill Smith (William G. Smith and Associates)
- Academic Data Experts

These people are the experts in my field and I want to know what they are thinking, where they are heading, and what value are they creating. What do they offer in the form of products and services? What do they bring to their online environment? How are they marketing themselves? These questions help me understand the competitive environment and perhaps if I could bring the best of the best then I might be able to create a new competitive offering to the table.

Summary

We talk of skills as the foundation of employment and in today's world the majority of those skills are computer related. As technology continues to evolve, we must all stay focused on increasing our exposure. We must be honest with out evaluations in order to build a solid development plan. For most people, this can be a challenge in a world that still places more emphasis on your network versus you actual accomplishments. What are you good at? What are you passionate about? And, what is the value of impact of these things in the business world. You must be able to communicate this value to the world in a clear and concise message.

Did you discover what your are good at, what creates value, and what you have a passion for? Does your skill inventory and passion analysis align with this view of where you are going? The basic idea of this chapter is to get you to think about your value equation and how you are going to begin to develop that personal brand.

6

More business decisions occur over lunch and
dinner than at any other time, yet no MBA courses
are given on the subject."
- Peter Drucker

Networking Connections

oes it seem odd that we start with the one trademark class
that really doesn't have a physical representation that you
can touch and feel? The days of the fat rolodex sitting on
someone's desk are long gone and replaced with password
protected software. We all know people that are well connected.
These people get things done; they seem to know everyone in the
organization. Networking is a fairly easy thing to accomplish but
like most trademarks, you must develop the habit of networking in
order to deliver long term value.

Theme
The theme of this chapter is to make connections. Six degrees of
separation is the theory that all of us can be connected to any other
person on the planet through a chain of acquaintances that has no
more than five intermediaries. The theory was first proposed in
1929 by the Hungarian writer Frigyes Karinthy (1929) in a short
story called "Chains." In 1967, American sociologist Stanley
Milgram (2001) devised a new way to test the theory, which he
called "the small world problem." He randomly selected people in
the mid-West to send packages to a stranger located in
Massachusetts. The senders knew the recipient's name, occupation,
and general location. They were instructed to send the package to a
person they knew on a first-name basis who they thought was most

likely, out of all their friends, to know the target personally. That person would do the same, and so on, until the package was personally delivered to its target recipient. Although the participants expected the chain to include at least a hundred intermediaries, it only took (on average) between five and seven intermediaries to get each package delivered. Milgram's findings were published in Psychology Today and inspired the phrase "six degrees of separation."

The term networking was first used in the 1500's to describe the utilization of fishing nets versus the traditional line and tackle. What these early fisherman figured out that by using a net you could catch more fish in a shorter period of time; not to mention the least amount of effort. Today, networking has similar characteristics in that the best way to find a job is to utilize your network. In fact, 70% of jobs are landed through various forms of networking. One of the best success stories that I know of personally, is an individual that came to America with little more than a dream and technology skills. Today, he owns 8 businesses and perhaps the highest net worth in my inner circle. What makes this person so successful? His network and ability to utilize it on a daily basis is his secret of success. This utilization creates an environment where everyone looks at him as the go to guy in any project or program. Even though, 90% of the time someone else actually does the work. Now that's fishing with a huge net. What this person understands is that people need direction and his success draws you in to helping in these major projects. The interesting part is that his direction is not always right nor does his quick draw mentality always generate the greatest value. Still, doing something and learning from the experience is far better than studying the landscape for 3 months.

Networking is a lifelong relationship-building process that develops a wide range of interpersonal connections or contacts that you can contact or communicate. Networking is a social process that many of us are not very good at. This is especially true in the information worker where the skills of the introvert are valued higher than those with extrovert soft skills. Networks act as a kind of informal, highly customized, personal 'knowledge business yellow pages', providing a handy expert to fill in the brain-powered workers knowledge gap.

Benefits of Networking
There are many benefits to networking including:
- Allows you to communicate your message and value-add
- Allows you to receive insight and information from people who sincerely want to help you
- Enables you to help others; once people feel comfortable with helping there is no end in what they will do for you
- The size of your network allows you measure the penetration of your message
- Generates new ideas and innovate concepts when you can bounce your ideas off experts
- Develops life-long relationships with people
- Develop collaborative relationships where co-production emerges

Start with People You Already Know
The first step is to start with people you know which might include family, friends, associates, and professional acquaintances. This is the fun part of this exercise so go hog wild and include everyone you can think of including:
- School mates and Professors
- Former Employees or Managers
- Church Pastors and Members of the Flock
- Doctor, Dentist and Vet
- Insurance Salesman
- Neighbors
- Charity Committee Members
- Industry Conference Contacts
- Vendors
- Subject Matter Experts

This list could go on and on; the point is that you should start with people you already have some type of relationship even if you haven't contacted then in years. Where should you look for these contacts? No worries here; the network trails are everywhere: email, Christmas cards, family tree, church directory, organization charts and many others.

Information Collected
The key to collecting information is to not make it a pain to collect or manage. Also, you don't have to collect everything the first time you meet someone. Think of the three layers of information that you can collect and manage about someone in your network: contact information, context information, and relationship management information.

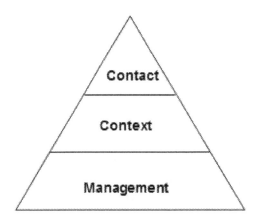

Figure 6.1: Layers of Information Collection

Each of these efforts can be layered upon each other. Unfortunately, the amount of effort required at each layer increases exponentially.

Contact Information
Open up your desk drawer and pull out someone's business card. The information held on that card is all you really need to stay in touch. While it may seem a little old fashion in this "beam me" your contact information world, you should always have a business card handy. The business card contains your name, address, phone, email, title, and even web address.

When ever you meet someone in a professional or personal setting, try to get as much contact information as possible. Business card exchange is expected and should be encouraged by all senior level management. Business cards establish the first form of communication. Just the simply act, creates a warm environment where you can express your interest in the other person. Ironically, this may not be the case in all organizations. Routinely, I have had to beg, borrow, and steal to try to get business cards printed over the past 20 years. I have even offered to pay the entire expense myself, if I could get my new address printed after a physical move. Sadly, management still looks at this type of effort as a perk for only the most important or highest ranked in the organization.

What if someone doesn't have a business card, then provide them with yours and ask for their email address. I have found that this is the easiest request that is rarely considered an invasion of privacy. Asking for someone's email address opens the door for other opportunities to collect elements of the contact information. Many people do an excellent job at providing information in their email signature. For example, here is one example of a signature that I got from an individual within our organization. Here, this person was willing to provide every conceivable contact information component.

John "J.J." Doe
BellSouth - Architect
AIO – Organization Group
Address Line 1
Address Line 21
Atlanta, GA 30308
ph: xxx-xxx-xxxx
fx: xxx-xxx-xxxx
email: john.doe @bellsouth.com
ipage: jdoe@imcingular.com
MySite (Personal Profile Page)

It is amazing how creative and informing an email signature can be if you pay attention. The key is to capture that information in order to retrieve it at the most opportunistic time.

Context Information

One of the issues with business cards is that you have very little context around how you received the contact information and the potential of the contact to integrate within your network. Each year, I attend as many as 15 conferences around the world. In each session, people approach me to ask questions, discuss points of conflict or establish a communication relationship. This communication relationship is critical to extending my network and I generally get 5-10 business cards per session. Over the course of a year, I can get as many as 100 business cards and contacts.

The challenge is to remember which session and what context this person approached me. In the same light, I approach great speakers as well to extend the business card olive branch. One thing that I try to do during the evening before going to bed is to write down a few things on the back of the card.

- How I meet the person
- What they seemed interested in
- What was expected of me
- What I expect of them
- When I promised to get back with them
- Who the common thread was during our conversation

Each of these questions addresses the context in which I met this person. First, I want to know what the context is when I met the person. Was it in a presentation session that I was presenting, one that I attended, or conversations after another speaker's session. Second, what follow up is needed? In most cases, there is no actual follow up required on an initial meeting. In other cases, the individual may need something from me. In the rare occasion, people will use my contact information to gain inside information about the organization. We all need to be wary of this type of networking abuse. Finally, I want to make a few notes on this person's expertise. As selfish as it sounds, I want to know what their level of experience and expertise is in case I need some information or guidance. I expect this person is doing the same with me.

While I have focused on a conference situation, the same is true with an online inquiry. When you become an industry expert, you will get numerous inquiries via email. Most of them are on the up and up, and I try to answer every inquiry within a few days. In the vast majority, people just want to know where to start or any insight to get beyond a sticky situation. In the past ten years, I can only name one occasion where the author asked a question that seemed out of bounds. The question was how do I implement metadata in my organization? While metadata is my area of expertise, it was clear the person hadn't put too much thought into the question nor the expectations from me.

Management Information
The final information collection level is the relationship management. Harvey Mackay is perhaps best known as the author of five business bestsellers, including Swim with the Sharks (Without Being Eaten Alive), Beware the Naked Man Who Offers You His Shirt, and Dig Your Well Before You're Thirsty. He is a nationally syndicated columnist, and one of America's most popular business speakers. In his first book, Mr. Mackay developed the MacKay 66 and the MacKay 33 for Managers. Both of these frameworks collect information about people. The first framework focuses on your customers while the second focuses on your employees. We live in a world where, even inside the corporation, we have customers, suppliers, managers, and employees. Here are some of the questions from the Mackay 66 profile.

Customer
1. Name; Nickname
2. Company name

3. Address; Home address
4. Telephone; Business; Home:
5. Birth date; Place; Hometown
6. Height (approx.); Weight (approx.)

Education
7. High school; Year graduated; College; Year graduated
8. College honors; Degrees
9. College fraternity/sorority

Sports
10. College extracurricular activities
11. If customer didn't attend college, is he/she sensitive about it?
12. Military service; Discharge rank; Attitude toward being in the service

Family
13. Spouse's name and occupation
14. Spouse's education
15. Spouse's interests
16. Anniversary
17. Children; if any. Names and ages
18. Children's education
19. Children's interests (hobbies, problems, etc.); Business Background

Professional
20. Previous employment: (most recent first); Company; Location, Title, etc/
21. Previous titles at present company, Title, Dates
22. "Status" symbols in office
23. Professional/trade
24. Offices held or honors
25. What business relationship does he/she have with others in our company?
26. Who are they?
27. Is it a good relationship? Why?
28. What other people in our company know the customer?

29. Type of connection; Nature of relationship
30. What do you feel is his/her long-range business objective?
31. What do you feel is his/her immediate business objective?
32. What do you think is of greatest concern to the customer at this time--the welfare of the company or his/her own personal welfare?
33. Does the customer think of the present or the future?

Special Interests
34. Clubs, fraternal associations or service clubs (masons, Kiwanis, etc.)
35. Politically active? ; Party; Important to customer?
36. Active in community? How?
37. Religion; Active?
38. Highly confidential/sensitive items not to be discussed with customer (i.e.: Divorce, AA member, etc.)
39. On what subjects (outside of business) does the customer have strong feelings?

Lifestyle
40. Medical history (current condition of health)
41. Does customer drink? If yes, what and how much?
42. If no, is customer offended by others drinking?
43. Does customer smoke? If no, object to others?
44. Favorite places for lunch?; Dinner?
45. Favorite items on menu
46. Does customer object to having anyone buy his/her meal?
47. Hobbies and recreational interests
48. Vacation habits
49. Spectator sports interest: sports and teams
50. What kind of car(s)
51. Conversational interests
52. Whom does the customer seem anxious to impress?
53. How does he/she want to be seen by those people?
54. What adjectives would you use to describe the customer?
55. What is he/she most proud of having achieved?
56. What do you feel is the customer's long-range, personal objective?
57. What do you feel is the customer's immediate personal goal?

The Customer and You

58. What moral or ethical considerations are involved when you work with this customer?
59. Does the customer feel any obligation to you, your company or your competition? If so, what?
60. Does the proposal you plan to make to him/her require the customer to change a habit or take an action that is contrary to custom?
61. Is he/she primarily concerned about the opinion of others?
62. Is he/she very self-centered?; Highly ethical?
63. What are the key problems as the customer sees them?
64. What are the priorities of the customer's management?
65. Can you help with these problems?
66. Does your competitor have better answers to the above questions than you have?

When you review Mr. Mackay profile framework, you will notice the importance he places on knowing what the customer is like as a human being, what they feel strongly about, what they are proud of achieving, and what status symbols can be found in their office. When you know your network to this level of detail then picking up the phone and having a conversation is easy. For example, a good friend of mine and I have worked together on and off for the past twenty years. At any point of the day, I can pick up the phone and call him to reflect on a shared experience. Over the years, he has helped me land great jobs and make additional contacts within the industry. The same is true about another business associate that loves to play golf. At least one a month, I can email him about some great shot hit or how the golfing Gods took revenge on me during the last round. Both of these individuals have help, enhanced and promoted my career.

Do you have to keep this type of management information on everyone you meet? The obvious answer is no, but think about this for a moment. If I were to ask you to complete the questionnaire on as many people as you can without contacting them, I would be willing to wager that we all could do 5-10 people.

As business people, we tend to rotate our co-workers but the people we are really too close remains. All of us gather data or have the opportunity to gather data; the question is if we take advantage of the opportunities when they arise.

Recently, I was invited to visit a vice president of the company. I as entered the office, I took a look around the office and picked up on a few things that might come in handy in the future as conversation points.

- Stock Certificates (The last three companies he had worked which were the same as my last three employers).
- Pictures of the Alabama Crimson Tide (As an Auburn fan, this provided more topics of discussion or controversy. Both invite commuication).
- Family (two sons like me)
- Thomas Friedman's Book (I had read two weeks prior to the meeting).
- Pictures of the BellSouth Golf Classic Pro-AM
- New Tablet PC (I had just converted three weeks prior)

Within 3 seconds, I had six topics of conversation that could be used to break the ice or start down a more collaborative road. At the end of the day, we are all just people doing a job the very best that we can. And believe it or not, we all would rather do business with people we know and respect. Having the ability to pick up or manage information about our network is critical to get the greatest value. The main thing to understand that what ever model you use for your network, you don't have to collect every piece of information or pepper the individual for their Birthday. Simply pay attention to the information you have and act upon it when presented.

Future State
Forming new habits take time and energy. Have you ever wanted to loose weight and vowed to exercise daily and change your eating habits? Many of us go through the New Year's resolution

ritual only to forget by early March what ever commitments we made. Researchers say that it takes 21 days to form a lasting habit. To place that fact into the context of this chapter, it will take 21 contacts in order to create the habit of networking.

The first thing we need to do is write down the word networking and post it somewhere you can see it everyday. If you sit at a desk then take a 3x5 Index card and write in big bold letters: "Networking Goals". Now, decide on how many people you will contact in the following categories:

1. Make new contacts that you have never communicated with in the past
2. Old Contacts that you haven't spoken to in a long time
3. Correcting a damaged relationship and repairing some conflict
4. Taking someone to lunch this week that you don't normally spend time with
5. Review the deluge of emails you get on a daily basis and see where you might have an opportunity to network
6. Update your Rolodex with at least X number of entries

This will take a few minutes of time during the day, so schedule that time into your day planner and keep it as a commitment. Remember, the 21 days are important so place that on your calendar as soon as possible. Once you have reached the 21 days, then don't let anything get in your way of your commitment.

There are three keys to forming new habits which include consistency, rewards and motivation. Networking has to be something you want, done regularly for a decent period of time (21 Days). The key for you is to find ways to integrate all three elements at once. Setting the calendar entry helps with the consistency and your career should be enough motivation. However, rewarding yourself is also a critical element in networking. The relationships will certainly be rewarding but I would still think of some reward that you can integrate into your networking routine. For example, you may set Rolodex goals where by when you reach that number you buy yourself a music CD or computer game. Another idea may be to institute an escalation type rewards like they do in my childs school. If he sells 10 rolls of wrapping paper he gets a flashlight, 25 rolls bags him a spy kit, and 50 rolls and we get a new CD player. While this may sound cheesy, keep in mind that your Rolodex is your future and the source of future income. So, don't get cheap on the rewards. Talk about it with your better half, and make these rewards substantive.

Gap Analysis
Where do you want to be and where are you now? These are fairly straight forward questions that should be asked by all of us. Technically, gap analysis is the study of the differences between two different information systems or applications, often for the purpose of determining how to get from one state to a new state. A gap is sometimes spoken of as "the space between where we are and where we want to be." Gap analysis is undertaken as a means of bridging that space.

Quantity and Quality Gap
Clearly, the number one gap that we can identify is the number of contacts we have and the quality of those individuals. Placing these two components together emphasizes the importance of not becoming the leaning tower of Pisa. You should never look at networking as a number game where your main focus is to increase the number of individuals you communicate with. While many people boast of a Rolodex of 5,000 names, there is no real way to stay in touch with that many people on a routine basis. Yes, you should increase your numbers but you should also focus on ensuring that those contacts are critical to the success of your game plan. In addition, you should ensure that you are important to their game plan as well. A relationship that is one sided will not last very long.

All that being said, you shouldn't focus 100% of your efforts on a single group of individuals for fear of over whelming them with your attention. There is a fine line between networking and becoming and pain in the behind. Perhaps the best example is to think about the different types of people that attend conferences. Every now and then, I will meet someone early in the conference and I can't get away from them. After a 15 minute conversation, we are now the very best of friends. They show up to breakfast, lunch and dinner. During the conference sessions, they will find the seat right next to me and continue the conversation we had during the break. Short of insulting the individual, I find it very difficult to shake a shadow. The point is that you should make contact and try to determine the level of interaction required and move on. What we are talking about is the art of the conversation. A wonderful antidote, recalls how a good networking professional will work a home and at the end of the night, you can't help but think that person is the smartest person in the room. However, a really great networking professional will make you think that "you" are the smartest person in the room.

Process Gap

What do you do when you meet someone for the first time? Based on what you have read so far, is there anything different you do? Even small adjustments can pay off over the long run. Study after study indicates that 80% of our emails / communications go to a small audience of co-workers or friends. Knowing this, I like to send follow up emails to people I meet within the organization. Of course, this is a good idea bit more importantly what happens to the email environment? That person's name is automatically, entered into the type ahead feature within Outlook. Say for example, I routinely send email to a co-worker by the name of John, Smith. Every time I key in smith in the email field, a drop down appears with John's name. In addition, every "Smith" I have emailed also appears in the list. This functionality serves as a gentle reminder of my network. A simple change in a process increases my network.

By my nature, I am more of an introvert type person that an extrovert. I tend to prefer small group communications versus large groups. Introverts seem to get energy from reading, studying or learning by themselves. Extroverts prefer people and the interaction of events. That being said, the world isn't black and white and introverts can act like extroverts on occasion. I know this is true since I regularly address large groups presenting keynotes and tutorials. I don't have to enjoy the process, just knowing that there are things in life that you must do, irregardless of the discomfort. Altering the process of your network is the first step in improving the basic utility and expanding the community.

After reading the prior sections, you could easily walk away with the "what's in it for me" mentality. Should you add or create a relationship when you are 100% sure that the person will never be able to be of service? Networking is more about what you can do for the community versus what the community can do for you. There are no scorecards in networking and you should never think that you need to get into a quidproquo with anyone. Perhaps Dale Carnegie said it best "You can make more friends in two months by becoming interested in other people than you can in two years by trying to get other people interested in you".

Managing the Network
After the initial inventory, you need to begin thinking about a management plan. Up until now, we have talked about what happens when someone pushes information at you but how do you operate the network once you have built it? How often should you contact someone in the network? Of course, that all depends on you and the amount of time that you have.

Each year, my wife and I send out a Christmas letter describing the activities of the family and what each member has been up to. We send out about 250 of these letters to friends, family and business associates. Over the past 12 years, not a single person has ever complained about the letter and most respond with positive feedback or comments. The letter serves as a high level summary of personal and professional activities within the family. Christmas cards, photos, and letters connect people that may not have the time to stay in touch. Many of the letters go to people we haven't seen in 10 years but in the world of networking, all contact is good contact.

You should take the time and place you network into various classification or describe them with metadata elements. One of the first descriptors is your comfort zone of talking to this person. There are many people that I have no issue of picking up the phone at any time of the day and calling. The same holds true with email; some people I will just fire off a comment or feeling just to get their response and start a conversation. Instant messaging and mobile devices create an environment where this is much easier than in the past. Here is an important point to make. We are all human and for some of us this effort doesn't come naturally. There is a tendency to talk ourselves out of meeting new people. When we enter a meeting room, we tend to look for familiar faces instead of trying to focus on the individuals that we don't know. Old habits are hard to break but you need to focus on the important aspects and long term value of your network. Learn the art of small talk; from the book *How To Do Just About Everything in the Office (Rosen, 2003,)* here are a few tips on small talk.

- Practice. Converse with everyone you encounter: cashiers, waiters, people you're in a queue with, neighbors, co-workers and kids. Chat with people unlike yourself, from the elderly to teenagers to tourists.
- Read everything: cookbooks, newspapers, magazines, reviews, product inserts, maps, signs and catalogues. Everything is a source of information that can be turned into interesting conversations.
- Force yourself to get into small-talk situations, such as doctors' waiting rooms, cocktail parties and meetings at the office. Accept invitations or host your own gathering.
- Immerse yourself in culture, both high and low. Television, music, sports, fashion, art and poetry are great sources of chat. If you can't stand Shakespeare, your dislike of the bard is also a good topic for discussion.
- Keep a diary. Write down funny stories you hear, beautiful things you see, quotes, observations, shopping lists and phone calls you made. That story about the time when the

operator at the call centre misunderstood you could become an opening line.

- Talk to yourself in the mirror. Make a random list of topics and see what you have to say on the subjects. Tennis, Russia, butter, hip-hop, shoes - the more varied your list, the better.
- Expand your horizons. Go home a new way. Try sushi. Play pinball. Go online. Paint a watercolor. Bake a pie. Try something new every day.
- Be a better listener. Did your boss say that she suffers from migraines? Has your doctor just had twins? These are opportunities for making small talk.
- Work on building up your confidence, overcoming shyness and banishing any feelings of stage fright. Remember, the more you know, the more you know you can talk about

10 Minute Conversation

You need to be able to communicate with people effectively and within a very period of time. As information workers, we are trained to get to the point as quickly as possible. We are trained that we may only have 30 seconds to get our point across. That being said, in most situations this isn't true. Learning the art of small talk can help your brand in so many ways. Suppose that I am at a technology conference and approach someone with the following ice breaker.

"Hi, I'm Todd Stephens and I do metadata"

Yikes, the vast majority of people have no idea what metadata is or why they should be interested in the subject. A better comment might be:

"Hi, I'm Todd Stephens and I perform the function of a librarian. We catalog technology assets and make them available to the business in the form of electronic card catalogs"

Who couldn't relate to a library and the card catalog? The key is to place the other person at ease and not intimidate them. Networking is like giving a speech. While it is essential that you come off relaxed and honest, you should never wing your conversations. Just as a great speaker thinks about what they want to accomplish, message they want to convey, and have a solid plan of what you want to accomplish. Before you attend a session or meeting, do your homework. Try to determine who will be there and what value they will provide. For an internal meeting, this information is generally published in the employee directory. Decide who you would like to meet and what you might say to open the door. Recently, I attended a meeting where one individual had the title "User Experience Director". As someone with a doctorate in human computer interaction, I was eager to discuss usability techniques with this person. I immediately went to Google to see if they were published in order to get some insight to their area of expertise. In addition, I had worked with an individual the year before that currently worked for this person. By placing a call to them, I was able to gain some insight into this person's interests and skills. Decide on what you want to walk away from the meeting with; a minimum would be the contact information.

Do what you need to do to remember the names of everyone you meet. Write them down on 3x5 cards or collect their business cards. I am the world's worst in this area. I am truly amazed at my sons Karate teacher. He can have a class of 40 students and knows each one of them by name.

Finally, be sure you follow up with the individual. An email thank you note is essential to provide your information to the individual. Let the person know that you enjoyed the meeting and thank them for any tips that might help you in the future. Everyone enjoys feeling appreciated so be sure to make a habit to thank people you meet.

Networking in a 2.0 World

Online social networks, such as Friendster, LinkedIn, and Spoke1, have rapidly acquired millions of users and assist them in forming new social or business contacts through those they already have. These existing contacts are either entered manually or gathered automatically, e.g., from email, instant messaging, and the web of trust for decentralized cryptographic keys (Adamic & Hogg, 2004). Online networks allow people to explicitly articulate their social network, present themselves through a Profile (interests and demographics), post public testimonials about one another, browse a network of people, and establish themselves as subject matter experts with features and answers from LinkedIn. Like any network, the environment must be managed in order to gain the greatest value. LinkedIn now boasts 10 million members and is adding 120,000 per week. Along with many other online networking sites, LinkedIn provides you the ability to crate, manage, and own your online identity.

One of the basic differences between the traditional business environment and the Web 2.0 is one of anonymity. The web allows you to become anonymous by created fictitious names or even organizations. Prior to the 2.0 environment, you could sing in the shower, talk to yourself in the car, or even have a family discussion without anyone else ever knowing your thoughts. Today, you can post it online and if it is outrageous enough, you will get enormous publicity. In some cases, great ideas emerge and catch a wave of momentum but many others do not. When you review blog posts, many authors simply use code names such as "Mike", "Peter J." or "/xx". People are more adept to share information when there isn't much of a chance to actually find out who they are. From a networking perspective, this can be a challenge. Most blogs to allow you to include a email or web address which can point back to your online representation.

Social Networks within the Enterprise
While social networking applications have taken off outside the corporations, many organizations have started to embrace internal networks as well. Natural teams form along lines of hierarchy, location, and areas of interest. For smaller organizations, social

networking can be accomplished by the "management by walking around" philosophy. Simply, walking around the office or floor, you can create networks.

In the Enterprise 2.0 world, the ability to walk around is limited since most of the work force is distributed. Today, employees may very well work in India or Georgia. With the advent of communications, we are able to work anywhere in the world. Additionally, more and more work is being moved to outsourcing firms which creates additional barriers for social networking. However, formal structure does not limit the informal networks forming on the basis of technology or personal interests. These network type structures are more prevalent in today's environment versus earlier periods when technology and communications were scarce. Organizations are providing several tools that enable the social aspects of virtual organizations. Many of these were discussed in Chapter three including blogs, wikis, and tagging applications. The one element not covered is the concept of a personal profile type application. Traditional employee directories include contact information, reporting structures, and human resource type information. In most cases, the employee has little control over the information presented. More importantly, they had limited ability to update the information and customize toward their interests or job function.

IBM's Bluepages is an excellent example where an organization has extended the employee directory to include more social networking components. IBM's intranet has been selected as one of "The Year's 10 Best Intranets" by the Nielsen Norman Group in 2006. Specifically, the report indicated "If the average employee directory is a hill, the IBM BluePages would be the Matterhorn . with a plethora of features and pertinent information, the IBM BluePages is probably the most robust intranet employee directory we have ever encountered" (Coyne, Nielsen, & Schwartz, 2006). The pages include information pulled from the employee database but also areas where the employee can update the information such as previous jobs, experiences, qualifications, prior projects or teams, and communities of interest. The system allows for tagging as well as global search which makes finding like minded employees a simple process. They are now moving this technology to a software solution that can be purchased called "Lotus Connections". Connections is social software for business that empowers you to be more innovative and helps you execute more quickly by using dynamic networks of coworkers, partners and customers.

Not to be out done, Microsoft has their own product for social networking that is embedded into their Sharepoint Portal software. In addition to the traditional social networking tools, SharePoint allows you to create collaborative workspaces, content pages, and both public and private views within "MySite".

Summary
The specific expectancies are attributed to the trustee based on the personal belief and institutional factors. The two drivers of the specific expectancies are the attributes of trust and incentives of both parties to participate in a trustworthy relationship. Researchers have identified five key attributes of trust, which include: belief, benevolence, integrity, openness, and predictability. The trustee must believe the other party has the ability to perform the task with or without confirmation of such ability. Seligman (1997) indicates that the ability to perform an action without confirmation of ability, character, or intentions is central to the definition of trust. Benevolence raises a judgment on the character of the other party. People that are thought of as benevolent are considered genuine and truthful. Individuals cannot be thought of as trustworthy if they are perceived as operating behind a façade or have a history of dishonesty (Arceneaux, 1994). Cannon and Doney (1997) describe benevolence as the extent to which a partner is genuinely interested in the other party's welfare and should be motivated to seek joint gain. The integrity is similar to the benevolence of the individual with the addition of respected values and keeping promises. This idea that people will act in a predictable fashion follows the core definition of trust by Gefen and Straub (2000). Expanding this view of predictability is the idea that trust creates a social environment in which business

function with or without contractual governance. Finally the idea of openness, which reflects good communications and the willingness to share information that will enable trust within the relationship, should be considered in the formation of expectations.

All things being equal, you will do business with people you know and trust. All things being unequal, you still will do business with people you know and trust. Networking has always been critical in the world of business and the advent of 2.0 technologies simply increases the need of communicating your trustworthiness.

7

If there's a book you really want to read, but it hasn't been written yet, then you must write it.
- Toni Morrison

Publishing Your Expertise

Publishing is by far the most important trademark that you need to develop. I challenge you to name one industry expert that hasn't been published or had someone else publish about them. There are no short cuts in the world of publishing and with the new media formats, you will have a much harder time in getting your voice out there. With 71 million blogs, 50 million mySpace accounts and millions of web sites, the communication noise is deafening.

Theme
The theme of this trademark is recognition. You must be recognized for your expertise if you are going to gain a competitive advantage. As the saying goes, even if you are one in a million there are still thousands of people just like you in the world today. Getting recognized as an expert in your chosen field is critical to your long term branding effort.

Over the past 20 years, I have come to the conclusion that no one really cares what you did five years ago or five years from now. Update your resume and take it into your boss and ask her what you did three years ago? What project did you work on that was the corporate priority in 2001? Why did you do to deserve that outstanding annual review? Assuming you still work for the same person which is rare, I doubt they will remember or can recall at a moments notice. Maybe you are between jobs; does anyone ask what you did five years ago in an interview? Our industry is very short term focused due to the changes in the business and technology. Reflecting on the past, as the saying goes, isn't what it uses to be. The point is that most of our work activities are temporal in nature; they have a limited value over a long period of time.

Amazon.com has millions books available for purchase and the vast majority of these are not best sellers. Chris Anderson (2004) wrote an interesting article on a concept referred to as the "Long Tail". The long tail is basically the products and services that have lost their "sale" ability within a geographical area. Online retailers can carry a much larger inventory than physical stores which allow them to generate more sales along the long tail of popularity. For example, Barnes and Noble bookstores carry around 120,000 titles while Amazon.com boasts 2.3 million titles. The obvious reason is that shelf space inside Wal-Mart, Blockbuster, and Books-A-Million is limited and these organizations only have so much real estate to display their products to the customer. This physical constraint forces organizations to focus their marketing and promotion on the top selling items. Online organizations do not carry shelf costs and therefore an additional item is simply an update to the online catalog. The advancements in technologies such as search, social software, and product comparison sites allow for more fragmented channels and niche products. Interestingly, 57% of the sales at Amazon.com come from titles not available at your local book store. This phenomenon seems to be true from books to application software. There are more than 4.5 million books in print, indicating even a published book, doesn't guarantee success. With Web 2.0, you can publish in just about any format including blogs, wiki's, slideshare, LinkedIn answers, and many others enable you to publish your ideas to millions of readers.

Obstacles of Publishing
Hardly a week goes by without a conversation with someone about publishing. I want to take some time to discuss the most common excuses for not publishing:

- I have too many commitments and I don't have the time
- This is not a good time to be trying something new; I need to focus on the job
- I don't have the talent to be an author
- I have nothing new to say or to add to the body of knowledge
- My grammar skills are horrible and I would be embarrassed

Limited Time
This is by far my favorite excuse of the lot. Time is an interesting commodity; people that make the worst use of their time are the same ones that complain that they don't have the time. I remember an individual telling me about all the activities they had going on with work, kids, and church. There simply wasn't anytime left to devote to enhancing their career. Yet within 6 months, this individual found the time to return to school and spend 20 hours on class assignments. The question that popped into my head was if you had 20 hours a week to spare why couldn't you have utilized that time over the past five years. Robert Hastings said it wonderfully "The great dividing line between success and failure can be expressed in five words: I did not have time".

Funny think about time, we all have the exact same amount of hours in a day. Yet, a few people simply get more out of their day than others. Some people focus on action while others wait to be acted upon. When one individual remarked their limitation of time, I asked them what they did during their lunch hour? Like many of us, this gentleman went to lunch with his co-workers on a daily basis. What would happen if he spent three days of the week working on an article? Those three hours could easily produce an article or several blog comments. How about the two hours you spend commuting everyday? They now have voice recognition software that actually records and converts your voice to text. The bottom line is that time is a choice that we must make. We choose to watch Desperate Housewives or that Auburn football game on ESPN. These are easy choices to make. It is much harder to sit in front of your computer after working 12 hours and dealing with the kids. The point is that you have the time, you simply need the motivation to allocate that time to what truly maters in your long term employability. Life begins at 60 has much more implications when you are talking about hours in the week.

Timing is All Wrong
If not now then when? A friend of mine published a small article in a local newspaper. He commented how late he was to the publishing game at 53. Of course, that's better than 63. We wish we had written up that project three years ago or the integration effort at our last job. Everything in life is a matter of timing. Success is a matter of timing, preparation (planning) and action (execution). There may be some ideal combination, but waiting for "perfect timing" will inevitably mean you never make a move, so finding the balance between planning and execution means finding the point in time which gets you on the road to success (Strickland, 2005).

The truth of the matter is that the perfect timing excuse is really a fear of failure. We all fear failure and we all regret things that we have done. However, most successes are built on top of failures. You will never get better at publishing until you dive in and learn from your mistakes. Conrad Hilton said it best "Success seems to be connected with action. Successful people keep moving. They make mistakes, but they don't quit." Failure is a natural consequence of trying, the difference is your perspective. In the academic world, I hear it over and over again: what if they reject my paper? So what you your paper gets rejected eight times? What happens when the ninth publisher accepts your article in an industry journal? Does anyone else in the whole world need to know of the eight rejections? No, all they need to know is that you are a published author. Since we are talking about a brand, you can keep the failure metrics to yourself but publish the successful ones. Like time, timing is a poor excuse for not publishing your ideas and thoughts.

No Talent

Who among us hasn't thought that we didn't have the talent or skills. At the age of five or six, I was playing pee-wee league football where my timid nature placed me as a tackle or guard. I can't remember how the running back got hurt but the coach asked me to run the ball since I knew most of the plays. To make a long story short, I wimped out because I didn't think I had the skills to do it. The coach's second choice did a great job and he continued to play fullback all the way through high school. That was a mistake that I never repeated. When I told people that I was going to back to school at the age of 36, not many supported the idea or could think of a reason for doing such a thing. While you may not be the next Hemmingway or Tom Clancy, you can write about your area of expertise. Albert Einstein once commented that didn't have any specific talents, he was simply inquisitive. The truth is whatever you lack in talent can be overcame with persistence and commitment. All of us have talent in spite of being told otherwise. Many of us grew up in families where achievement wasn't rewarded and talent wasn't allowed to blossom. Others of us were not pushed hard enough to discover those hidden talents and instead allowed to focus on conformity. The truth is that many people with average talent go further than those with great talent, simply because they have more drive and ambition.

Nothing to Say

You can't sit there and think you have nothing to say on technology, work, family, or politics. Everyone has an opinion on something. I will also say that you can never claim to be an expert in any field if you can't carry on a detailed discussion of the topic. I would argue that metadata is perhaps the dullest topic on earth but I have been able to write a monthly column as well as monthly magazine article on this very subject for well over 4 years. When you immerse yourself into the topic, you will never be at a loss for words.

Grammar is an Issue

Authors are not born they are created though trial and error. My English SAT scores kept me out of most major universities. This should be attributed to my lack of interest in the subject more than anything else. However, through perseverance and failure I have been able to publish books, book chapters, articles, and numerous academic publications. Grammar, spelling, and style can be aided by new software but you should always have someone help you with. If you don't know someone that majored in English then you can hire an editor or proof reader. For one of my first papers in school, I hired an editor and she did a very good job. Colleges and universities have plenty of starving English majors that need some side cash. They would be more than willing to help you in this area.

Getting Started

How can you get started writing about you topic of choice? The easy answer is just write, there is no other solution more important than just sitting down and pull a Nike; just do it.

State the Obvious

The first step is to write down what you think everyone else already knows. The "Dummies" series of books are not ground breaking work nor introduce new information that hasn't already been said 1,000 times. The real innovation comes from delivering the same information that everyone else has been publishing but in a user friendly way. The goal of any publication is to have the reader understand the topic. One of the biggest mistakes we make in academic writing is that we write for the top 1% of the readers. Papers won't get published it they are not groundbreaking. Unfortunately, this misses a great opportunity to educate and expand the body of knowledge. One of the best transformations away from this type of thinking is Harvard Business Review. In the 80's, Harvard Business Review was a painful magazine to read and really was only of use for the elite of the business world. Today, the magazine is perhaps the best business reference out there.

Writing about what we think everyone else knows helps us form thoughts and trains us to write in an understandable way. The truth is there is always someone that doesn't understand the obvious and instead of looking down on them, we should try to educate them. Over the past four years or 48 issues, I have written a monthly column about one of the simplest technologies in the world. That would equate to over 150 pages musing over the topic of metadata. The truth is that I write about things people already or have experienced. For example, the following excerpt was taken from my May article of 2004: The Metadata Experience.

What is "The meta data experience?" Over the past 20 years, I have come to realize that meta data is not a technology but a philosophy. While we tend to focus our efforts around the "data about data" definition, the reality is that meta data spans much further into the multitude of dimensions around information technology. Perhaps the easiest way to think about these dimensions is to relate them to the four different sectors of business: raw materials, products, services and the experience. For example, the coffee business can be segmented into these four different areas.

Pine and Gilmore (1997) open their discussion of "the experience economy" by tracing the value added to the coffee bean in its various iterations from pure "commodity" to pure "experience." In their evolutionary construct there are four stages - in ascending order of sophistication the stages are commodity, good, service, experience. They point out that coffee is traded on the futures market at roughly $1 a pound (thus, about 2 cents a cup at the "commodity" level). After manufacturers roast, grind, package and distribute the bean for retail, the price jumps to between 5 and 25 cents a cup (the "goods" level). At a "run-of-the-mill" diner a cup might run from 50 cents to $1 a cup (the traditional "service" level).

Pine and Gilmore contend that one can, "Serve that same coffee in a five-star restaurant or espresso bar, where the ordering, creation and consumption of the cup embodies a heightened ambience or sense of theater, and consumers gladly pay anywhere from $2 to $5 for each cup." Thus, by creating value at the "experience" level, the seller is able to charge an extremely high premium over that charged by the "service" provider. In defining their terms they argue that, "When a person buys a service, he purchases a set of intangible activities carried out on his behalf. But when he buys an experience, he pays to spend time enjoying a series of memorable events that a company stages - as in a theatrical play - to engage him in a personal way.

The article took a concept that is an everyday occurrence and applied it to the core technology of metadata. The raw material was associated with the metadata information that describes the variety of assets in the technology community. The product was associated with the metadata repository or registry. The service was associated with the huge collection of add-on services our group applies to the environment including metrics, project management, naming standards, operations, security and many others. The "experience" was a designation of integrating collaborative or Web 2.0 functionality to the environment which would bring the producers and consumers of metadata into a single frame of mind. Just as Starbucks does for the "third place" designation, we developed another dimension of metadata delivery and truly expanded the body of knowledge. Stating the obvious is not a bad strategy for building a portfolio of writing topics.

Applying Frameworks
Personally, I am a visual type person and I seem to think, dream, and remember in snapshots of time. When I see an image or pattern, I tend to remember that much more than text or video. Frameworks are visual models that represent ideas such as the Zachman Framework, or Michael Porter's Business Model framework. You can hardly pick up a magazine or book that doesn't have a framework worthy of review. Can you apply this framework to your area of interest and provide a different way of thinking about it? Many technologists are more logical or numbers oriented but that needs to change. Visual learners prefer graphs, pictures, and diagrams. They look for visual representations of information, data, and knowledge.

Take for example a simple sitemap. Most organizations simply list core pages arranged alphabetically as can be seen in my own site map shown in Figure 7.1.

Index:		
Academic Portfolio	Feedback	Reading Favorites
Articles	Future of Information	Reading Room
Biography	Home Page	Resume
Blog	Interview	RSS Feeds
Blog Overview	Languages	Speaking
Book	Library	2002
Branding IT Programs	Metadata Experience	2003
Curriculum Vitae	News	2004
Data Professionals	Online Articles	2005
Developing Trust	Patents	2006
Downloads	Portfolio	Teaching Philosophy
Enterprise Metadata	Privacy	Top 10 Designs
Enterprise Reuse	Professional Portfolio	Usability and Design

Figure 7.1: Sitemap for http://www.rtodd.com

However, other organizations like Dynamic Designs make a living by taking the logical representation and presenting that same information in a more graphical model.

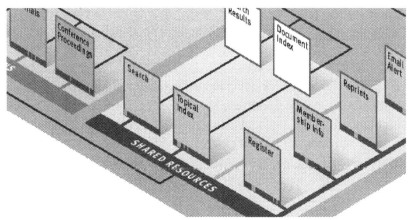

Figure 7.2: 3-D Model of an Online Environment

Here, the company has depicted the entire environment in a simple to understandable model. The three dimensional model of the content and functionality communicates more about the environment than the alphabetical listing.

Real World Events and Experiences

Another option for writing is to write about your experiences. One of the things that I hear over and over again is the universal applicability of the authors experience within the areas of business, technology, or volunteer lessons. For me, I see metadata everywhere. Have you ever thought about what life without metadata would be like? Not the traditional database metadata but retail metadata; the kind of metadata that appears on every product inside Walmart, Kroger, and Publix. Imagine a simple bottle of Bayer aspirin where the metadata on the box includes the manufacturer, ingredients, volume, quantity, directions, safety warnings, etc. Open the box up and there is an insert with even more metadata on how and when to use the product. Not to mention, the bottle repeats much of the metadata on the box; only smaller print. Imagine walking into your local Kroger grocery store and as you enter the store all of the traditional taxonomies have been removed since product classifications are a form of metadata. The isle signage has been removed and replaced with emptiness. The only thing you can see are the blank containers designed for the products themselves. Let's suppose you need a can of soup to go with Saturday's dinner. You grab a can and begin to shake it in hopes that the weight and movement can provide you some indication of the contents. Is it tomato soup or a can of beans? Perhaps, this is a can of peaches or mixed vegetables. Ok, maybe you're an experienced shopper who can distinguish between soup and other products; is it chicken noodle soup, vegetable soup, or clam chowder? Frustrated, you head over to the dried goods area but your problems don't seem to fade away. This time you pick up a blank box which may contain laundry detergent, dish washing cleaner, or cereal. Of course, these uncertainties have little impact as compared to the pharmacy where you may be taking Viagra or Tylenol for your now, splitting headache. Can you imagine any business that would actually run their store in such a manner? Can you imagine any retail environment without the information or information architecture required to do business? Neither can I, but the real world offers a litany of subjects to write about and experiences to draw upon.

Co-Authors

You don't have to go it alone. Writing can be one of the loneliest times and professions to enter. I remember leaving school after the doctoral core curriculum was complete. My fellow students left the university to enter the isolated world of writing a dissertation. It was essential to stay in touch with the people within your class to help motivate you to stay focused on the goal.

Many people look at writing as an overwhelming activity that requires years to complete something of value. Co-authoring may be an option, if you find someone that shares your level of commitment. I can't tell you how many times I have had someone signup to help write a book or paper, only to see them drop out once the hard work started. However, co-authors can cut the effort and time as well as provide you someone to bounce ideas off of. The communication alone may be of tremendous value to you as a publisher.

After several years of going solo in my writing, I decided to contribute a book chapter to an academic book. In December of 2006, the book "Architecture of Reliable Web Applications Software" was published. The book presented new concepts regarding the reliability, availability, manageability, performance, scalability, and secured-ability of applications, particularly the ones that run over the web. My chapter focused on my subject matter of enterprise metadata. I joined 15 authors to publish a truly wonderful book. Based on that success, I went on to contribute to books on Open Source, Virtual Workspaces, and Web 2.0. Bottom line is that co-authorship is another option for those that want to get published.

Simple Rules for Writing

Philip Bourne (2005) published a great list of ten simple rules for getting published. While his rules were applied to the field of Biology, we should be able to adapt them for the information worker.

Rule 1: Read Tirelessly

One of the keys to becoming a better writer is the ability to know when your material is good enough to be published. Notice, I used the phrase "good enough" versus perfect. Reading quality work will help you in your writing, not only in the idea generation but your ability to communicate in an effect way. I highly recommend the Harvard Business Review magazines, academic journals and books. These sources have great writers and in most cases, the authors understand how to communicate their message in a clear and concise manner. Everyone one is a critic, so you should become one yourself. Send the editor a note or comment about the article and see if they will publish your response in the following issue. Being able to recognize quality work will help you becoming more objective in your own writings.

Rule 2: Objectivity is the Key

Most authors seem to fall into two camps. The first camp is for those of us that are way too harsh on our writing and the second is not being harsh enough. By reading other authors, you begin to develop a sense of what quality is acceptable. Needless to say, academic writing is different than professional writing; the levels of critique are very different. Perhaps, you can develop both styles and expand your portfolio even more. In the past, I have used my wife and fellow students as readers to get a sense of quality. They also help me judge if the message is coming out clear and understandable. This is very important for all authors. When we write we tend to write to a certain level of knowledge and understanding. This can be very dangerous in our own field of study. Remember, you are the expert and no one else in the world has your level of knowledge. Clarity is essential as well as your ability to lead the reader to your conclusion with stories and analogies.

Rule 3: Find a Good Editor and Reviewer
Most academic publications will have predefined editors and they can be cruel. Never submit research that you haven't read 100 times as well as had someone else review the material. You don't want to be rejected for grammar or spelling mistakes. While reviewers can be cruel, they can also be fair. When I was working on my dissertation, I always remembered my response when the first feedback came in; I was pissed. After awhile, I realized that they were improving the dissertation not hurting it. Their comments were not personal but constructive. It may be hard to accept that kind of feedback but I will tell you, just accept it and move on. Keep your eye on the bigger prize of getting published.

Rule 4: Take a Writing Class
If you don't write well then take a class or continuing education program. The best papers are those in which complex ideas are expressed in a way that those who are less than immersed in the field can understand. Have you noticed that the most renowned scientists often give the most logical and simple stimulating lectures? This extends to their written work as well. Note that writing clearly is valuable, even if your ultimate career does not hinge on producing good scientific papers in English language journals. Submitted papers that are not clearly written in good English, unless the research is truly outstanding, are often rejected or at best slow to publish since they require extensive copyediting (Bourne, 2005).

Rule 5: Learn to Live with Rejection
Let us clear up one thing from the outset. **YOU WILL BE REJECTED!** Make no mistake about it; rejection is part of the game. Every author has been rejected. Dr. Seuss's first children's book was rejected by twenty-three publishers. The twenty-fourth publisher sold six million copies and Dr. Seuss died having known his perseverance resulted in entertaining, challenging, and educating millions of children. If a reviewer or editor rejects your work for poor quality then learn from it, build on it, and improve on it. There will always be another conference, another

publication, or another book. The only person that can force you to quit is you.

Rule 6: Ingredients of Good Writing
What does it take to produce a good article, research paper or even a book? Clearly, something novel or innovative can push you material over the edge. We can see this idea in recent books like *The Long Tail* by Chris Anderson or *Blink* by Malcolm Gladwell. Other authors will tell you to ensure that you have supporting research like Jim Collins had with his groundbreaking book *Built to Last*. More importantly is your ability to make your writing interesting. Not many authors can get away with a writing style that is designed to confuse and make it impossible to understand. In 1687 Newton published *Philosophiae Naturalis Principia Mathematica*, surely the greatest scientific book ever written. The motion of the planets was not well understood before Newton, although the heliocentric system allowed Kepler to describe the orbits. By design, the book was written to be difficult to read unless you happen to be a mathematician.

Rule 7: Start Now
The best time to have started writing your publication was yesterday and the worse day will be tomorrow. The bottom line is that writers write, developers code, and painters paint. Dreamers and wanna-be's think about it. Here are a few famous quotes on writing that seem to make the point very well.

> "One hasn't become a writer until one has distilled writing into a habit, and that habit has been forced into an obsession. Writing has to be an obsession. It has to be something as organic, physiological and psychological as speaking or sleeping or eating." - Niyi Osundare

> "If you're going to be a writer, the first essential is just to write. Do not wait for an idea. Start writing something and the ideas will come. You have to turn the faucet on before the water starts to flow." - Louis L'Amour

"Successful writers are not the ones who write the best sentences. They are the ones who keep writing. They are the ones who discover what is most important and strangest and most pleasurable in themselves, and keep believing in the value of their work, despite the difficulties." - Bonnie Friedman

"Writing is easy: All you do is sit staring at a blank sheet of paper until drops of blood form on your forehead." - Gene Fowler

Ok, maybe it's not that bad but the point is you need to write and there is no better time than right now.

Rule 8: Become a Reviewer
Without a doubt, reviewing other peoples work will help your writing ability. Start with others writers in your field. Believe me they will appreciate the help. Writing a monthly article or journal paper is a huge challenge and authors will appreciate your help and feedback. Once you have established yourself as an Industry expert you may be asked to sit on award committees or chair conference panel discussions. This type of event can be an enormous opportunity for you to get your ideas into the minds of others.

Rule 9: Set Goals
As they say, goals are dreams with deadlines. You need to take time to think about what you will publish on and the related topics. In addition, where these concepts will be published is just as important question that needs to be asked. In the persona chapter, we will take a deep dive into the production of long lasting publications but for right now, let's just say that not all publications are the same. Just as interesting is your audience may dictate the critical locations for publication. For instance, I have found that academics rate journal publications and patents high, while professionals rank books and conference proceedings high.

Opportunities to Get Published

There are a plethora of opportunities to get published outside the organization as well as inside. Many of these will be covered in detail in Chapter 9.

Professional and Academic Opportunities
- Conferences
- Journals
- Magazines
- Letters to the Editor
- Newsletters
- Books
- Textbooks
- Community Service or other Volunteer Efforts

Web 2.0 Opportunities
- Weblogs
- Wikis
- Social Networks
- Ranking, Rating, and Reviewing
- Posting Content (Slideshare)

Enterprise Opportunities
- Organizational Newsletters
- Patents
- White Papers
- Collaborative Technologies
- Intranet Publishing
- Industry Awards

Publishing in the New Media

Getting published in the new media is easier than ever. While there are plenty of choices, we are going to focus on the Weblog. In Chapter eight, we will spend some time discussing usability and the user interface. Here, I want to focus on how you can write an effective blog from a content and metadata perspective. When you understand the basic concepts of metadata, you begin to see a larger picture where how you write something is as important as the content itself.

Metdata Tags
By now you have a real good idea of your topic or area of interest. What are the keywords that are best associated with it? Keep these handy and use them when ever possible. This is especially true in the title of the blog post. For example, suppose I wanted to post something about writing blogs. I could say "Helpful hints in writing blogs" which would be better than "Writing Hints". What about "Effective Writing Techniques in Web 2.0 including Blogs and Wikis"? Here you have highlighted terms like "effective", "writing", "web 2.0", "blog", and "wiki", all of which are great keywords in the social software area. The same holds true in the post itself, utilize your knowledge and embrace the usage of keywords and key phrases.

Another example of effective utilization of metadata is to choose your keywords or classification words effectively. If subject matter experts are using the term XML then you should do so as well. Even though you prefer Extensible Markup Language, stay with the masses on this one and utilize XML. When I first got started, I was a purist, and assumed people wanted to locate information based on tags that fully represented the subject matter. So I used "Enterprise Metadata", "Human Computer Interaction", and "Reusable Architectures" to represent my posted content. I realized that I wasn't generating any traffic because people couldn't find the information I was providing. Eventually, I realized that "Metadata", "HCI", and "Reuse" were far better terms. Sometimes you have to go with the flow to stay in the game.

Keep in Short and Simple
It goes without saying that people prefer to browse content versus actually reading and trying to comprehend every word. While I am guilty of not doing this very well, you should try to keep you posts to a paragraph or two. Learn to write in a succinct, clear, and

effective manner. If you can say it two sentences then do so, wordiness isn't a virtue in the online environment. If you have more to say then try to break up your posts into multiple posts which will not only help your readers, you help yourself by increasing the possibility of an external link or Goggle result.

Utilize links and images where possible; this will help in the Goggle race to the top. Images shouldn't be any larger than a quarter of the page; you can always link to the image in a PDF or PowerPoint document.

Use Microsoft Word

Unless you are an English major, use a word processing program that can check your spelling, punctuation, and grammar. While programs like Microsoft's word isn't perfect it's better than trying to write in a text editor. The reason for using Word is to ensure that people don't get distracted with you writing ability but stay focused on your content. People sometimes have habits that create patterns; you see this is public speaking all of the time. When people get nervous or need to pause to think about what to say next they tend to use words like "Um". One senior level person at our company always used the phrase "the fact of the matter is". It got so bad that people would actually count the number of times that the phrase was used. This meant that the actually content was ignored. The one thing you need to be careful of is transferring the content from word to the editor. For my software program, the apostrophe never translates well and is replaced by special characters. So "You shouldn't comment on the Customer's" gets translated to "You should@*t comment on the Customer@*s". The point is to work around the short comings of your software or application as best you can.

Mixing Media

One of the techniques that I use is to actually mix the media. For example, each month my column appears in a trade magazine. The very same day the online environment reflects the new content then I will update my site. In addition to the web environment, I update my blog to reflect the new information as well. If you are counting, that would be seven different references to a single column.

- Placed on the home page for two months
- Added to the Monthly Column inventory
- Converted to PDF and posted online
- Article is announced on the News page with links
- Article is announced on the Weblog with links
- Original article can be found on the web page of the magazine
- Article is published in the magazine itself

It's All About the Content
At the end of the day, your blog is all about the content. You want to demonstrate your passion, commitment, and expertise in your area of specialty. Remember, people will judge your blog by the ideas and innovation they find. This keeps them coming back time and time again. You should try to post two or three times a week to keep the content fresh. Take a look around at the other people posting about your subject; are you unique or simply spitting out the same information? You have the experience and you have the knowledge, so utilize the blog to present that voice. Develop a sense of personality and know what your readers are looking for.

Utilize other techniques like bulleted lists. People love lists, top ten this and top ten that. Some people have written books with the sole purpose of producing lists. Mark McCormack was great at this and his book collections make great references for anyone that wants to know how to write with lists. In the spirit of Mr. McCormack's style, here are ten things you need to remember to blog effectively:

1. Simplicity and Clarity at all times
2. Post 2-3 times a week
3. Stay on topic; other topics may be interesting but people come to you for your expertise not political opinion
4. Collaborate and link to others

5. Use proper grammar and spell check. Read Twice, Publish Once
6. Metadata Rules; understand the impact and relationship of good metadata practices
7. Demonstrate your passion, understanding, and commitment to the topic
8. Find a niche; all great blogs have one
9. Encourage comments and clean up the spam
10. Add your personality, experiences, and vision to the topic; Be the Leader

Summary

There simply is no better way to establish your expertise than to publish your ideas and thoughts. Regardless of medium, you have the opportunity to communicate to the largest audience ever in the history of mankind. Every day, the Intranet and social applications grow which open up new opportunities for communicating your expertise. This chapter focused on providing you with some best practices and ideas to move beyond the writer block. The key is simply to write and write; ensure that you get in the habit of developing the written word.

8

There is no on so bound to his own face that he does not cherish the hope of presenting another to the world.
- Antonio Machado

The Persona Principles

Throughout the process of writing this book, I have patiently waited to write this chapter. My excitement and enthusiasm for this area has no boundaries. This may be the most critical aspect of building your trademark in the 21st century. This chapter will focus on building the core building blocks for communicating your brand: personal website, blog, Curriculum Vitae (CV) or Resume. All of these communication mediums will be the cornerstone of your message. You may be world class in your area but if you can't communicate that in a professional manner no one will know. You might lose your chance for the job, for the contract, or for the recognition that you deserve. This single chapter can't tell you everything you need to know and the truth is that you must get into the game or hire the best to do it for you. Please don't skimp on the investment of time or money in order to deliver your message to the world in a clear and professional manner. Simply put, you will lose the game of attention.

Theme

The theme is obvious; perception. Here are the cold hard facts; people will have a perception of you. Your boss has a perception. Your co-workers have a perception as well as your employees. The only real question is that perception managed, developed, and maintained by you or is it based on a collection of random events. Here is a silly question, would you rather be perceived as the world greatest knowledge expert on X but the truth is that you're only slightly above average or the other way around? Personally, I can fix the first one by working hard but changing perceptions is near impossible. This chapter is about building that online communication medium that will define you as an industry professional.

18% of Harley owners are willing to get the brand logo tattooed in places that are better left unsaid. Branding is the process of developing, guiding, and managing the perceptions of the organization. Selling, marketing and branding yourself is about creating a perception of value. You or your organization will have a perception, either by design or by default. What does your management or architecture community think of your program? What have you done in the last three weeks to impact or alter that belief? Can you create a yellow page ad for who you are? The totality of your brand includes the visual, emotional, rational, and cultural image associated with you as perceived by your customers, suppliers, management and architecture community. The whole idea is to manage the total package and value-add of the program.

Universal Resource Identifier (URL)
The URL is the unique identifier that serves as an address to your online environment. There has always been questions on what makes a good URL or web address so I'll add my two cents. First and foremost, you want the ".com" extension irregardless of the type of business you will be in. The main reason is that by default, people will assume a ".com" address even if you specifically state the address is one of the many other suffixes available like ".net" or ".org". My first URL I purchased was www.inc2.net. This first attempt wasn't bad; it was short, easy to remember, and allowed me to get in the game. Unfortunately, I could never get the .com so I had to give it up.

Another suggestion is to try to keep it below 12 characters. This is clearly not a hard and fast rule, especially with the advent of

Google and the other search engines. The reason for the limitation is that you want an address that most people can easily spell. While shorter than 12 characters, many people would struggle to spell Reveleus, which is a technology consultant company. Other examples might include: Semantix, Fortent, or Inxight. These are all great companies but they chose names that are a challenge to spell. The good news is that if you get the spelling correct it's very easy to be number one on the Google search engine. Many web experts are also suggesting that you try to invent a word that would place you in the forefront of the search engines. I struggle with this suggestion since made up names may not represent who you are and what value you bring to the world. That being said, if you have time and can break into the culture you could turn ziggybytes.com into a household name like Amazon and Yahoo.

What about "cookies.com", is this a great URL or what? On the surface, this sounds like a great domain name and well worth the enormous expense. The problem with this domain name is that it doesn't work very well in the search engines. Search engines perform over 200 million searches per day. If you purchased the cookies.com and customers searched on your business name, "cookies", the odds of you coming up in front of Mrs. Fields, Pillsbury, and the Keebler Elves are slim to none. Common names are great when customers want to type directly into the address bar of the browser but they are terrible when utilizing search engines. A better name might be CookieTrails or CookiesByDesign. These names add context to the search which may be more valuable than having a simply name like cookies.com. The key is simplicity; can you create a memorable domain that is unique or context specific?

When searching my own domain name, I took a look at "ToddStephens" but not only was that owned by someone else, the results set was well over a million. Another Todd Stephens, a film director, seemed to own that keyword set. This would take a lot of work to move in the top ten results. Since 2nd grade, I have always used my middle name. In the context of business, I differentiated myself by referencing my first initial followed by my middle name (R. Todd). Wouldn't you know it, rtodd.com would be available in

3 months. The domain rtodd.com was simple, short, memorable, easy to spell, and created context in the search engines. Think of other successful businesses that have used context and simplicity in their names: JetBlue, SouthWest, IBM, Starbucks, and Applebees. The Internet is well over 10 years old, so domain names can be a challenge to locate one that fits you or your business. Keep in mind, there are many people that are willing to sell you domains names since that is why they purchased them in the first place. The previous owner of http://www.rtodd.com actually allowed the domain to expire and I simply picked it up on the open market. What ever name you pick, spend some time on it and ensure that you believe in it and what it represents.

You can check the availability of your domain and step through the registration process at several different places.   In fact, most hosting companies will guide you through the process. A couple of resources that I have used in the past include:

- Register.com (Availability and Registration)
- Network Solutions (Availability and Registration)
- Great Domains (Buy or Sell Domains)

Another service that might be of interest is domain backorder. When you register a domain you pay the fee for a specific time period; 1-3 years. Many people allow these domains to expire and companies will allow you to back order the domain which means you get first shot and the purchase once the expiration date had passed. What are some good examples of URL's that other trademark professionals are using to brand their products and services. Here are some of my favorites:

- http://www.tompeters.com
- http://www.jimcollins.com
- http://www.stevehoberman.com/
- http://www.answerthink.com/
- http://www.davidco.com/
- http://www.lexonomy.com/

- http://www.thomaslfriedman.com/
- http://newparadigm.com/
- http://www.danpink.com/
- http://www.harveymackay.com/

Each of these sites represent the owner or founder of the business. They are also really great examples of design and ease of use that will be covered later in this section.

Getting Started

Ok, you have registered you domain name and are ready to proceed, now what? You are going to need a hosting company where your site can be stored. In most cases, this can be obtained for $8.00 - $12.00 per month depending on the amount of services or add-ons you might need. A web hosting service is a type of Internet hosting service that allows individuals and organizations to provide their own websites accessible via the World Wide Web. Web hosts are companies that provide space on a server they own for use by their clients as well as providing Internet connectivity, typically in a data center. Web hosts can also provide data center space and connectivity to the Internet for servers they do not own to be located in their data center, called co-location.

The scope of hosting services vary widely. The most basic is webpage and small-scale file hosting, where files can be uploaded via File Transfer Protocol (FTP) or a Web interface. The files are usually delivered to the Web "as is" or with little processing. Many Internet service providers (ISPs) offer this service for free to their subscribers. People can also obtain Web page hosting from other, alternative service providers. Web page hosting is typically free, advertisement-sponsored, or cheap. Web page hosting is generally sufficient only for personal web pages. A complex site calls for a more comprehensive package that provides database support and application development platforms (e.g. PHP, Java, and ASP.NET). These facilities allow the customers to write or install scripts for applications like forums and content management. For e-commerce, SSL is also required. The host may also provide a

Web interface control panel (e.g. cPanel, Hosting Controller, Plesk) for managing the Web server and installing scripts as well as other services like e-mail. Some hosts specialize in certain software or services (e.g. e-commerce).

Personally, I have used a variety of hosting services over the years including:

- Alentus Corporation
- Living Dot
- A couple that are no longer in business or have been bought out

Software

Discussing software is like discussing your favorite football team, everyone has their preference. For the personal computer, the two leading applications include Frontpage and Dreamweaver. Personally, I have been using FrontPage since 1999 and can honestly say that it is a great tool. Both Dreamweaver and FrontPage are WYSIWYG (What You See Is What You Get) web page editors. For basic web page development, either one will do the job. Most software developers will say to start with FrontPage but move to Dreamweaver as your skills progress. I say, if you are not going to become a web developer then FrontPage will work just fine. You can build really solid sites with this tool which include several built-in components that can make your life much easier like the include pages, reporting, metrics, and impact analysis. One warning is that your hosting company will need to be able to host the FrontPage extensions in order to access these add-ons.

The design tools in FrontPage 2003 generate efficient and clean Hypertext Markup Language (HTML), and give you more control over the code. Or you can use the scripting and coding tools to create an interactive experience for your audience.
Here are a few features that FrontPage excels in:

- Use a split view to see modifications made in the Design View automatically updated in the Code View.
- Select, modify, and manipulate tags easily using the Quick Tag Selector and Quick Tag Editor.
- Simplify code writing and make it less prone to errors with Microsoft IntelliSense technology. The technology is available for HTML, cascading style sheets, XSLT, Microsoft JScript, and Microsoft ASP.NET.
- Remove extraneous code generated by Microsoft Word or other Web authoring programs.
- Enhance interactivity on your site without writing a line of code by using behaviours to author JScript.
- Take advantage of support for IntelliSense and scripting tools for authoring JScript and Microsoft Visual Basic Scripting Edition (VBScript).

The next version of FrontPage is called SharePoint Designer. SharePoint is a collaborative solution that integrates Web 2.0 technologies with traditional Internet delivery. Think about the traditional Internet communication medium. Information is controlled by a few people but published to a world-wide audience. SharePoint is a collaborative application that integrates some of the Web 2.0 functionality into an easy to use environment. The cost of hosting a collaborative site is less than $30.00 which is small price to pay for Web 2.0 integration.

Simplicity in Design
Web sites don't have to be complicated to be of value. Do consumer products define success by the complexity rule? What about the IPod? The IPod has a simple interface that does one thing exceptionally well; play music. The IPod is more expensive and has less features that most MP3 players but who cares? Those trademark white earphones are everywhere. The Google interface isn't overloaded with ads or links; just a search box. The interface simplicity hides the complexity of the network, search algorithm and infrastructure. The key is to hide the complexity behind an interface of simplicity.

Usability

Usability is a term that has been batted around more and more these days. This is a great sign, especially for the world of branding. What is Usability? Other terms such as usability testing, information architecture, human factors, or human computer interaction all basically point the focus of how the individual interacts with the application. Mark Pearrow (2000) provides a great definition:

> Usability is the broad discipline of applying sound scientific observation, measurement, and design principles to the creation and maintenance of applications in order to bring about the greatest ease of use, ease of learnability, amount of usefulness, and least amount of discomfort for the humans who have to use the system.

Clearly, usability is an important aspect of application delivery. One might even go so far as to say usability is an imperative to the long term success to your brand development. But why is it that some applications are not very usable? It would short-sighted to think that software developers don't care about the end user or that the release schedules don't allow time to apply a few design principles. Unfortunately, the reasons go much deeper than that.

1. Usability is a moving target. The principles of usability keep evolving as the world-wide-web becomes more pervasive. Design principles that worked five to ten years ago won't make in today's world. Perhaps we can thank companies like Amazon.com, Dell, Ebay, and many others for continually raising the bar.
2. Application vendors spent an enormous amount of time on functionality. Functionality and utility is what sells the product. Unfortunately, it's usability that creates the environment usage of the entire organization and not just for a small set of power users.
3. We still live in a world where complexity rules the day. Products, solutions, trends, fads, and methodologies that

168

are complex and layered with confusion still sell while simple solutions are overlooked. Simplicity should be one of the driving forces application development.

4. Most people assume they are usability specialists. Perhaps our egos get in the way of admitting that we need help in the visual placement of information and the construction of a solid information architecture. In the development of web environments, I tend to agree with Clint Eastwood. The environment is littered with the good, the bad, and the ugly. And like some super bowl half time shows, the good is getting harder and harder to find.

5. Upper level management won't make usability a priority. This is astonishing since 68% of us find it difficult to locate information and 50% of us spend more than 2 hours a day searching (Frappaolo, 2003).

Design Elements
There are various schools of thought on which design elements make a successful web site. Scanlon, Schroeder, Snyder, and Spool (1998) collected qualitative and quantitative data on key design factors, which included: searching, content, text links, images, links navigation, page layout, readability, graphics, and user's knowledge. Each of these design elements makes an important contribution to a successful website. Websites are built to provide information or sell a product or service. Experts indicate that usability is about making sure that the average person can use the site as intended. Well chosen names, layout of the page, text, graphics, and navigation structure should all come together to create instantaneous recognition (Krug, 2000).

Becker and Mottay (2001) developed a usability assessment model used to measure a user's experience within a web environment. The authors defined eight usability factors, which included page layout, navigation, design consistency, information content, performance, customer service, reliability, and security. Usability and design can play an important role within the electronic commerce market. Design consistency has been defined as the key to usability (Nielsen, 1998). Karvonen (2000) reported that experienced users admitted to making intuitive and emotional decisions when shopping online. Some users simply stated, "If it looks pleasant then I trust it". Even if developing trust is not that simple, the research clearly shows how important design is in the area of trust. There are a variety of web design elements that can have a positive impact on a website's image, effectiveness, and trustworthiness. Design elements like well-chosen images, clean and clear layout, careful typography, and a solid use of color can create an effective site. In addition, a solid navigation structure and continuity in design can provide the user with the control and access required within an electronic commerce interface (Andres, 1999). Although, design elements may take on the form of a visual cue, the true value comes from a combination presentation, structure, and interactivity. A solid website is a collaboration of design, content, usability, and a back end system that is integrated into the processes of the business (Veen, 2001). Krug (2000) defines a set of tools as location indicators, which are design elements of the site that tells the user where they are. This can be in the form of a page name, header, sitemap or page utility. The page utility should be used within a list type program, which allows the user to know where they are within the list of elements. Indicators like "Page 1 of 12" can be extremely helpful informing the user of their location. Nielsen (2000) describes the need for the user to know where they are, where they have been and where they can go.

In this section of the research paper, the researcher will review six basic design elements that encompass a web design.

Page Layout
The page layout is the visual presentation of the web page by means of background color, white space, horizontal and vertical scrolling, font size, color combinations, and other deign elements (Becker & Mottay, 2001). Graphical layout is a prime consideration in the design of a functional website. Designers must consider the font size and placement, scrolling versus hypertext linkage, sentence and paragraph lengths, and several other factors that are logically integrated into a structure (Palmer, 2002). Page layout is one of the strongest contexts used by designers today.

These layout-based contexts have grown or evolved based on the experience of web designers and the current user base (Veen, 2001).

The majority of web pages can be broken down into the parts that make up the screen real estate. Nielsen (2000) indicates that the content of a web page should take up to around 80% of the screen real estate while the navigation structure should be around 20%. Nielsen's description is at a very high level, by breaking down the contents of a page design we can see that the designer has many other elements to contend with.

The web designer's ultimate role is to place these elements into a page layout that works for the first time user, intermittent, and frequent users of the website. Shneiderman (1997) provides a clear understanding of the importance of design on these three categories of users. "First-time users need an overview to understand the range of services and to know what is not available, plus buttons to select actions. Intermittent users need an orderly structure, familiar landmarks, reversibility, and safety during exploration. Frequent users demand shortcuts or macros to speed repeated tasks, compact in-depth information, and extensive services to satisfy their varied needs."

By structuring a web page into a familiar convention, the user will be able to scan the more easily and faster. Every publishing medium develops conventions and continues to refine them and even develop new ones over time. The web already has several conventions derived from newspaper and magazine standards (Krug, 2000). Generally speaking, the top section of a web page is used for branding and site navigation. The left-hand side navigation section is also used to provide the user a more detailed navigation structure than can be provided within the top sections. The use of a blue font color and underlining for external links is a convention that most web pages use. These are a few of the page layout conventions used today and with the newer technologies and additional designers these will no doubt change over time. Another convention is the differences in the home page and the other informational pages within the site. The home page is the most important page on any website, getting more views than any other page (Nielsen & Tahir, 2002). Designers should understand the differences and needs of the users for both of these page layouts.

Navigation

The concept of navigation covers a broad spectrum of concepts described in the current literature. Eismann, McClelland, and Stone (2000) describe the navigation structure as a framework for providing viewers the information required to know where they are and a method of getting where they want to go. In addition, navigation quickly becomes intuitive when you use consistent treatment, placement, weight, and behavior of navigation web elements. Navigation is a goal-centered and action-oriented activity that revolves around the user experience. A navigation system should be easily learned, consistent, provides visual feedback, appear in context, offer alternatives, and provide an economy of action and time (Fleming, 1998). Nielsen (2000) defines navigation as the basic user interface by which users click on navigation links or icons in order to move around the site. Navigation in this context should be able to answer the questions:

- Where am I?
- Where have I been?
- Where can I go?

A solid navigation structure is important since it is easy for users to get lost in web applications because there is less structure than in other applications. Page design can help a user keep track of where they are. As a best practice, Meehan and Shubin (1997) indicates that the use of clear and consistent navigational aids like page names, logos, banners, icons, background color act as visual clues for the user. Morville and Rosenfeld (1998) published:

> "The foundation of almost all good information architectures is a well-designed hierarchy. In this hypertext world of nets such a statement may seem blasphemous, but it's true. Hierarchy is ubiquitous in our lives and informs

our understanding of the world in a profound and meaning way." (p. 65)

A web application is a series of nodes that are linked together. These web applications can also be linked together and the combination of all of the web network nodes make up the World Wide Web (WWW). Within the web environment, four key information structures exist. Figure 8.2 provides an example of each of these structures.

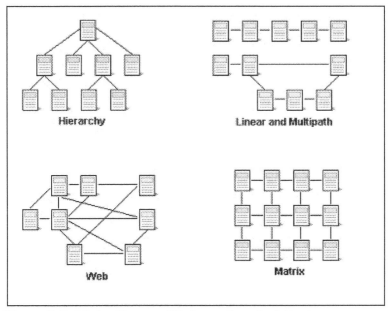

Figure 8.2: Major Types of Information Architecture

The hierarchy structure is by far the prevalent structure on the web. The reason for this is because human beings naturally order their world by establishing categories and subcategories (Farkas & Farkas, 2000). The navigation system should be constructed in order to replicate this structure and provide a cognitive approach to the information architecture defined within the web. A navigation scheme that works should be consistent. Users who rely on the navigation framework will begin to predict the location of the navigational elements and performance will improve over time (Fleming, 1998)

Consistency
As Fleming (1998) indicated, navigation should be consistent as well as the design of the entire web application. Shneiderman (1998) defined eight golden rules of interface design. The first rule is the designer should strive for consistency. The actions of the user should be very consistent as related to specific activities. Identical terminology should be used in the navigation, menus, help screens, and prompts. In addition, the designer should be consistent in the selection of color, font, layout, and the use of headers. Every major button, icon or navigational instruction, should have only one meaning. This meaning or function should not change within the web application. When designers fail to develop consistency in the application, user confusion, and frustration will follow (McClain & Sachs, 2002).

Design consistency is the consistent placement of page components within and across the Hypertext Markup Language (HTML) pages. Various components of a web application require a level of consistency. These components can range from the textual descriptions and labels to the error messages that are presented to the user. A level of consistency with the links, background, and text give the impression of a professional designed web application (Becker & Mottay, 2001). Consistency influences learnability positively when a design is consistent within the web application. A consistent application will impact the performance of the end user. The main source for improving the consistency of an application is the design knowledge of the developer (Eliens, Veer, & Welie, 1999).

Consistency is nothing new in the world of design. A newspaper is an excellent example of design consistency. The name of the newspaper is located at the top of the page with the lead stories taking the front page. The front page will also contain a table of contents, which can lead the user to additional sections of the newspaper. Like a newspaper, the consistency built in the web application can help the reader understand the content as well as the information architecture.

Web Style
A web style guide is a collection of principles, guidelines, and conventions brought together into a single medium and present a consistent look and feel (Ohnemus, 1997). Although style guides have a history in the documentation field, in this context the researcher focused on issues of the formatting, structure, graphics, color, and fonts. These are some of the broad categories defined by Forsythe, Grose, and Ratener (1996). The objectives of a style guide are to promote visual and functional consistency, promote good design practice, and reinforce the organizational brand (Gale, 1996). The Cascading Style Sheet (CSS) is one of the technologies on the web that helps to enforce a certain style consistencies. Although HTML encompasses font and layout, keeping the level of consistency needed in good design is difficult. The CSS is a powerful tool for specifying how the content should look. For example, the CSS can specify the size, margin, font, and type for header text (Veen, 2001). This look and feel for the header text will be consistent throughout the site unless overridden by a browser or the HTML code. Style sheets have two main advantages over HTML only based applications. First, CSS separates the content from the design. The content markup reflects the logical structure of the information and the style sheet provides the presentation instructions. Second, the style sheet provides efficient control over large document sets (Horton & Lynch, 1999).

Graphics
Faulring, Morrison, Pirolli, Rosenholtz, and Woodruff (2001) provided research comparing search engines where the results were presented in text and enhanced images. The enhanced image view provided the best and most consistent performance. Nielsen (2000) indicates that the use of graphics should be minimized due to the download requirements. However, users want to see images of the products to get a sense of the context in which they are being offered. In order to determine which graphics are important and

175

needed within the website, McClain and Sachs (2002) provide the following principles:

- Does the graphic highlight a feature on the page and does the graphic draw the attention of the user?
- Does it make a feature more usable, for example, illustrating how to use a specific function or color combination?
- If associated with content, does the graphic enhance the user's understanding, similar to the way photos are used in articles?
- Does it reinforce the brand?

If the image does not fit in these criteria then the graphic should be removed in order to increase the download speed. Good design and usability indicates that images should be reused where appropriate, sized based on function, and alternative text-only methods of access provided (Siegel, 1997).

Content
The main reason customers will come to your site is for information or content. The content of a website is not limited to the subject, product or services provided. Rather, content includes the solutions and strategies employed to make it easy for the user to accomplish important tasks, such as information retrieval, search, and navigation required in making a purchase, and obtaining feedback (Calongne, 2001). Becker and Mottay (2001) define information content to include timely and correct error messages, prompts, button labels, textual description, help, and customer service information. For a global perspective, web designers should be careful not to lose specific meaning in the translation or the use of specific symbols such as the shopping cart. The website gives an organization the ability to present almost limitless information on their product or service. This information or content should include the product and service quantity, quality, and relevance to the customer (Palmer, 2002).

Writing for the web is an important aspect of web-based content. Nielsen (2000) defined three core guidelines for writing for the web. First, information content should be succinct. Information provided on the web should be about 50% less than the information printed in a document. If additional information is required the user should link to a document or another web page. Second, the designer should write for scannability and not require the user to read long continuous blocks of text. Morkes and Nielsen (1997) reported that 79% of users simply scanned web pages versus actually reading line by line. Based on this research, articles should be structured with two to three levels of headlines. Finally, web designers should use hypertext to break up information into multiple pages. Keevil (1998) indicated that users prefer writing that is concise, easy to scan, and objective in style. In addition, the following guidelines can enhance a users experience within a usable website:

- Adding tables of content and section summaries;
- Adding bullets, numbered lists, and headings;
- Using boldface and colored text to highlight keywords;
- Writing shorter paragraphs, and
- Removing buzzwords and marketing objectives.

Effective content writing is one of the most critical aspects of all web page design. Most users will simply scan online content, rather than carefully reading each line (Nielsen & Tahir, 2002).

What content you put on your site will reflect your level of maturity in developing your trademark. You may start with just a vanity page of introducing yourself and describing your area of interest. Over time, you should be able to grow the content and built the online environment from the ground up. The content on my site falls into the following categories:

- Home Page: Overview, Latest Updates, Blog, and Featured Publications
- News: Current and Historical News

- About: CV, Resume, Roles, Responsibility, Projects, Programs, and Biography
- Speaking: Current and Historical Sessions, Handouts, Slides, Topics and Feedback
- Library: Books, Podcasts, Articles, Monthly Column, Downloads, and Interviews
- Portfolio: Academic and Professional Publications, Patents, and Dissertation Artifacts

Other items of content include the sitemap, privacy policy, book reviews, and other related content or sites of interest. There is no such thing as the perfect site. This site has evolved over a long period of time and will continue to evolve as I learn more and my trademarks change.

Building a Search Friendly Site
How do you create a search engine friendly site? Unfortunately, there are many different search engines that use a variety of different techniques. Let's review some of the techniques of improving your site ranking.

MetaTags
It isn't mentioned much in most Web design and development books. The vast majority of people will give you that deer in the headlights look when you bring the subject up. Without it, you have a snowball's chance in the south of succeeding in the world of electronic commerce. What is it? Allow me to introduce one of the newest members of the metadata family. Metatags are not exactly new, but they really came to the forefront in the early 2000s. One of the issues people have been struggling with is the ease and success of the Internet. There is simply too much information with only a limited ability to find what information you are looking for. A simple search for "metadata" delivers 2,380,000 hits. I think my site is in that list, probably number 2,125,361. The bright side of this is that you will only have to hit the "next" button 212,536 times to get to me. Undoubtedly, most of these hits won't provide you with even the basic understanding

around the concepts of metadata. The metatag is not only part of the problem but also part of the solution.

Metatags can fall into two categories. Site tags define characteristics for the entire site and are usually found on every page with identical values. Page tags are specific for each page being described. Metatags play a critical role in the development of web sites. Metatags can assist in the process of knowledge management by cataloging information and organizing content. This information can document the relevance of the document without actually reading the content and attempting to interpret the meaning. This, in turn, allows for greater management of the web site (Watchfire 2000). Over the past 20 years, software has grown extremely complex and difficult to maintain. HTML is now approaching the same complexity and growth. Even today, Web sites are becoming a burden to maintain. Some of these problems are physical in nature while others are not.

It sounds like metatags are a great idea. Well hold on, there are several authors that disagree. Danny Sullivan (2003) of Search Engine Watch describes the death of the metatag in his October article. Saying "Given that Inktomi is the last major crawler to still support the meta keywords tag, I don't think it was worth the time or bother for many Web masters to use." In a recent study, Hodgson (2001) presented information that 84 percent of the Web pages that contained metatags and comments contained little or no semantic content. Why are the search engines now looking away from the metatag? Metatags are part of the HTML source code that is invisible to someone viewing your site in a browser. Search engines can see them and in the early days used them to position sites. Unfortunately, this was an easy way for people to take advantage, and soon search engines had to adjust their algorithms to use the content of the site, not just what a programmer or optimizer wanted them to see. The point is that the metatag is a great idea that was simply abused. The search engines realized they couldn't trust the information placed in the tags.

Cross Linking

Google is one of the most popular Web search engines at this time. But getting your site indexed is just one step to getting promoted by Google. You need to improve your ranking in order to show up higher in the Google search results so that people actually find your site. While there are no "magic bullets" to improving your Google rankings, there are ways to help make sure that your site looks okay to the Googlebot. Combine this with some luck and some cross linking and you'll get higher ranking in Google (Kyrnin, 2006). That is to say, that you should strive to look for people that can link to you and your content. The more people link or associate you with an area of expertise the higher ranking you will have. At one point, I owned the term "Enterprise Metadata". I always appeared number one and two. Eventually, I lost that lead to IBM and BEA but that's not bad competition.

Content Techniques

Taken at face value, much of the Web 2.0 removes the technology barriers to publishing information. As stated before, you can utilize free Blog and Wiki services that virtually eliminate the need programming expertise. This means that the information or content you provide will be the sole determinate of your credibility. With blog technology, you can author a paragraph, click a button, and it's posted on the Internet. No need for visual design, page design, interaction design, information architecture, or any programming or server maintenance. Prior sections of this chapter disputed that but let's move forward. As with any content you publish you should put forth some thought and effort on what you're going to say and how. Page titles, headers, and blog titles should be clear and concise. Readers should be able to understand what you're writing about simply by reading the title. This is critical if readers come from aggregator of content, like Technorati where only tags, titles, and the first line of content are presented to the user.

Each and every month, I review my site statistics in order to see what terms or keywords people are locating my site with. A good metric system can tell you a lot about the people accessing your content. Anyway, inevitably the search phrase "Stu Leonards" is in the top ten. Just to be clear, I have no association with Stew Leonards which is a grocery store in the northeast part of the United States. One month, I wrote an article that misspelled the companies name but apparently a lot of other people do the same. The point is to select your page titles, blog entries, image descriptions, and headings strategically so that you can draw in customers or interest. I see nothing wrong with making a list of 15-20 keywords and ensuring that you use them in your content regularly. Why not do some name dropping; authors don't mind and you might get some second hand traffic. The point is to use the content as a means to generate traffic and enhance your search results.

Other Items for Persona Representation
All of us will face job transition throughout our careers whether through new opportunities, buyouts, layoffs, or the impact of globalization. Most of us spend countless hours thinking and acting upon metadata in our jobs. But, how many of us think about our personal metadata? The metadata of you is critical to manage like any other metadata and fortunately, we already have a collection of repository meta-models to choose from: Resume, CV, Portfolio, and extended online models. Like all other metadata efforts, personal metadata has an enormous ROI opportunity, when done right.

Resume
When was the last time you updated your resume? Last year? Five years ago? Basically, if you don't update your resume every six months then you may be losing the value of your personal metadata. What happens when your metadata goes out of date in the data world; your value-add goes to zero. The resume is a snap shot in time which is constrained by a page limit imposed by tradition. For those that publish a lot, this may seem like a hindrance. There are a million formats out there and most include: identification on every page, objectives, qualifications, education, employment history, and certifications. Personally, I try to keep this information on the first page which allows me to highlight

specific accomplishments and organizational impact on the second page. Figure 8.3 provides the page layout for the resume and includes the high level section headers.

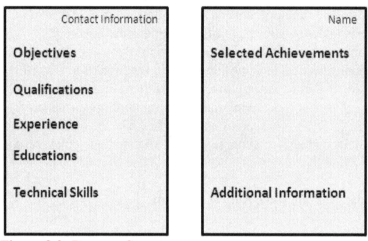

Figure 8.3: Resume Structure

These accomplishments will underscore both my skills and competencies. Skills focus on the knowledge of "what" I can do including specific tools, techniques, or business processes. Competencies focus on "how" I perform the different roles and responsibilities assigned. The skills and competencies focus on the information or knowledge work we have performed over the past decade. This format works well since it provides a single page reference of who I am as well as the differentiation elements of success on page two.

Curriculum Vita (CV)
The CV is the academic equivalent to the resume with the major exception that the CV has no page limit. In fact, most people pride themselves on the length and work very hard at extending it. The major sections of the CV include: education, research interest, honors, awards, experience, books, publications, patents, service, and associations. The CV is obviously more comprehensive than the resume and presents accomplishment over the long haul. More importantly, the CV provides the professional another way of

reviewing the progression of their career. For the first 15 years of my career, the resume was the tool of choice but something happened in 1999. I can't remember why I converted my resume but I did and the results were sad. From a two page resume plus 15 years experience, I got…. drum roll please…. a one page CV. That was an eye opener for me. How could it be possible for me to have worked in IT for 15 years and have such a great resume but have such a lousy (empty) CV? That revelation changed my career planning model and how I evaluate myself in a high performance world.

The point that had escaped me was that new jobs, responsibilities, promotions and organizational changes made only small incremental improvements in the CV. What I needed to do was to focus my attention, not on the corporate ladder, but extending the CV with long-term value-add additions. For example, the addition of a patent to your portfolio places you in a unique club. No matter what happens in the corporate environment, with globalization or industry consolidation, you will be part of history. More importantly, no one can ever take that accomplishment away from you. After reviewing hundreds of CV samples, this is the framework that seems to work the best. Figure 8.4 provides the page layout for the CV and includes the high level section headers.

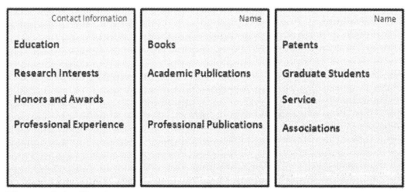

Figure 8.4: CV Format

Portfolio

Most of us know the secret of a great interview is to take control from moment you walk in the door. If you can take control of the interview then you can guide the interviewee to your strengths and successes while secretly avoiding your weaknesses. The only person I can remember that successfully took control away from me was a college graduate who walked into the office with a leather bound portfolio. This young man understood what every artist, actor, and model understands; the portfolio is a powerful weapon. Every time I asked a question on his background he was able to open his portfolio to a page and take a deep dive into his strengths and I was mesmerized. The secret is the power of the written word. While I didn't have a job for that young man, I will never forget how far ahead he was of the curve and I'll bet today he is a huge success.

The portfolio is a collection of articles, awards, or any physical evidence of your success. Do you have a logical model that would work in demonstrating your expertise or would you rather just keep on trying to use meta-physical descriptions? What better way to demonstrate your expertise in Data Warehousing other than by reviewing the press release of your previous organization winning the Data Warehousing Institute Best Practices Award. Any physical representation of your work could be moved into a portfolio and considering the current job environment, this may very well be an advantage for you. Consider that a few years ago InfoSys had 9,000 job openings in India with one million applicants (Use your best Dr. Evil voice). Not too many years ago, one job opening here would produce a thousand resumes. Maybe a portfolio is not such a bad idea in a highly competitive environment.

Why are these tracking system important and more importantly, why should we invest so much time in them? In the global economy, these are the products that represent you. They represent your very soul and value-add to the world. They create an environment of trust; people must trust you and what you represent. Trust is the central component of business and it's more important in a world that can be described as meta-physical. In the physical world, I could count on prior employers to provide a good reference but with HR and Legal issues, you can expect a luck warm recommendation, at best.

Trust and Influence
Trust is a concept that most people understand but have trouble defining. Brick and mortar companies establish trust by providing personal service, one-on-one contact, and creating an environment that communicates trust to the customer. In the electronic commerce environment, many of the face-to-face experiences a shopper receives from the physical store are missing. The online shopper must develop a level of trust based on the web representation of the company or organization. Only through good experiences are the bonds of trust solidified, making the user more comfortable sharing information and engaging in extensive forms of commerce. With online commercial transactions, the user is vulnerable to two specific trust violations: the loss of money in the transaction and the loss of privacy with the information provided (Friedman, Howe, & Kahn, 2000).

Trust plays an important role in any customer relationship or transaction. This is especially true in the world of commerce. Buyers and sellers must make a conscious decision whether or not to trust the other party. Trust is an integral part of commerce and has been in existence since the beginning of human social interactions. Most aspects surrounding trust are embedded in the social contact between the two parties or institutions. A buyer trusts the seller will deliver goods or services based on experience or "word of mouth". The seller in return trusts the buyer will pay for services rendered. Commerce trust can be defined in terms of uncertainty, risk, and vulnerability of the transactional relationship (Cannon & Doney, 1997).

The online world differs from the face-to-face world in several ways that are relevant to trust. Specifically, the online world lacks the dimensions of character and personality, nature of relationships, and institutional character on which we normally rely to form an attitude or base decisions about trust. Therefore, a framework of developing trust in an online environment is required in order to form the trust needed in electronic commerce. Christensen and Tedlow (2000) define the Internet as a collection of disruptive changes in the way retailers conduct business. The business model of the average discount department store has a margin of 23% with an inventory turnover of 5 times per year. The business model for an online vendor produces a margin as low as 5% and a turnover rate of 25 times per year.

Researchers have identified five key attributes of trust, which include: belief, benevolence, integrity, openness, and predictability. The trustee must believe the other party has the ability to perform the task with or without confirmation of such ability. Seligman (1997) indicates that the ability to perform an action without confirmation of ability, character, or intentions is central to the definition of trust. Benevolence raises a judgment on the character of the other party. People that are thought of as benevolent are considered genuine and truthful. Individuals cannot be thought of as trustworthy if they are perceived as operating behind a façade or have a history of dishonesty (Arceneaux, 1994). Cannon and Doney (1997) describe benevolence as the extent to which a partner is genuinely interested in the other party's welfare and should be motivated to seek joint gain. The integrity is similar to the benevolence of the individual with the addition of respected values and keeping promises. This idea that people will act in a predictable fashion follows the core definition of trust by Gefen and Straub (2000). Expanding this view of predictability is the idea that trust creates a social environment in which business function with or without contractual governance. Finally the idea of openness, which reflects good communications and the willingness to share information that will enable trust within the relationship, should be considered in the formation of expectations. An example of the type of information that would be valid in the formation of trust within a business relationship would include consumer feedback, financial information, pricing policies, and information from neutral resources (Lundgren, Seelen, & Walczuch, 2001).

Risk and vulnerability are two essential features of trust. Trust involves a vulnerability occasioned by some form of ignorance or basic uncertainty as to the other's motives (Seligman, 1997). In other words, vulnerability refers to the susceptibility of being taken advantage of by another party. In the absence of vulnerability, trust is not required since the outcome of the relationship cannot do harm. Trust must stipulate that at least one party has something meaningful at stake and is cognizant of the potential harm. There must exist the possibility of exit, betrayal, and defection (Bigley & Pearce, 1998). Risk is a function of the level of uncertainty perceived and the stakes involved. Risk is one of the core conditions considered essential in the psychological, sociological, and economic definitions of trust. Once again, trust would not be needed if the actions of the two parties could be undertaken with complete certainty and without risk (Burt, Camerer, Rousseau, & Sitkin, 1998). In summary, trust is the willingness to be vulnerable under conditions of risk and interdependence.

Design and Usability are Irrelevant in Web 2.0
Wait! I can hear every reader out there saying that in the Web 2.0 world design and usability are not big issues. The contribution will be based on the value of the content not the look and feel. Of course, that's why we buy a Lexus versus a dune buggy because we only want to get to point A to point B. Please, give me a break; you can't honestly believe that.

Imagine for a moment that web communications is like owning a home and the original web was like living with your parents. If you didn't know how to landscape a yard then you just cut it as your Dad told you to do. If you didn't have an inkling of interior design then that hand-me down furniture with neon posters worked fine. If you didn't understand the architecture of remodeling then you shared a bathroom with your three sisters. Same thing with Web 1.0 design and usability, if you didn't understand Human Computer Interaction, HTML or Metadata then you stayed at home and used whatever your management told you.

Early or Pre 2.0 applications like discussions threads or community sites was like leaving home and renting an apartment. Of course, you felt the freedom and exhilaration of being on your own and being able to say and do whatever you wanted to do. However, you couldn't change the infrastructure even if you had skills in design, the landlord would have kept that 2 month security fee. Rules were everywhere; no parking, no parties, no noise, no boats, etc. It was better than living at home but your freedoms were limited.

The emergence of Web 2.0 is like moving into your own home. You are now responsible for the look, the design, the content, and the perception decreed by the environment. If you want to plant Kudzo in the front yard because you have childhood memories of failure then that's ok. If you want to paint your house with a giant "Wonder Bread" design then knock yourself out. Do you like that seventies look? They still have those Forrest Green and Harvest Gold appliances available and shag carpet may be making a comeback. The point is that you control things now and you don't need to know HTML or .Net programming but you still have an image or brand to protect. Design and usability don't become irrelevant, they become distinguishing. There are 70 million voices out there and you are just one of them, you are going to need all of the help you can get.

Summary
While technology comes and goes over time, the simplicity of design never does. This chapter focused on the physical representations of you persona which must indicate professionalism. Maybe a full scale web site is too much time and effort, if so then simply create a blog from one of the many free sources. The key is to get that professionalism out in the public. At the heart of a professional representation is to see that the individual has differentiated themselves from the pack, a diverse set of skills and talent, and a history of delivery. If you can communicate that in a simple and concise manner then you are at the top of your game. Antoine de Saint-Exupéry said that "Perfection (in design) is achieved not when there is nothing more

to add, but rather when there is nothing more to take away". Often times people confuse complexity with performance or features but the true value comes when everyone one can gain value from your ideas and concepts. The fact remains that simplicity follows the natural evolution of complexity, not the other way around.

9

> Management is doing things right; leadership is doing the right things.
> - Peter Drucker

Portfolio Management

T he prior chapter focused on the scorekeeping aspects of the trademark effort. The web site, resume and CV are all methods of tracking your portfolio of accomplishments as they evolve over time. While we touched on the trademark elements, this chapter will take a deeper look at the various elements of your portfolio.

Theme

The basic theme of this chapter is achievement which can be directly associated with action and accomplishments. While you will make mistakes during your career and may even take steps backwards, your ability to continually press forward on your goals is the corner stone for achievement. The key is the ability to keep going, having small victories, and not letting the road blocks get in your way. Helen Hayes had an interesting quote on achievement: "My mother drew a distinction between achievement and success. She said that achievement is the knowledge that you have studied and worked hard and done the best that is in you. Success is being praised by others. That is nice but not as important or satisfying. Always aim for achievement and forget about success". Achievement is not a matter of chance or luck; it's the result of a constant focus and making the choice to achieve.

How do you rank and classify your trademarks? This chapter is going to provide a list of notable achievements that you can use as a reference. In most cases, these achievements can be added to one of the tracking mediums described in the prior chapter. The idea is that we can take an achievement and classify it as high, medium, and low depending on the impact to your brand. For example, adding a comment to a weblog, like Fast Company's, is great and will get you plenty of exposure but not really add much to your portfolio. On the other hand, a patent can establish you as an expert in your field and have a tremendous impact, both professionally and financially.

Low Impacting Components
Low impact components are contributions to your portfolio that may not add a line item to your Resume or CV. While you might mention that you comment on Seth Godin's weblog or edited of a Wikipedia entry for Business Process Management, you wouldn't necessarily add this to your portfolio. Still, these items can have an impact to your trademark over an extended period of time.

Letters to the Editor
Every magazine and journal provides you with an opportunity to give feedback. In August of 2005, Gary Beach asked what we can do to make a difference in the U.S. education crisis. I had to comment on the quality of our education and specifically the education system in Georgia, which at that time ranked 50th. While not specifically tied to my trademark, the comment was published online as well as in the following issue of the magazine. Within two days, I received three comments from people I know about seeing the magazine.

Another side benefit was that Google indexed this article which added to my ranking within the search engine world. With the enormous collection of magazines in the world, I am sure there is one that focuses on your area of interest. Email the author or send a note to the editor; there is no telling what might happen to your ideas.

Weblogs or Blogs Comments
Weblogs (Blog) and Wikis were covered in detail in Chapter three. Weblogs are basically journal applications that allow you to post your thoughts and ideas as well as provide the ability of others to contribute. As part of low impact area, this trademark revolves around your contribution to other Weblogs. With 71 million Weblogs, there should be plenty of sites associated with your subject matter. Not to mention, most authors and magazines have this type of communication and would really appreciate your input.

Wikis Contributions
Unlike Weblogs, where you can add content, wiki's allow you to alter and add content. For example, at Wikipedia, I can go into the "Metadata" area and add content on recently published articles or upcoming conferences on the topic. I can also alter the information if I don't agree with the original author. Of course, everyone also has the same ability to add, subtract and alter the content. So what happens when twenty different people, with different experiences get together to discuss a topic; confusion or chaos? No, what actually happens is that the subject converges into "common" knowledge which may be more accurate than having a single editor. This item is considered to low impacting one due to the fact that you wouldn't normally add your contributions to your tracking devices.

Personal Volunteer Efforts
Not sure if we should add volunteer efforts to the catalog of accomplishments but many people look at these as great learning experiences. John Maxwell stated that if you wanted to learn about leadership then you should observe people in volunteer positions. When there is no financial or political reason to lead, real leaders will emerge. Perhaps the best example of this type of trademark is volunteering for non-profits or religious organizations.

However noble this type of effort is, it won't make it to the Resume or CV. Perhaps a key is to try to marry your volunteer work with your area of expertise. Suppose that you were really into web design and active server page development. Your church may have a web site that is in need of drastic overhaul. If Web 2.0 is your area then why not integrate a collaborative solution for the entire church body. By combining your area of interest and volunteer work, you may be able to create a total different value model than just volunteering your time.

Press Releases
A press release is an important marketing tool in any business. If you have a product or service, a press release is a cost-effective and practical way of letting your targeted audience know about the product or service. Press releases are also a very important tool in the process of spreading the word about yourself or publications. They serve as an introductory letter to those who may wish to purchase or review your work. Traditionally, press releases were for large organizations with very little attention paid to the individual or small company. As with most things, time changes everything and most of the barriers associated with press releases have been removed. Online services like erelease.com will help you distribute your press release to over 30,000 journalists for a relative small fee.

Peer Accolades
Who among us doesn't want to hear positive opinions about ourselves, our products or our services? This feedback may come as the result of an article or conference presentation. My monthly column generates two to three comments from readers every month. Not all of which are positive, but feedback none the less. I view the criticism as constructive and the complimentary ones as branding material. These can be great marketing tools when added to your online presence. While solid content is important peer review can generate huge advantages over the long term. The fact is that in order for you to become the defacto standard, you will need the support from the industry segment. Peer accolades should be added to your web site in order to help your credibility and enable the trust that you are going to need.

Trademarks or Copyrights

Trademark rights may be used to prevent others from using a confusingly similar mark, but not to prevent others from making the same goods or from selling the same goods or services under a clearly different mark. Trademarks which are used in interstate or foreign commerce may be registered with the United States Patent Office. Trademarks are all around us including the Starbucks logo, the Coca-Cola swirl, and the Nike swoosh. Most trademarks are combination of words or symbols that define the company and represents the corporate brand. Not all trademarks can be seen; Harley Davidson has been able to trademark their rumble sound that comes from their motorcycles.

Graduate Students

Many from the academic community would rank graduate student work much higher. To which, I remind the reader that this is a framework that you can alter to best fit your situation. While some of my work has been to help graduate students within the academic setting, I would also add that most universities are looking for case studies and case work that students can engage in. They want to bring in the real life of business and integrate it into the world of research. In most cases, the students will work for free and provide valuable insight into your program.

Peer Reviewing

Once you have established yourself as a subject matter expert, the offers for reviewing will be overwhelming. Journals will ask you to review appropriateness of the research. Conferences may ask you to sit in on sessions in order to provide insight. In all cases, when you contribute a paper or chapter of a book, you will have the opportunity to review other contributions which can really help you in your publishing. One author asked me to review his book where I provided feedback and advice on how to simplify the writing. The topic was extremely complicated for the average person to understand. The author was nice enough to mention my name in his book which made it to one of the top 200 books sold on Amazon.com; quite an achievement for this technologist.

Many of us find professional peer review very useful: it suggests different perspectives and provides valuable feedback on what is compelling and what is problematic in a publication. Just as you want and need peer reviews, you should also be willing to provide feedback. You want to give the writer information that will help to improve the publication. You should try to be honest, but not personal or unnecessarily harsh in your reviews.

Network associations
As described in a previous chapter, networking is essential. Even those that seem to contribute the least to your career should be acknowledged and recognized on an annual basis. These are classified as low impact only from a trademark perspective. Make no mistake about it, your network is your livelihood. When Harvey Mackay was asked what one thing he would save from his office if it was burning down; the rolodex.

Medium Impacting Components
Unlike the low impact elements, the medium impacting ones should be added to your online persona, Resume or CV. While they may not carry as much weight as the high impact ones, they should be viewed as a welcome addition to the portfolio.

Professional Affiliations
Professional affiliations, memberships or associations are where groups of people within your industry come together to share similar interest. Professional organizations may have standards and processes that you must adhere to in order to be a member. Other organizations, like IEEE, have member classifications which can add to your credibility. For the data professional, the Data Management Association (DAMA) leads the field. Every discipline will have some sort of association where you can communicate with like minded people and pick up on the industry news. Professional organizations offer a place for learning and performance issues. They provide information, research, analysis and practical information derived from its own research, the knowledge and experience of its members, its conferences,

expositions, seminars, publications and the coalitions and partnerships.

Newsletters

Much like a web site, a newsletter is used to communicate to a large audience. Unfortunately, most people that publish newsletters make them too technical or too hard to read and apply the information. There some really great newsletters from financial companies like Vanguard, T. Rowe Price, and 20th Century. These organizations understand that they have to communicate with a wide variety of readers with enormous diversity and financial knowledge. Ultimately, the newsletter is about generating leads for your products and services or building your credibility. Newsletters should be short but don't try to do it alone; there are plenty of people that want to publish their expertise. One of the more successful online newsletters in my field is *The Data Administration Newsletter* edited by Robert Seiner. This newsletter draws in 100,000 readers per month and has established Bob as one of the premier experts in the field of information asset management.

Professional Articles

It seems like every industry has a trade journal or a magazine. Technology may be the worst of the bunch, from Data Management, to Disaster Recovery; we have a magazine for just about every genre of technology. Each month, these magazines produce mounds of information contributed by people just like you. Not to mention the growing number of online magazines where folks are begging for contributed content. The key is to generate an inventory of publishable material that you can use. This is a lot easier said than done. On average, I will publish about 20-30 articles a year than span across professional and academic publications. The key is to stay focused and continue to write.

Another good strategy for publications is the element of reuse. No one says that a publication can only be used by a single publisher. The academic world has been doing this for ages. Dissertations may produce five different academic publications in a variety of locations. Charles Betz used his Masters Thesis to produce a wonderful book on ITIL called *"Architecture and Patterns for IT Service Management, Resource Planning, and Governance: Making Shoes for the Cobbler's Children"*.

Academic Articles

Professional articles are great but academic ones are just as important. At a very high level, professional publications need to be simplified and applicability while academic ones need more rigor. There is tremendous value in both of them. For the professional, academic work may seem to be overbearing and have little impact on the career. The key is to not look at the academic side as a negative but rather another investment medium. A collection of academic articles can't hurt your professional career and they support your claim to expanding the body of knowledge.

Monthly Columns

Monthly columns are similar to professional articles in subject, length, and content. The major difference is that a monthly column forces you to deliver on a more frequent basis. There are no excuses; you must deliver 12 quality papers on time to the editor. Some columns write themselves while others require agonizing effort to complete. I can't tell you the number of times I thought I had a great idea which ended up only producing a half page of content. The key is to get started early and make sure your column has a actionable point. The magazine that I write for has 10-15 other writers who want to grab the reader's attention. Using current events, known frameworks, or associated writing from other authors will get you more mileage.

Professional Volunteer Efforts

Volunteer efforts may not always be in a church or civic group. Industry organizations are constantly looking for people to help organize or lead meetings and social gatherings. Conference boards may need help in reviewing awards organizing the actual conference proceedings. Like many of these medium impacting components, they add up over time. I once made the comment that we hire, not on the basis of technology experience, but on the basis of customer service. Serving others is central to building a long term business model around technology. This is especially true when dealing with the business side of the organization. Volunteer efforts help people understand the need and the gratification of serving others.

Professional Conference Sessions

Speaking in front of a group of people is one of the hardest things we do in life. From Tony Robbins to your Minister, everyone get butterflies before addressing a group of individuals. Remember, the attendees have selected your session to attend. They may have paid to see your presentation but you can bet they want to see you succeed. Nobody goes out and buys a car in hopes that it will break down. Every professional conference is looking for speakers with a story to tell. The hardest step is simply putting together 20 slides that tell that story and submitting it.

By far, conferences are the easiest method of getting published. There is always a conference that would like to hear about your case study or observed best practices. The reason is simple; most professional conferences are littered with vendors and consultants. Theory, products, and research are great, but when you have a story to tell, the world will beat a path to your door.

Academic Conference Sessions

Academic conferences are a little different since they require you to publish a research paper. The truth is that the real value from an academic comes from the paper that is published, more so than the presentation. In fact, I have seen conference tracks with as few attendees as five; four of which are presenters. Conferences sessions may last for 20 minutes or up to 8 hours depending on your role. Also, these conferences really need volunteers to help organize and facilitate the tracks. In the vast majority of the cases, if you have a session then the conference will pick up the conference fee. While this isn't true for an academic conference, the price is usually much lower than a professional one.

Patents Pending

Patents go through a long process with various process steps. We could easily add a trademark opportunity for submitting a patent. In fact, the majority of the work comes during this stage. Corporations that have a patent program will place greater importance on this step than any other. Patent pending is a declaration used to describe a patent application that has been filed, but prior to the patent being issued or the application abandoned. You are entitled to some protection once the patent application reaches this stage.

Weblog or Blog Ownership
One point to make is that while weblog entries may have a low impact, the existence of an industry weblog will have a huge impact. The key is to be sincere and post often. Readers need a reason to return to your weblog and expressing your thoughts and expertise is a great method. A weblog is an online diary or journal that sits on a web page and can be read by anyone with access to the internet. The most popular bloggers update their blogs on a daily basis, with diary entries and comments on the issues of the day. They also recommend other blogs that share similar interests, and offer visitors the chance to respond via e-mail or message board facilities. What you see happening is a community of interest forming and your taking an active role within that community.

Wiki Ownership
Under most Wiki type collaborative efforts, you can progress through various roles. Since most Wiki's are updateable by anyone, the base role is a contributor. You may also take on an editor role which corrects things like grammar, poisoning, and tagging information. The editor is ultimately responsible for the quality of the information while the Administrator has overall responsibility to the wiki element. The Administrator is one who makes the decisions of the validity and accuracy of the information. For a medium weight trademark, one should be an administrator for one or more areas of a major industry wiki.

Past Positions

Do positions and titles mean anything in today's world? I may be a bit cynical but in the new world, history, legacy and tradition seem to have very little to do with hiring. In fact, one might say that working for a single organization is a detriment to one's career. Employers wonder if you have spent too much time within a bureaucracy where high performance is discouraged and conformity encouraged. Traditionally, I liked to see where an individual progressed through the rank and file with positions like:

- Operator
- Programmer
- Analyst
- Architect
- Manager
- Director

This would indicate a natural progression and success all along the way. However today, very few organizations participate in internships with local community colleges. They are so focused on this quarter's financials or this months deliverables, long term planning has been dumped out with the bath water. If you stay in a single trade and move around then you will have a variety of positions. Some will look good and some won't pan out as planned.

Roles and Responsibilities

Throughout these jobs and positions, you will have a variety of roles and responsibilities. Your span of control will be narrow and other times much broader depending on the job. In some cases, you will be performing the work and in others you will have a staff to do the digging. What ever role you have, ensure that you are observant to all the different roles that are happening within the organization. Management roles and responsibilities are structured and assigned but generally change over time. Be sure that you have this documented. Many information workers forget about keeping their roles updated in the various Human Resource systems. For example, a gentleman worked for me for well over seven years and while his job responsibility changed several time his official job title remained "Data Warehouse Manager".

Usually your responsibilities are worked out with your manager, but you should always understand that you control a great deal of this. By working hard or volunteering, you can literally define your own job. Generally speaking, roles and responsibilities define the job and the requirements of success.

Projects and Programs
While titles and roles are important, it's hard to create a story or develop folklore around those elements. What is your story? What are your stories of success? As you move through the various projects, do you leave a path of success? If you return to the prior chapter you see that I focused the second page of the Resume on a few sample stories of success. Can you articulate how you made a difference? You must be the one to document your successes since in most cases no one inside the organization will remember.

Projects contribute to the overall business model and create such an impact that we can develop stories from them. Many projects are hot today and cold tomorrow. If possible, we want to choose our projects and programs carefully. I want to end this section with a collection of quotes from various authors on storytelling:

"Narrative imagining—story—is the fundamental instrument of thought," says cognitive scientist Mark Turner.

"Most of our experience, our knowledge, is organized as stories."
Donald Norman writes,

"Stories are marvelous means of summarizing experiences, of capturing an event and the surrounding context that seems essential. Stories are important cognitive events, for they encapsulate, into one compact package, information, knowledge, context, and emotion."

"The fusion of memory, metaphor and story enables consumers to create meaning around, or to see personal relevance in, a company or a specific brand," notes Gerald Zaltman.

Dan Pink concludes, "We are our stories. We compress years of experience, thought, and emotion into a few compact narratives that we convey to others and tell to ourselves." What's your story?

Courses Taught

Even if you are not a professor at a major university, there are plenty of opportunities to teach and give back to the community. An Adjunct professor is someone who does not have a permanent position at the academic institution; this may be someone with a job outside the academic institution teaching courses in a specialized field; or it may refer to persons hired to teach courses on contractual basis (frequently renewable contracts); it is generally a part-time position with a teaching load below the minimum required to earn benefits (health care, life insurance, etc.), although the number of courses taught can vary from a single course to a full-time load (or even an overload).

An adjunct is generally not required to participate in the administrative responsibilities at the institution often expected of other full-time professors, nor do they generally have research responsibilities. The pay for these positions is usually nominal, even though adjuncts typically hold a Ph.D., but most adjuncts also hold concurrent positions at several institutions or in industry.

Consulting Projects

While not all of us work for consulting companies, we all have opportunities to consult within our area of expertise. The idea is that consultants perform work worth paying for. We must understand this concept of "work worth paying for" and apply it to every function we provide. This is especially for those of us in traditional roles within an enterprise. Consultants live and die by their engagements and the stories that are generated from that effort. They get paid for results not activities. While many of us study and actually perform ROI analysis, we don't generate an invoice and charge back for our time. And even if we did, we hold a kind of monopoly over the organization. Consulting projects should be looked at carefully and chosen wisely. The industry has a very good network and a few failures could result in the destruction of your brand.

Books Edited or Reviewed
Most authors are looking for people who can edit or review their book. Since you are an expert in the field, they will seek you out which in turn can enhance your brand. Not only can you gain access to the information early, you can setup a rapport with the author which can payoff in the future. Even if the author doesn't ask for your review, you can certainly contribute to the various sites like Amazon.com and become an "Expert" reviewer.

High Impacting Components
High impact entries are essential in your long term trademark plan in that they continuously contribute long after the physical effort has past. Most of the medium elements have a one time value and require a continuous effort in order to deliver over the long term. You should also notice that these high impact elements require a much larger effort in order to make it happen.

Industry Awards
A quick search on Google for industry awards reveals over 53 million hits. The advent of the web created an environment where awards were easy to obtain. For a few dollars or cross-linking, you can post the world's best web site. These type of awards are not the kind of the awards we are talking about here.

For my industry, the Wilshire Metadata Award is the most visible and recognized award for metadata. This award is handed out every year and attracts some of the best implementations in the world. The award judges the metadata programs based on the following:

- Overall business impact/benefits
- Return on objective
- Measurable return on investment
- Scale of the solution (i.e. enterprise, business unit)
- Number and breadth of applications served by the solution
- Length of time the solution has been in place
- Innovative problem solving
- How well the submission addresses the questions asked above
- Sponsorship, Planning and Frameworks
- Business Requirements and Taxonomy Development
- Architecture
- Resource Utilization
- Metrics

This is an excellent award that you want to try to obtain for your organization. The award speaks volumes and can be considered a peer-review type recognition. The weight of this type of recognition is enormous. One past winner said the award helped his company document its worth to management. Another saw his system become a model for other organizations doing similar work.

Organizations like IEEE also award individual designated honors. To recognize its members for their outstanding accomplishments, the Computer Society sponsors an active and prestigious awards program. The awards honor technical achievements and service to the computer profession and to the society. The IEEE Computer Society sponsors a robust program of awards designed to recognize both technical achievement and service to the society and the profession. In the technical area, recognition may be given for pioneering and significant contributions to the field of computer science and engineering. Service awards may be given to both volunteers and staff for well defined and highly valued contributions to the society. The Awards Committee must take care to preserve the integrity of the evaluation and selection process to assure that it is both open and rigorous, and that it contributes to the prestige of the society and the award recipients. The focus of the awards program is the value and quality of the contributions. In most cases there are no eligibility restrictions on the nominee or nominator. The society encourages nominations of and by its members for appropriate IEEE awards. No award is automatic or given by reason of an individual simply holding a position.

Designated Honors

Closely related to awards, designated honors include special recognition that organizations have bestowed upon you. I still have on my desk at home a letter written in 1984 recognizing my efforts on a specific project. It isn't that fact that it was the first of such awards but the impact it had on me professionally. The letter reminds me of the importance of focusing on the details and those little things that make a difference. Designated honors may include honor programs or honorary degrees that are bestowed on people that have made large contributions to a particular field.

Certifications

Another trademark is the certification and there plenty to choose from in today's market. Certification Magazine published a list of top certification programs (Tittel, 2003).

- Cisco Certified Internetwork Expert (CCIE)
- Red Hat Certified Engineer (RHCE)
- Novell Certified Directory Engineer (CDE)
- Oracle9i DBA Certified Professional (OCP)
- Oracle9i Database Administrator Certified Master (OCM)
- Field Certified Systems Engineer (FCSE)
- Field Certified Systems Administrator (FCSA)
- Field Certified PC Technician (FCPT)
- Certified Professional Information Technology Consultant (CPITC)

- Cisco Career Certifications (Associate, Professional and Specialist)

Additionally, the magazine published a list of vendor neutral certifications.

- National Association of Communication Systems Engineers (NACSE)
- National Association of Radio & Telecommunications Engineers (NARTE)
- Project Management Institute (PMI)
- Field Certified Professional Association (FCPA)
- Information Systems Audit and Control Association (ISACA)
- BICSI
- Service & Support Professionals Association (SSPA)
- Linux Professional Institute (LPI)
- The Computing Technology Industry Association (CompTIA)

The key point here is that you should combine both solid education with certifications to build an unbeatable combination of trademarks.

Educational Degrees
It goes without saying that I am a big believer in education and certifications. I truly believe that one of the variables in the success of the United States is the availability of the education system. Education can create bonds, relationships, knowledge, and provide the skills one needs to move up the social ladder. Education provides mobility where as you move up the social ladder you have more freedom and more choices. Not to mention that education improves you chances at getting a job with higher pay. Take a look at the table on the following page.

Unemployment Rate	Education Attained	Median Weekly Earnings (% of High)
1.6%	Doctoral degree	$1,421 (100%)
1.1%	Professional degree	$1,370 (96.4%)
2.1%	Master's degree	$1,129 (79.5%)
2.6%	Bachelor's degree	$937 (65.9%)
3.3%	Associate degree	$699 (49.2%)
4.2%	Some college, no degree	$653 (45.9%)
7.6%	High-school graduate	$583 (41.1%)
7.6%	Some high-school, no diploma	$409 (28.8%)

Table 9.1: Education Levels

Clearly, education is the key to earning more, having more, and College degrees are great professional trademarks. Today, more than 25% of the population will complete a Bachelor's degree and more than 75% will complete High School. In 1950, 17 percent of the older population had graduated from high school, and only 3 percent had at least a Bachelor's degree. The access and availability of education should continue this trend, especially considering the fact that many degrees can now be obtained over the Internet. The Sloan Consortium (2003) Survey on Online Learning found that complete online degree programs are offered by 34 percent of institutions. Among public institutions, 49 percent are offering full online degree programs. 80 percent of public and 37 percent of private institutions offer both online and blended programs. For profit institutions expect to increase their online programs more rapidly than any other type of institution, anticipating an increase of more than 40 percent. In addition, according to Consortium findings, three quarters of academic leaders at public colleges and universities believe that online learning quality is equal to or superior to face-to-face instruction.

Traditionally, the MBA was the ticket into the management ranks of the Fortune 100. Of course, as the saying goes "what happens when the special is no longer special"? Today, we see fewer and fewer companies investing in their management layers. Why would you, if you are working so very hard to reduce those ranks through advanced technology. That being said, every research organization is expressing the need for technologist to obtain more business knowledge. The MBA is a great way to quick start this process and gain the basic foundations of business.

Patents Granted and Trademarks
From the United States patent office, A patent for an invention is the grant of a property right to the inventor, issued by the United States Patent and Trademark Office. Generally, the term of a new patent is 20 years from the date on which the application for the patent was filed in the United States or, in special cases, from the date an earlier related application was filed, subject to the payment of maintenance fees. U.S. patent grants are effective only within the United States, U.S. territories, and U.S. possessions. Under certain circumstances, patent term extensions or adjustments may be available.

The right conferred by the patent grant is, in the language of the statute and of the grant itself, "the right to exclude others from making, using, offering for sale, or selling" the invention in the United States or "importing" the invention into the United States. What is granted is not the right to make, use, offer for sale, sell or import, but the right to exclude others from making, using, offering for sale, selling or importing the invention. Once a patent is issued, the patentee must enforce the patent without aid of the USPTO.

There are three types of patents:
1. Utility patents may be granted to anyone who invents or discovers any new and useful process, machine, article of manufacture, or composition of matter, or any new and useful improvement thereof;
2. Design patents may be granted to anyone who invents a new, original, and ornamental design for an article of manufacture; and

3. Plant patents may be granted to anyone who invents or discovers and asexually reproduces any distinct and new variety of plant.

A trademark is a word, name, symbol, or device that is used in trade with goods to indicate the source of the goods and to distinguish them from the goods of others. A servicemark is the same as a trademark except that it identifies and distinguishes the source of a service rather than a product. The terms "trademark" and "mark" are commonly used to refer to both trademarks and servicemarks.

Trademark rights may be used to prevent others from using a confusingly similar mark, but not to prevent others from making the same goods or from selling the same goods or services under a clearly different mark. Trademarks which are used in interstate or foreign commerce may be registered with the USPTO.

Published Books
Just by the fact that you are reading this book demonstrates how easy it is to get published. The Internet has helped this by lowering the distribution and inventory costs in such a way that online book retailers can carry millions of titles which would be impossible for the physical book store. See Chapter one for a detailed discussion on the Long Tail. Traditional book publishing required large amount of resources and distribution channels. Another option is to go with one of the self-publishing services like iUniverse. Depending on the volume of sales you expect, this might be a better option.

Contributed Chapters
Certainly, books are the cream of the crop and nothing beats a best seller to kick start your brand. That being said, writing a full book can be daunting and an enormous time commitment that many people just can't make. An alternative path could be to contribute a chapter to a book which will save plenty of time. There are plenty of groups that issue "Call for Chapters" around a specific topic. Keeping in mind that my area of expertise is in Information

Architecture (Metadata), Collaboration, and Knowledge Stores, I was able to contribute chapters on Web Applications, Open Source, Virtual Environments, and Knowledge Management. Book publishers like Idea Group routinely have 10-20 calls active at any given time.

Academic Journals and Professional Journals
From an academic perspective, the journal is the ultimate trademark. An academic journal is a regularly-published, peer-reviewed publication that publishes scholarship relating to an academic discipline. The purpose of such a journal is to provide a place for the introduction and scrutiny of new research, and often a forum for the critique of existing research, whether as journal articles or as books. These purposes are most often manifested in the publication of original research articles, review articles, and book reviews. Earlier, we mentioned that articles and columns were an important contribution but only a medium impact. Academic and professional journals are different in that they are designed to expand the body of knowledge. The amount of effort is far greater and peer review is tremendous. The rigor of the research will be put to the test and you must be able to back up the information presented. Your paper must be formatted correctly according to one of the standards dictated by the publishing journal. Generally, you are constrained to length, ranging from 5-10 pages. If you receive a rejection slip, send your manuscript out again soon to another journal with some adjustments especially if reasons were given for the rejection. Rejection doesn't necessarily mean that an article is a poor one; it may simply indicate that the journal has another article on a similar topic in the works or that the article's literary genre does not match the journal. Most articles that are accepted for publication will be "re-writes"; the editor typically asks an author to resubmit the piece with some indicated changes, shortening of manuscript, etc. Then the editor will do some copy-editing for stylistic elegance, punctuation, capitalizations, etc. (Fahey, 2006).

Portfolio Management Techniques
This chapter has produced a list trademarks where each one has the potential of expanding your brand. Taken with the prior chapter, you have all the tools you need for portfolio expansion. We simply need to bring these components together and produce a working governance model.

Ideally, we want a balanced portfolio of trademarks. Like financial investments, you should never put all of your eggs in one basket. A balanced portfolio would ensure that you focus on the many different levels as well as different categories. What is needed is a high level tracking device that can be customized to fit your methodology of measurement. While one hit wonders do exist, most people that enjoy a solid brand have built it up over time and continue to support it with publications, speaking engagements, and consulting practices. In order to actually track trademark activity, we are going to need to collect an inventory type system where we can log our activities. Keep in mind, if you are already keeping your Resume or CV up to date this effort should be relatively small. Starting with a simple inventory of trademarks and classifications, I can begin the process of building a simple tracking system.

Trademark Inventory	
Low Impact Components	**Quantity**
Letters to the Editor	1
Weblog Comments	120
Wiki Contributions	1
Personal Volunteer Efforts	4
Press Releases	0
Peer Accolades	60
Professional Affiliations	3
Network: Low Value Contacts	10
Technical Reports	3
Trademarks	1
Graduate Students Supervised	2
Peer Reviewing	3
Totals	208

Table 9.2: Quantity View of Trademark Management

Table 9.2 presents an image of the low impacting trademarks with quantity cells added. The time you want to spend on your evaluations will determine how complex you make the formula. By focusing on the quantity alone, you will be able to see your progress over time. This type of analysis is a great starting point in tracking and analyzing your brand progression. Appropriately, the tracking system separates the high, medium, and low classifications which can also have weights assigned in order to define a better numeric image of your progression. In other words, we can take the total score for the low components and multiply by a weight such as 1.00. The medium component score may be multiplied by 2.00 and the high value multiplied by 3.00. Again, you as the owner of the model can adjust these weights as you see fit.

Can this model be expanded? Are simple classifications, weights, classes, and quantity enough to develop a deep understanding of your brand image? We can expand the model by adding weights to each individual line elements. By using the 10-20-40-20-10 rule we can improve the model and scoring system. The rule states that 10% of the components will receive weight of 1.00 as well as a 5.00. Correspondently, 20% of the components will have a weight of 2.00 and 4.00. Finally, 40% of the components will have the middle weight of 3.00. This allows us to distribute impact across the portfolio.

Low Impact Components	Quantity	Weight	Total
Letters to the Editor	1	3.00	3.00
Weblog Comments	238	2.00	476.00
Wiki Contributions	1	2.00	2.00
Personal Volunteer Efforts	2	3.00	6.00
Press Releases	0	1.00	0.00
Peer Accolades	8	4.00	32.00
Professional Affiliations	7	4.00	28.00
Network: Low Value Contacts	10	3.00	30.00
Technical Reports	1	5.00	5.00
Trademarks	1	3.00	3.00
Graduate Students Supervised	3	3.00	9.00
Peer Reviewing	0	3.00	0.00
Totals	272		594

Table 9.3: Low Impacting Comments

Based on Table 9.3, the weights actually change the impact order which is what we were hoping for. Any distribution of weights could be used and it is really up to your experience to alter them as you move forward. There are still two problems with the model in that it doesn't take into account time and repetition of elements.

Based on the prior paragraph, we might also want to add a "regression" factor which reduces the value of each subsequent addition of that specific trademark type. This would be important in determining what we should be working on and the value of any additional effort. For example, suppose we have 25 professional publications with a regression factor of 0.95. This would indicate that the trademark value of the first publication was 1.00 and the second 0.95. However, the 25th publication would only have a trademark value of 0.29. What this tells you is that at some point the value of adding a trademark within this category is fairly low and you might be better off spending your time in other areas. In other words, you have only invested in small cap stocks and you need to diversify.

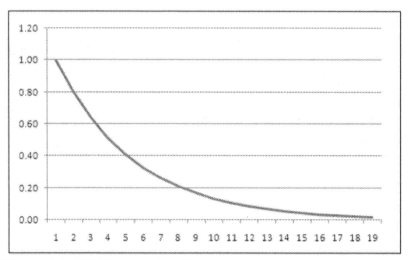

Figure 9.1: 80% Regression Factor

Figure 9.1 presents the value equation of each subsequent trademark which has a regression factor of 80%. After about 8, the value obtained seems to be low relative to the amount of effort required.

Another factor in calculating the value contribution is currency. The more current a trademark is the more valuable it is to your portfolio. This passes the common sense test since a Computer Science degree received in the past few years is more valuable than the one I received during the 80's. Especially since Pascal, Snobol, Lisp and other programming languages are no longer viable. However, by not individually listing the trademarks, we are going to need to make a judgment call on how these trademarks sit along the distribution timeline. Figure 9.2 presents four possible options.

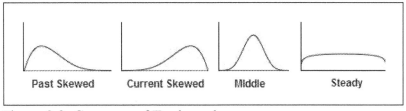

Figure 9.2: Currency of Trademark

Assume that the diagram represents your publishing distribution. The first image (Left Skewed) indicates that the majority of your publications were early in your career and you really haven't focused on this in some time. The second image (Right Skewed) indicates that the majority of your publications have been within the last few years. The third image (Middle Distribution) indicates a slow start but advancement later in your career. However, lately you production has fallen off the norm which could be a result of family additions, areas of interest, or employment changes. The final image represents someone that has steadily produced publications over a long period of time. Keep in mind the diagrams will change based on the amount of time you use as a base. For me, if I look at my 24 year career, then my publication distribution looks like the current skewed image. As with all measurements you just want to be honest with your valuation. Mathematically, we would think that the right skewed (current) distribution would have the highest contribution to your trademark portfolio with the past skewed being weakest. In our model, we are going provide a ranking system 1 to 4 where 1 is a past skewed inventory, 2 is middle skewed, 3 is steady, and 4 would represent current skewed trademark production.

Now, we have a trademark model that goes beyond simple quantity evaluation and adds the concepts of time and regression. Table 9.4 provides an example of an Excel template for the medium classifications.

Medium Impact Components	QTY	Weight	Regress	Curr	Total
Newsletter Articles	13	1.00	60%	2.0	2.51
Professional Articles	3	3.00	75%	2.0	8.63
Academic Articles	0	3.00	80%	0.0	0.00
Monthly Columns	45	3.00	75%	4.0	12.0
Network: Medium Value Contacts	5	2.00	100%	4.0	40.0
Professional Volenteer Efforts	7	3.00	95%	2.0	22.6
Professional Conference Sessions	35	3.00	95%	4.0	64.6
Academic Conference Sessions	11	3.00	95%	1.0	25.8
Patents Pending	11	3.00	85%	2.0	18.76
Wiki Ownership (High Profile)	0	1.00	80%	0.0	0.00
Weblog Ownership (High Profile)	1	2.00	80%	1.0	2.00
Past Positions	8	5.00	75%	4.0	20.0
Professional Projects and Programs	0	5.00	100%	0.0	0.00
Courses Taught	3	2.00	95%	1.0	5.71
Consulting Projects	0	4.00	100%	0.0	0.00
Book Editing or Reviewing	2	4.00	95%	2.0	11.6
Totals	144				234

Table 9.4: Medium Trademarks

The quantity (144) and trademark valuation (234.34) won't mean much without context or comparison information. Since there is no national standard or publication of other people's trademark score, you can only really compare yourself to yourself. Figure 9.3 provides a career long view of the trademark valuations. This chart takes the low, medium, and high rankings and presents them as a stacked chart which should give you an idea of the growth and allocation of the trademarks.

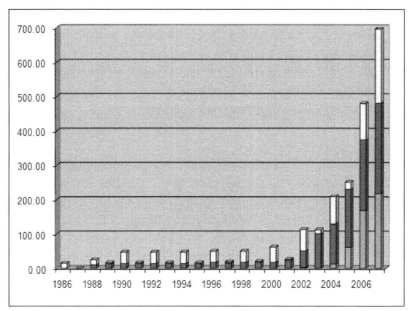

Figure 9.3: Year by Year Review of Trademark Portfolio

For the first 15 years, my own trademark portfolio was weak and without growth. In 2002, the program started to have an impact and progress was being made. Today, my overall score is approaching 700 with a fairly equal distribution between low (blue), medium (red) and high (yellow) trademark components.

Regardless of what type of management tracking tool you use, you want to see this type of progression. Make no mistake about it, this stuff takes time and isn't going to happen overnight.

Choosing Trademark Opportunities
With your tracking system in place, now we need to turn our attention on the trademark opportunities themselves. I define an opportunity as any situation that opens itself up to you which you can then evaluate the impact to your brand. Examples of opportunities might include:

- Should you go back to school and earn another degree?
- Should you obtain a Microsoft Certification?

217

- Should you patent your new idea on portfolio management?
- Should you build a blog on collaborative computing?
- Should you take your boss to lunch?

The following categories and questions allow you to evaluate each opportunity for developing new trademarks.

Strategic Alignment

Strategic alignment focuses attention on how the trademark opportunity impacts your overall direction. Clearly, you want alignment of your efforts to your strategy in order to reduce the amount of wasted time. While I might be tempted to write a fiction novel, the success or failure will have little impact to my overall brand. Worse yet, it may very well confuse the customer and actually reduce the value of the brand. Strategic alignment is not optional and if you don't have a strategic brand then your trademarks will fail to deliver the value promised in this book.

- Does the opportunity fit with your goals and strategic direction?
- Does the opportunity leverage your core competencies?
- Does the opportunity support a balance among other opportunities?
- What is the long term strategic value of the opportunity?

Trademark Alignment

While the strategic alignment focused on the high level plan, the trademark alignment is more tactical. You want to be sure that the opportunity can be leveraged or even reused in various areas. Once you have completed the trademark task, what do you expect to happen?

- Does the opportunity create an advantage over the other SME's?
- Does the opportunity create unique benefits and value in the future?

- Does the opportunity align with your current tactical direction?

Industry Attractiveness
Every one of us are different from the perspective of the brand. We believe and focus on different things at different times of our career. Our industry has expectations and assumptions of value that you need to recognize. This fact is hard to argue when you see the differences between the academic and professional communities.

- Does the opportunity meet the minimum expectations of the industry?
- Does the opportunity provide opportunity for growth?
- Does the opportunity create a competitive advantage?
- Does the opportunity present a branding opportunity?

Feasibility
Can you pull off this trademark? Most of us hate to think about failure or even the possibility. We are all dreamers and if properly motivated, nothing is impossible. That being said, you have to be honest with yourself and what you are capable of. Most of the trademarks are going to be developed above and beyond your current position. If your wife just delivered twins and you started a new job, I doubt that you will have any free time to focus on this branding effort.

- Is the opportunity feasible to complete in an appropriate amount of time?
- Do you have the foundation of knowledge and experience?
- Can you manage the effort with all that is currently happening?
- What is the amount of effort required; time, money, resources?

Risk
Risk is an important issue in that you need to take a look around to
see what might influence or prevent you from completing the
effort. Job uncertainties, topic popularity, or industry standards
may influence your progression. Take a book as an example. It is
always possible that someone else will beat you to the punch and
deliver the best seller on your topic. The first book out the gate
may set the standard and also may influence the success or failure
of any subsequent book.

- Is there anything or anyone that would hamper your effort?
- Are there any uncertainties that need to be considered?
- Is there anything or anyone that you must depend on to
  complete the opportunity?
- Can you manage the progression and detailed tasks?

Return on Effort (ROE)
Ok, not exactly Return on Investment (ROI) but we should ask if
the effort that is required worth it. What can you reuse or utilize in
other areas where value can be extended? Truth be told, not all of
the trademarks are going to generate any kind of revenue. I once
asked an author about his return on the books he had authored. His
response was about 5 cents an hour; not quite minimum wage.
Still, you might want to think about how many of these trademarks
you can pay for or do free of charge. Most conference
organizations will gladly pick up the fee but may not include travel
until you become a known commodity.

- Can you reuse the trademark material?
- Is the ROI good relative to the risk associated?
- Will the Opportunity generate revenue or have associated
  revenue?

Current Inventory
Finally, you want to be sure your additional efforts work with your
current inventory. This goes back to the idea that if you already
have 100 patents is one more going to make a difference. You

want to be sure your portfolio compliments itself and really creates a solid resume or CV.

- Does the addition of the opportunity complement your current portfolio?
- Do you already have an abundance of this level of opportunity (High, Medium, and Low)?
- Do you already have an abundance of this type of opportunity (i.e. Publications)?

Trademark Measurements
The prior section focused on providing you with an internal tool for measuring your progress but what about the penetration of your brand into the market? How can we measure or track the progress of our brand over time?

One of the innovations that Google developed was utilizing the connections between web sites in order to determine relevancy and ranking. The PageRank system evaluates the importance and relevance of a information source by the number of other people referencing that source. PageRank is the algorithm used by the Google search engine, originally formulated by Sergey Brin and Larry Page (1998) in their paper *The Anatomy of a Large-Scale Hypertextual Web Search Engine.* The concept is based on the premise, prevalent in academia, that the importance of a research paper can be judged by the number of citations the paper has from other research papers. Brin and Page have simply transferred this premise to its web equivalent: the importance of a web page can be judged by the number of hyperlinks pointing to it from other web pages. While we won't provide a mathematical formula for measuring our brand, we can take this principle and apply is to the various trademarks presented earlier.

Web Analytics
A web site is simply collection of objects called pages. We designate our web address to point to a single entry page and from there branch out to the various areas of interest. Most hosting

companies will provide web analytics which include unique users, visits, hits, pages, and bandwidth. The following figure presents one year's worth of metrics for the authors own web site.

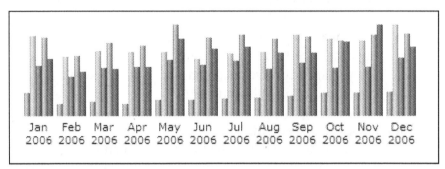

Figure 9.4: Web Metrics

The key is to look for growth. Take the last column in Figure 9.4, each month I can review the bandwidth used by the community. The higher the bandwidth, the more traffic I am generating with the web site. Same is true for visits and users, we want to see an element of growth over time. In order to represent the expansion of the brand, we want to see these metrics obtain a sustainable increase. We can judge the brand itself, by the increased traffic on the web sites. For example, suppose you publish a book online and offer it free to subscribers. Using web analytics you can monitor how much traffic the product generates as well as the number of subscriptions. From there, we might be able to track sales conversions. This is commonly referred to as a "conversion rate". The key is to establish a base line of metrics and monitor the growth in order to gauge the expansion of your brand. We may also review the country of origin in order to determine the global impact of our brand. We can review the difference between visitors and unique visitors in order to calculate return business. Did the user come from a search engine? If so, what keywords or phrases led him to your environment? Did they come from other sites that reference your work? If so, what's the percentage of this type versus utilizing the search engines or word of mouth? Keep in mind, early in your effort these numbers will be relatively low and that should be expected. You can also review what pages people are reviewing, the length of time, and the time of day. These too may provide some insight into where your brand is heading. One might argue that if you have heavy traffic in the early morning hours, then your brand is growing overseas. You may also conclude that heavy traffic during the office hours indicates the appeal of your brand to organizations, universities, or corporations is increasing. The longer you can hold peoples attention, the greater interest people have in your product, service, and expertise. By analyzing the average length of stay, you can get a pretty good idea.

Weblog (Blog) Analytics
Like web pages, weblogs can also have analytics which operate similarly to the traditional ones described above. Additionally, aggregators like Technorati provide ranking, ratings, and comments. An aggregator is like a newspaper that pulls in content from various writers, subjects, and types. Much of the content you see in Newspapers is syndicated which means that the news paper pays for the content. In the Web 2.0 world, many of the applications (i.e blog, wiki, podcasts) have built in feed components. This would be analogous to a writer writing an article and then informing various newspapers that they could pick it up if they like. Only in the 2.0 world, this is an automatic process that is done for you. Technorati allows bloggers to post information to their own Weblog but have the software ping this aggregator type site. The aggregator will show all of the latest posts as well as allow end users to search across all blogs. The key area that I want to highlight is the blogranking. Figure 9.7 provides an example of the O'Reilly Media blog. Notice that this blog ranks 30th out of 71 million.

oreilly.com -- Welcome to O'Reilly Media, Inc.
Rank: 30 (19,936 links from 8,616 blogs)
URL: http://www.oreilly.com
Updated: 29 minutes ago
Favorited by: 7 members   Favorite this Blog

Search this blog

gure 9.5: Technorate Ranking

The good news for my blog is that I made it to the top 2% of all blogs. The bad news is that I am still number $1,836,000^{th}$ in the entire blogsphere. Still, this system allows me to monitor my progress over the long term.

Other methods of measuring a blog's impact is the number comments, trackbacks, or feedback you get from the readers. The larger your brand grows, the more people you will attract. While I am not privy to the metrics, I can easily see that tompeters.com can get as many as 50-60 responses from his readers. Assuming metrics tell the whole story, I would expect to see him pull in 500 readers on a single post which would be a great goal for all of us.

Search Engine Ranking
As industry experts, we define a collection of keywords that best describe our area of expertise. For example, in the collaboration space we can use terms like Web 2.0, Enterprise 2.0, virtual workspaces, collaborate, collaboration, collaborative, etc. Where do we rank when people use these keywords and can we improve those rankings? There are some tools on the web where you can provide you web site and a few keywords to determine where you rank. Google provides a very nice tool called "GoogleRanks" which will also search other search engines like Yahoo. For example, if I ask where my site ranks using the search phrase "Enterprise Metadata" then you will see that my site comes up with four of the top ten hits. In Yahoo, we own three of the top ten hits. You want to monitor this to ensure that you are staying on the forefront of your industry. If you are not too sure what terms you

should be monitoring then check you site metrics to see what people are searching for in order to locate your web site.

Referencing
For the academic side, getting your research published is great. Ultimately, you want to see others reference your work. The more people that reference your work, the higher valuation can be associated to the material. You can review this by reviewing web sites like IEEE and ACM. For none academic work, you may have to work harder to search for references. Many people believe that if you can find information on the web, then it is open for the taking. In my opinion, you should always reference other people's work regardless of where you find it. For me, most people ask if they can use or reuse the information. All I ask is that they reference the material or provide a link to my web site.

Other Ideas
Depending on what your goals are with the trademark program, you can clearly measure the number of leads or additional revenue you generate from this exercise. Ultimately, you want ensure the effort produces results based on your overall strategy. When consultants give conference speeches, there are primarily looking to generate leads for their business. The same is true for building ones brand.

At the end of the day, the truest measure of your success is how you feel about yourself. Building up your trademarks will improve how you look at yourself and the belief in your abilities. If you think your business is growing or you think your reputation is improving then the effort was completely worth it. Whether you call it self-esteem, self-confidence or self-worth, if you don't think highly of yourself, you will struggle with this effort and the results.

Zeus Jones
Up to this point, we have focused our attention on you, the individual. Our research, framework, and solution has strived to improve your environment but a question emerges. Can these techniques be applied to organizations and has anyone actually

tried it? In many cases, when an individual markets or brands their expertise it is in an effort to generate business. Many speakers attend conferences in order to develop leads to further their consulting practice. Book s and articles are written under the same guidelines. These are easy examples that we can point to but that don't really bring into account the Web 2.0 technologies. So to repeat, is there an example of where an organizations has gone full board on the trademark 2.0 program?

Zeus Jones is an interesting example of an organization that has fully embraced the foundational components of a trademark program. They are a company that understands the potential impact of Web 2.0 technologies and the ability to create viral marketing. They state on their web site that they believe that actions speak louder than words and are dedicated to solving business problems by helping clients use their marketing to do things for their customers instead of just saying things to them. Instead of the normal marketing efforts such as building an online web site, brochures, and product announcements, they have utilized several facets of the 2.0 world. Take a look at the following list which only compromises a small percentage of their efforts.

- Created a profile on LinkedIn to highlight their past experience and knowledge
- Created Music that could be downloaded on several music download sites (mp3.com)
- Created desktop art with the company logo strategically placed
- Created case study videos and posted them on YouTube
- Created and commented on blogs about business, brands, and special interests of the five members of the team
- Created cell phone ring tones
- Listed the company goals and values on 43 Things
- Entered an online sewing contest
- Created a "Zeus Jones" figure in one of the largest virtual worlds "World Warcraft"

- Made predictions at "Longbets.org" and placed $50.00 on the wager
- Created entries on people they would like to meet and places they would like to visit
- Developed RSS feeds to daily information

The idea is simple, they are developing an online persona and using the web to express and expand it. How effective are they? In a single month, they increased the number of Google hits from 43 to 11,700. Viral marketing describes any strategy that encourages individuals to pass on a marketing message to others, creating the potential for exponential growth in the message's exposure and influence. What this company is doing is trying to find the right combination of techniques that creates a sort of virus; attention virus. Is this new? Of course not, we can see plenty of examples of where organizations have created a sort of viral buzz: Harry Potter, IPod, Blair Witch Project, and the VW Beetle. The key is to understand that this viral activity was planned and executed. In a McKinsey study, 13% of products are largely driven by this type of phenomenon. Zeus Jones is simply utilizing the Web 2.0 technologies to do what would normally be done by large marketing firms and large investments.

Summary
Managing your portfolio of Trademarks is the most critical aspect of this book. You must, repeat must, managing this like you manage your financial portfolio. Don't pull a Clark Howard and go cheap, spend what you need to do in order to continue to move forward on your trademark journey. Ensure you have a balanced portfolio and don't over contribute to a single area. This will be key in diversifying the portfolio which may open some doors in others areas. While you might think that a single publication doesn't mean it much, it may very well be butterfly wings. The impact may be felt in Japan or 10 years from now. Persistence is the key, big accomplishments are simply the summation or the driving winds of little ones.

10 | A leader is a dealer in hope.
- Napoleon Bonaparte.

The Trademark Promise

Why should you put in the time and energy into the Trademark program? Simply to be a world class resource doesn't seem to carry much of a payoff based on the traditional measures of success. Does a bigger office, more money, or more power drive you to work long hours and sacrifice your home life? Personally, I am not sure that these are the types of rewards you will receive by following the plan in this text. Still, I can understand the pull of this type of mentality. Otherwise how would those commercials that promise you the lifestyle you deserve ever make in on air. The promise of an easy road without obstacles is not what this program is all about.

Before you can look at the trademark promise, we should spend a few moments reviewing what actually changes when we move to the Web 2.0 environment. The 1.0 environment was a great step forward in sharing information and exposing many outdated business processes. That being said, web 1.0 was still focused on the company or the individual. The communications was still basically one way in that you need some advanced technical skills in order to communicate with even the basic web environment. This communication medium focused on the "Home" page as the author's own personal web site which is static by nature, even though it is generally updated on weekly basis. The only hint of a community was sharing links of others but the primary business reason for this practice was to increase ones ranking within the Google search engine. The old environment rewarded the logical, the technical, the isolated, and the narrow focus of the traditional business model. This new environment is more about a community, the power of us if you will. Here the end user drives the product design and selection not the other way around. Web 2.0 is less about technology and more about the content. You don't need the technical skills but simply the desire to communicate. This environment is more for the right brained individuals, the collaborators, the transparent, and those that look toward a greater good. Table 10.1 provides a few of the key differences between Web 1.0 and 2.0.

Web 1.0 Characteristics	Web 2.0 Characteristics
Static Content	Dynamic Content
Producer Based Information	Participatory Based Information
Messages Pushed to Consumer	Messages Pulled by Consumer
Institutional Control	Individual Enabled
Top Down Implementation	Bottom Up Implementation
Users Search and Browse	Users Publish and Subscribe
Transactional Based Interactions	Relationship Based Interactions
Goal of Mass Adoption	Goal of Niche Adoption
Taxonomy	Folksonomy

Table 10.1: Characteristics of Web 1.0 and Web 2.0

Notice these are not technical differences per se, but more aligned with the functional differences. Perhaps the key difference for our context is the participatory based information. In the Web 1.0 world, there really weren't that many brands out there, at least from an information worker perspective. I doubt we would be overstating the case to say that less than 1% of the web sites were focused on the individual brand. In the 2.0 world, that changes since in most cases it's the individual that produces the content not an organization. Randy Baseler, vice president of marketing for

Boeing Commercial Airplanes in Seattle, is a central figure in Boeing's online presence. Just as he is enhancing the image of Boeing, he is developing his own brand.

One of the main reasons that hundreds of thousands of people freely contribute to this new world is the sense of belonging. Belonging to a specific culture or group has a very powerful draw and for many people a way of life. This chapter will focus on reviewing various reasons that information workers should focus on developing themselves a personal brand and steps you can start today.

Agility and Versatility
Agility and versatility are two dimensions that most information workers are familiar with. Agility describes your ability to adapt to different situations which comes from knowledge. Individuals should ensure that their development plans includes broad experiences and various skills as part of their career planning. Training, education, and a variety of roles are keys to agility development.

With the abundance of information workers available today, organizations have plenty of staffing options and are in a position to be more demanding than in the past. For the first 20 years of information work, the demand for services was far greater than the supply. Today, that trend is shifting and unless some new transformation occurs, the power will continue to shift to the employer. Employers want knowledge, skill, speed and ability across the board. Businesses need people that can enable them to react quickly to the changing demands of their business and to take advantage of opportunities.

Beardsley, Johnson, and Manyika (2006) reported that organizations are seeing faster pace of specialization, globalization, and technology change. The old strategies for efficiency improvements don't apply to employees whose jobs mostly involve tacit activities. These tacit activities create an environment where agility is paramount. Executives will have to learn how to compete, innovate, and manage in a world where clear lines of authority and roles are blurred at best.

Business agility can be described as the ability of the enterprise to cope with unpredictable changes, to survive unprecedented threats from the business environment, and to take advantage of changes as opportunities (Goldman, Nagel, and Preiss, 1996). The world of business is changing due to a variety of forces such as mobilization, collaboration, integration, and digitalization. Agility was once a term used to describe small and nimble organizations that could change their business model and internal processes very quickly. This agility provided a competitive advantage for the smaller organization but that's changing as more and more organizations implement agile technology, agile business processes, service oriented architectures, and ubiquitous communications. One example of a company already in the agility mode is Cemex; the third largest cement company in the world, based in Mexico. Creative thinking has led them to invent a concrete mix with added anti-bacterial agent which means that when used for flooring in low cost housing projects for poorer communities, dwellings have built-in health protection; when used in hospitals and clinics, the treated concrete not only helps kill germs but also means less expensive (and potentially polluting) cleaning agents have to be used. In addition, Cemex cut costs and delivery times by using global-positioning satellite technology in its delivery trucks and redefined its business model with online auctions.

Self-Actualization
Maslow's hierarchy of needs is a theory in psychology that Abraham Maslow (1943) proposed in his paper: *A Theory of Human Motivation*. His theory contends that as humans meet 'basic needs', they seek to satisfy successively 'higher needs' that occupy a set hierarchy. Maslow studied exemplary people such as Albert Einstein, Jane Addams, Eleanor Roosevelt, and Frederick Douglass rather than mentally ill or neurotic people, writing that "the study of crippled, stunted, immature, and unhealthy specimens can yield only a cripple psychology and a cripple philosophy. (Maslow,

1987). Maslow developed a theory of personality that has influenced a number of different fields, including technology. This wide influence is due in part to the high level of practicality of Maslow's theory as well as his focus on the high performers of his time. This theory accurately describes many realities of personal experiences. Maslow's basic needs include the following:

Physiological Needs
These are biological needs. They consist of needs for oxygen, food, water, and a relatively constant body temperature. They are the strongest needs because if a person were deprived of all needs, the physiological ones would come first in the person's search for satisfaction.

Safety Needs
When all physiological needs are satisfied and are no longer controlling thoughts and behaviors, the needs for security can become active. Adults have little awareness of their security needs except in times of emergency or periods of disorganization in the social structure (such as the L.A. riots). Children often display the signs of insecurity and the need to be safe.

Needs of Love, Affection and Belongingness
When the needs for safety and for physiological well-being are satisfied, the next class of needs for love, affection and belongingness can emerge. Maslow states that people seek to overcome feelings of loneliness and alienation. This involves both giving and receiving love, affection and the sense of belonging.

Needs for Esteem
When the first three classes of needs are satisfied, the needs for esteem can become dominant. These involve needs for both self-esteem and for the esteem a person gets from others. Humans have a need for a stable, firmly based, high level of self-respect, and respect from others. When these needs are satisfied, the person feels self-confident and valuable as a person in the world. When these needs are frustrated, the person feels inferior, weak, helpless

and worthless. The next generation of the web allows everyone to contribute and be a part of something regardless of position or class.

Needs for Self-Actualization
When all of the foregoing needs are satisfied, then and only then are the needs for self-actualization activated. Maslow describes self-actualization as a person's need to be and do that which the person was "born to do". A musician must make music, an artist must paint, and a poet must write. These needs make themselves felt in signs of restlessness. The person feels on edge, tense, lacking something, in short, restless. If a person is hungry, unsafe, not loved or accepted, or lacking self-esteem, it is very easy to know what the person is restless about. It is not always clear what a person wants when there is a need for self-actualization. The hierarchic theory is often represented as a pyramid, with the larger, lower levels representing the lower needs, and the upper point representing the need for self-actualization. Maslow believes that the only reason that people would not move well in direction of self-actualization is because of hindrances placed in their way by society (Simons, J., Irwin, D. & Drinnien, B, 2006). While Maslow's framework is a wonderful visual representation, the representation of a movement from one level to the next may be misleading. Most researchers now believe that many of these levels are fulfilled at the same time or in parallel.

Notice the words "Born to do" as a base description of self-actualization. That is the emotion that comes out when you are one of the best in the world. Self-Actualization fuels your commitment of excellence. John Wooden believed that the mark of a true champion is to always perform near your own level of competency.

Perks of World Class Designation
One of the perks of being classified as a world class expert is the travel opportunities. For most consultants, travel is a way of life but as an employee, my opportunities have been limited over the years. As time moves on, I get more and more invitations to speak

around the world. In most cases, the determining factor is for me is the location and the tourism opportunities. We have had to opportunity to travel all over the United States as well as Hawaii, Australia, and Europe. I doubt that I would have ever gotten to see Dover Castle if it hadn't been for the world class designation within the world of metadata.

Another benefit is the training you get from the other world class experts. Every keynote or tutorial that I present provides me the opportunity to attend the conference and learn new and innovative technologies. In most cases, professional conferences will pick up the tab for the conference; if you share your knowledge and experience. You cannot become world class by isolating yourself from your peers. Building upon the ideas and concepts of others helps you keep your message up to date and relevant to the audience. Of course, this gives you the opportunity to keep an eye on your competition. Conference sessions also provide you the opportunity to communicate with the vendor community or hold special sessions with other Fortune 100 companies. It is amazing how much people open up about their implementations and technology when they feel they are around like minded folks and away from corporate control.

Differentiation
What makes you different or unique? You work in a major corporation along with 20,000 of your dearest friends and I want to know what makes you unique? The program presented in this book will set you apart from the crowd. When you review this material, you will see that the concepts are fairly straight forward. Yet, so few people will actually take action in order to move beyond their comfort zone. Ask yourself these questions:

1. If your company would commit to buying you two books a year would you take advantage of the offer?

2. If your company was in difficult business cycle, would you attend training classes at your own expense?

3. If the company only paid for half your tuition would you go back to school and earn your MBA?

4. If your company paid you to file a patent would you do it?

Most people would answer "yes, of course" but you and I know the reality. Very few people will actually do these things because they require effort and commitment. Differentiation is doing what other people are not doing; the road less traveled. Don't get me wrong, the world doesn't want you to stand out. Our education system doesn't want you to color outside the lines and our corporations want moveable chess pieces with similar skills, knowledge, and background. Differentiation is not about being a rebel without a cause. It is a realization of one's uniqueness and the seeing one's role, goal, and calling with an "internal" eye. The goal of most organizations is to create sameness; you must break out of this environment and set your eyes on a bigger prize.

One question that I get sometimes is why I am not a consultant making the big bucks instead of settling for 1% corporate raises based on the equality mentality. The reality is that I am not playing the same game as everyone else. My success or failure will not be determined by an annual review but rather on a long term trademark program. If I get a 1.5% raise but generate 26 publications then was that a good year or a bad year? The essence of this program is to change the game you are playing.

Most people believe that the rules of business and career planning are fixed in stone. My grandfather who grew up at the turn of the century worked for a single company, he based his entire existence on one livelihood. He worked in a sawmill until the day he retired in 1990. Day after day, in the hot southern sun, he worked to survive. My father's career started much the same way where he went to work for a large electric supply company in Columbus, GA. The story did end differently, in that he became an entrepreneur after 20 years in the business. Eventually, my father owned two different companies and both were successful. As for myself, I have worked for a single trade (Technology) but for a variety of organizations. Over my 24 years in business, I have worked for seven different organizations, not counting mergers and acquisitions. The days of working for the same company for 50 years are over and most people are willing to move from trade to another two to three times in their lifetime. My father is also an avid golfer and one day we talked about golf and business. His wisdom was that in golf the rules of the game are fixed and governed by the United States Golf Association (USGA). However in business, if you can change the rules of the game then you can win. He wasn't talking about accounting rules or illegal activities, he was talking about products, costs, innovation, execution, and business strategy. The same thing applies in the world of career planning.

Returning to stories provided by John McCormack (1990) in his book *Self Made in America*, he tells a great story about an elderly gentleman he meets by the beach. After having a couple of conversations, Abe wanted to help John understand one of the core concepts of business. He challenges him to a 100 yard dash and offers up $100.00 to the winner. John, being physically fit, accepts the challenge and begins thinking of how he is going to take his wife out to dinner with the money. On the day of the race, Abe arrives carrying a sack. After marking off the 100 yards, Abe asks John if he thinks he can beat him. John responds, yes, of course. I agree, so what do people at the race track do to get you to bet on the slower horse? They give him the better jockey or add weights to the faster horse. Here, Abe hands John two ten pound barbells. Now, do you think you can beet me? Yes! Me too, here put these blinders on like they make horses wear. Now, do you think you can beet me? Yes! Ok, you run backwards. Ready, Set, Go... Of course, Abe wins by a mile and John hands him two fifty dollar bills. Abe asks John what he learned from this? That I was just taken by an 80 year old? No, keep thinking and let's get together tomorrow and discuss further. The next day John tells Abe that if you can change the rules of the game, you can win. John went on to become a multi-millionaire in the hair styling business.

Opportunities

Based on my experience, the best promise of the trademark program is the wide variety of opportunities that emerge. These opportunities will emerge inside and outside the organization. The leadership within your organization will recognize your talents and will want to take advantage of your unique value. A word of caution, when executive leaders see your potential they may want to move you to another area of the business. Of course, you will have to be careful and stay focused on your long term plan which may require turning down these offers. Trade organizations will seek you out to help fill their needs for communication. Volunteer opportunities will also be available for standard bodies, magazines, and many other areas. The point is that has your trademark grows the number of opportunities will also grow.

Trust and Credibility
The word trust has been active in human language throughout written history. Although the concept of trust is vital to our daily lives, most people have trouble defining trust in specific terms. Trust as the dependence of sources such as reliability, genuineness, truthfulness, intent, competence, and other similar factors. These factors can be applied to situations that either enable trust or destroy it (Bhattacharya, Devinney, and Pillutla (1998). Trust as an expectancy of positive outcomes that can be received from another party. Trust can be based on the expected actions within an interaction characterized by uncertainty. Trust can be viewed as the perceived credibility and benevolence of the other party. The credibility of the party is related to the documentation or statements made during the course of a business relationship. Benevolence is the conceptualization that one party is genuinely concerned for the other's welfare and is motivated by seeking a joint gain in the relationship. We can characterize trust into the basic dimensions of capability, commitment, and consistency. Within a customer and supplier relationship, trust is the customer's belief in the supplier's benevolence, honesty, and competence to act in the best interest of the relationship. Each of these definitions expands on the basic concepts of trust and enables a more thorough understanding of the emotion. People have a disposition to trust based on past experiences. This disposition is formed by the view

that people are generally trustworthy and should be given the benefit of doubt.

Social norms and opinions of certain reference groups have a powerful influence on the formation of individual's specific and general expectations of trust. For example, Asians point to their superior aspects of the oriental culture, such as deference to authority, emphasis on education, and family values, as a source of foundational trust. Trust exists in an environment of mutuality, where any given situation is person specific and built on the experiences and beliefs of the individual. The institutional factors are defined as the social networks and oversight processes put into place by the government, communities of trust, and the legal profession. Becoming a world class expert creates an environment where you benefit from the social trust that is supported by the trademark framework. This in turn, creates an environment where you get the benefit of the doubt on credibility.

Expanding the Body of Knowledge
The phrase expanding the body of knowledge comes from the academic side of the house. The trademark experience builds on the solid foundation of knowledge within your area of expertise. Your efforts are directly involved in the research and knowledge generation process, not only learning as you conduct research and experiments, but also expanding the body of knowledge with your publications and patents. The trademark program focuses on expanding the body of knowledge related to the business of creating and delivering knowledge within your discipline. This point is critical, since your entire effort focuses on differentiation. Eventually, your efforts will expand the knowledge base but keep in mind this expansion doesn't have to be three miles wide. Even a small contribution can be built upon by others.

In a famous remark made in 1676, Newton modestly declared in a letter to Hooke: "you defer too much my ability for searching into this subject ... If I have seen further [than the ancients] it is by standing on the shoulders of Giants". Clearly, expanded the body of knowledge, even just a little, is a great contribution to the world of science. We all must work together in order to continue to press forward as our physical, emotional and social needs continue to expand.

Influence, Visibility and Mindshare
Who does your organization turn to when they need help? As I have mentioned before that my area of expertise is enterprise metadata and collaborative technology. When the company needed help in the Information Worker space and the utilization of tools like Collaboration, Online Meeting, and Workflow, they turned to our organization. When they wanted guidance in data architecture, reuse, online ordering, and social networking, they came to our organization. Success breeds success and you need to be aware of how this impacts your brand. The more your brand grows the more visibility and influence you are going to have within the enterprise. Early in my metadata adventure, I would attend meetings and everyone would argue over the best strategy and even the definition of metadata. I had very little credibility, so my ideas and innovations were treated as every ones else's. Over the years, I have seen a change in that we get in very few discussions around metadata. Consultants know that if they come into the organization claiming expertise then they will be challenged. No matter what their credentials are, I will have home field advantage and don't mind exercising that fact.

Career Mountains
Development Plans have evolved as a particular approach to planning career and skill development activities for individuals within employing organizations. The concept of a development plan is the creation of a clear action plan for an individual for which the individual takes primary responsibility. Barber, Hirsh, and Tamkin (2005) describe the development plan as:

> *"A Personal Development Plan can vary considerably in focus. A plan may concentrate purely on development needed to perform better in the current job. It may extend to development required for the next career step. It may take a much more holistic or person based approach; encouraging the individual*

to consider their personal effectiveness and a correspondingly wider range of development needs. This issue of focus was very important to how the individual employees perceived their scheme. By and large, employees feel more satisfied by a development planning process which takes their wider personal aspirations on board."

I am going to use an analogy here in order to describe the corporate development planning environment. The world of development consists of two basic elements: mountains and valleys. The analogy of the mountain describes the enormous amount of effort required in order to develop and execute a true value-add development plan. The valley describes the area that 80-90% of information technology workers evolve too. I use the word evolve in the sense that we all, at one time or another, worked on developing skills, knowledge, and ability beyond the current scope of employment. For most of us, this was the college years where we went to school during the day and worked at night or vice versa. Eventually, we got into a job or career that has carried us to the valley.

Why do I use the imagery of a valley to describe where most people are in their development activities? While not exactly true, we see the valley as a peaceful place where flowers bloom, the grass is always green, and simple cottages paint the landscape. People that live on the plains will certainly work hard for those 40 hours that they are paid and sometimes stretch to 45-50 if the work demands it. They will go to training if the corporation pays for it and read the occasional industry article. They will focus on their weaknesses as pointed out during performance reviews all the while giving the illusion of an actual development plan. In no way am I saying that the people of the valley are lazy, lack ambition, or don't care about their career. The simple fact is that they are not climbing one of the four mountains. Is a mountain a representation of what we do for a living? No, the mountain represents what you do to develop your career when no one is looking. Mountains are not a representation of what you do for a living or what you get paid for, that is something else and we would not have valleys if that were the case. What do you do after you put the kids to bed? Do you watch the next episode of Desperate Housewives or do you read Fast Company or Harvard Business Review? When you are sitting in traffic, do you listen to talk radio or do you pop in the latest book by Tom Peters or Seth Godin? You see, the valley has a place for those that work hard and do a good job but the mountains are for those reaching to a higher plane where the future must be created not simply managed.

The four mountains that will be described include Mt. Academia, Mt. Professional, Mt. Corporate, and Mt. Entrepreneur. One early warning about these mountains is that the terrain is constantly changing and what looked like a solid career plan yesterday might not work today. Let's start with the mountain that the vast majority of performance reviews focus on and that's Mt. Corporate. The people that are climbing Mr. Corporate are obvious since we vilify these people daily and Dilbert has mocked them for years. They are the ones we refer to as workaholics, the ones that work 60 to 70 hours a week, the ones that are driving toward that corner office with conviction. We know them well since we sit at company outings and make snide comments about who is seen with them; "Hey look at Frank over there kissing up". Those of us in the valley enjoy sitting out in our lounge chair and laugh as they slip, get on failed projects, and embarrass themselves during town halls. That is, of course, until they reach the top and then we are amazed at their model of success. Make no mistake, these people want the projects no one else does, they want to be on the most challenging projects, and they want to be on the firing line. They understand medals of valor are not awarded to the cooks unless you're Steven Segal. The question remains that while you may want to "Be" a Director are you willing to "Do" Director. Life on Mt. Corporate is not easy and I admire those that travel this path.

The next mountain is one that I am very familiar with since I have spent the last seven years aimlessly wandering around. Mt. Academia is where education and the expansion of the body of knowledge take center stage. For some people, Mt. Academia is

241

getting a Masters degree while others it's the Associate degree. For others, publishing in journals, proceedings, and writing textbooks complete the challenge of the climb. Now, how does the corporation or the technology manager view people that are climbing Mt. Academia? It wasn't that long ago that an MBA was a treasured credential. Organizations not only paid for the degree they allowed employees to take time off to complete (often with pay). Today, many managers value experience over an education. Graduate business schools are churning out a record number of eager MBA holders, approaching 120,000 a year in the United States alone, according to the U.S. Department of Education. Because of the sheer volume of graduates, the status of a conventional MBA degree as differentiator has faded; instead, it has become the common denominator. However, I will argue that academic credentials can never be removed from your resume and publishing in a journal and proceeding is still very rare. The reason I like Mt. Academia within the corporate setting is that the accomplishments have a lasting value while project work does not. When you get a chance ask your current manager what project you worked on three years ago. Chances are they don't remember or care. Corporate America only really cares about what you did in the last twelve months or the next six. Whether you agree or disagree that this fact that this is good for business is up for debate but it is undeniable none the less.

Mt. Professional is out next adventure to discuss. Let me start with this comment; talent competes on a global scale while labor competes on a local scale. In other words, learning Microsoft's .Net is no big deal but being one of the top five .Net programmers in the world is. When I say Data Modeler, who comes to mind? (Graeme Simsion or William Smith?) When I say Metadata Management, who comes to mind? (David Marco or Adrienne Tannenbaum?) When I say Information Architecture, who comes to mind? (Louis Rosenfeld or Peter Morville?) And one more, when I say Enterprise Architecture, who do you think about? (John Zachman or Steven Spawek?) These people have climbed Mt. Professional and set themselves apart from the rest of us within our field of study. How do these people differentiate themselves? The most popular method is the publication channel. They spend an enormous amount of time writing articles, books, and presenting material at national conferences. They are letting their voice be heard across the vast channels of communication. To ask the same question as we did for Mt. Academia; how does corporate America look at people that are climbing Mt. Professional? I wish I could say they support people trying to get at the top of their game and becoming one of the top experts in their field. Unfortunately, fear over Intellectual Property, trade secrets, and simple lack of understanding by front line managers forces most people to sit at the base of Mt. Professional and never take that first step.

The final mountain is Mt. Entrepreneur. Who among us haven't thought about starting our own business or moving into the consulting environment. I enjoy the commercial where the lady is telling the story of how her and her husband vacationed in some exotic location and decided to stay and open a beach bar. In fact, many of us made that leap during the Y2K and Dot-Com eras to try our hand at the entrepreneur game. Sadly, many of these individuals have returned as these "Tulip" Mania events failed to deliver on the dramatic increase in demand for resources. Gerber (1995) makes the claim that the small business owner must be an entrepreneur and a manager as well as a technician. The technician is the worker-bee, the one who produces the product. The manager makes sure operations and finances run smoothly and consistently. The entrepreneur formulates the goals, and steers the business in the direction needed to reach those goals. Of these three personalities, the entrepreneur is the key. Without it, the technician will work himself or herself to death or bankruptcy. As the business grows, the business owner will need to draw away from the technician work and manager work and delegate this work, rather than abdicate this, to others. Clearly corporate America frowns on the obvious conflict of interest. Recently, a fellow enterprise architect changed jobs and was forced to stop blogging due to the "Corporate Policy". As Tom Peter's once said, if you're not willing to be fired for what you believe in then why get up in the morning. He found a new job and continues his climb on Mt. Professional.

So what are the implications of where you stand; mountain or valley? First, we need to understand and admit that the valley cannot compete with the globalization movement. We must bring together a collection of forces in order to compete: Innovation from Mt. Academia, Risk from Mt. Enterprise, Knowledge from Mt. Professional and the Commitment from Mt. Corporate. Only the combination of these skills will be able to turn the tide of automation, standardization, and globalization. Second, you need to commit that you will tackle at least one of the mountains described in this article. The new competitive framework requires a broader set of skills; "hard" (technical) and "soft" (interpersonal and communication) skills are equally important. The skills identified by a number of authors include managing information, resources, and relationships with people as well as self-management. In addition, "global" workers need flexibility, problem-solving and decision-making ability, adaptability, creative thinking, self-motivation, and the capacity for reflection (Kerka, 2004).

What can you do?
Assuming that you followed the plan laid out in this book, you should have a good idea of where you need to go. Granted, that journey may be a long one but those first few steps are critical. I encourage you to execute this action plan with. Felder (2006) publishing an interesting hypothetical interview that reflects the criticality of becoming the world's best.

Interviewer: *"Good morning, Mr. Allen. I'm Angela Macher— project engineering and human services at Consolidated Industries "*

Senior: *"Good morning, Ms. Macher—nice to meet you."*
I: *"So, I understand you're getting ready to graduate in May and you're looking for a position with Consolidated...and I also see you've got a 3.75 GPA coming into this semester—very impressive. What kind of position did you have in mind?"*

S: *"Well, I liked most of my engineering courses but especially the ones with lots of math and computer applications—I've gotten pretty good at Excel and Matlab and I also know some Visual Basic. I was thinking about control systems or design."*

I: *"I see. To be honest, we have very few openings in those areas— we've moved most of our manufacturing and design work to China and Romania and most of our programming to India. Got any foreign languages?"*

S: *"Um, a couple of years of Spanish in high school but I couldn't take any more in college—no room in the curriculum."*

I: *"How would you feel about taking an intensive language course for a few months and moving to one of our overseas facilities? If you do well you could be on a fast track to management."*

S: *"Uh...I was really hoping I could stay in the States. Aren't any positions left over here?"*

I: *"Sure, but not like ten years ago, and you need different skills to get them. Let me ask you a couple of questions to see if we can find a fit. First, what do you think your strengths are outside of math and computers?"*

S: *"Well, I've always been good in physics."*

I: *"How about social sciences and humanities?"*

S: *"I did all right in those courses—mostly A's—but I can't honestly say I enjoy that stuff."*

I: *"Right. And would you describe yourself as a people person?"*

S: *"Um...I get along with most people, but I guess I'm kind of introverted."*

I: *"I see...."* (Stands up.) *OK, Mr. Allen—thanks. I'll forward your application to our central headquarters, and if we find any slots that might work we'll be in touch. Have a nice day."*

The job market over the next 5-10 years will change dramatically as more and more organizations look toward the automation or outsourcing Information Worker jobs. Based on this hypothetical interview, we can summarize that the skills needed include the ability to think innovatively, holistically, and entrepreneurially. Design for aesthetics as well as function, communicate persuasively, bridge cultural gaps, and periodically re-engineer themselves to adjust to changing market conditions will be the keys for long term transformation. Here are 7 things you can do in conjunction with your trademark program to ensure long term success and viability in the market.

Get Involved and Engaged with Web 2.0 Technologies
You don't have to look far to see the emergence of Web 2.0 technologies within the organization. Corporations are deploying wikis, blogs, and social networking software throughout the enterprise. While organizations have plenty of communication channels like email, portals, and knowledge management systems, these new tools are opening up new possibilities for sharing and locating information. These tools are more open without the strict rules imposed by other mediums. Corporations like IBM, Oracle, and Microsoft have tools that enable the Web 2.0 functionality.

As stated in Chapter 3, Sharepoint is one of the fastest growing tools in their portfolio. The market continues to grow as both Microsoft and IBM has sold more than 100 million seats for their collaborative products. Our organization offers a plethora of products that can be used by the individual or work group. Individuals can build their own "MySite" which acts as a social networking platform where like minded or people that share interest can locate each other. The environment provides the ability for the end user to share their current projects, research interests, background, and skills. The system supports end-user application directory search, authentication, organizational structure, and provides multiple fields as search criteria. Integration into the typical business model includes presence, outlook, web conference, and the ability to call another employee right from the "MySite". The system even indicates whether people are currently online and available for an instant message. This integrated functionality makes it easier than ever for employees to find and connect with the colleagues who have the knowledge and experience they need to help answer questions, build designs and collaborate with others on business problems. Additional users can create their own web pages in order to communicate or process work with management.

By now, most organizations have some form of collaborative technologies in place that information workers can engage. Web, Audio, and Video conferencing applications allow you to meet with people around the world which is an excellent way of immersing yourself into a world without hierarchal structures. Additionally, organizations are adding many of the social applications like employee profile, instant messaging, blogs, and wikis.

The boundaries of the workplace are shifting, and are frequently less defined by organizational structures than by the value added to the business. As the work force becomes mobile, businesses embrace globalization and the speed to market becomes a better determinate of competitive advantage, collaborative solutions will play a more strategic role. Collaborative technologies can be defined as any application that allows more than two people to interact. Baltzan, Haag, and Phillips (2006) describe collaborative systems as an technology-based set of tools that support the work of teams by facilitating the sharing and flow of information. Most organizations collaborate with other businesses or customers through a variety of applications including Electronic Data Interchange (EDI) and the World Wide Web (WWW). Collaboration tools create virtual workplaces and include of a wide variety functional information categories including: knowledge management, content management, online meetings, discussion groups, weblogs, wikis, etc. Collaboration tools are actually a subset of a much larger tool palate denoted as the tools of the information worker. This expanded tool collection includes: security tools, enterprise applications, portals, office suites, client applications, process automation, and enterprise knowledge stores. Deploying collaborative solutions is different than simply implementing traditional enterprise applications which operate over structured data and generally focus on specific business processes. Collaborative environments operate over unstructured information and can span several business processes and organizational boundaries. Since the need for virtual workspaces emerge when organizational collaboration occurs, the ability to predict demand is nearly impossible. More importantly, when the business need arises for a virtual workspace, the technology cannot wait or the competitive advantage may be lost.

Collaborative workspaces are generally designed for distributed teams which can be defined as groups of people that interact through interdependent tasks guided by common purpose, and work across space, time, and organizational boundaries primarily through electronic means (Maznevski & Chudoba, 2000). In order to be effective in sharing information and working in an online environment, end users need to understand and develop knowledge sharing practices (Becerra-Fernandez & Sabherwal, 2001).

While there are many products in the world of collaboration, most organizations will implement a single product and then add additional components as the business demands new functionality. The collaborative tool defines how the information will be stored, presented, and integrated into the environment. The virtual workspace design will emerge from the various artifacts already produced which include the user requirements, research from the business case and the architectures described by the technical community. The workspace should be based on solid design principles and subjected to usability studies. Remember, virtual workspaces are not just a single function but rather a collection of utilities or applications. Knowledge management, information architecture, content management, search engine technology, and portalization are just a few of the evolutionary benefits of implementing collaborative solutions at the enterprise level. Collaborative products like Microsoft's SharePoint, WebEx, and IBM's WorkPlace deliver a set of solutions which include many of the following:

- Email, Task Management and Calendar
- Document Management and Publishing
- Intranet and Extranet Environments
- Discussions
- RSS Feeds

- Professional Profiles
- Taxonomy and Information Domain Constructs
- Personalization
- Wiki and Weblog (Blog) Functionality
- Form Management
- Workflow

With all of this functionality, you may see the opportunity to replace your Intranet applications with collaborative functionality. One of the most frequent requests is that the virtual workspaces integrate with the organizational Intranet and business applications. In many organizations, the technology group implements three different solutions that are rarely integrated. The most common form of integration problem is the search engine. Each technology may have their own internal search engine which requires the end user to decide before hand if the information is located on the company portal, corporate Intranet, knowledge stores or virtual workspaces. Part of the issue is technology, but politics and usability also come into play, which make it difficult to integrate the various knowledge environments.

Try Some of the New Technologies at Home
While work is a great place to try out Web 2.0 technology, you have plenty of options at home. Locate a weblog that interests you. With a simple search with Google or Technorati, you can locate a weblog on just about any topic you wish. Why not begin to contribute to the conversation and demonstrate your knowledge of the subject. You might be surprised by the number of people that agree with you and those that don't. Another option is to join LinkedIn and begin to build your social network or create an Avatar in Second Life. If you buy a book from Amazon or rent a movie from netFlix, then post your feedback and review comments.

Within this chapter, we have talked about Wikipedia, YouTube, Second Life, and many other Web 2.0 environments. The easiest way to get involved is to try these technologies and see what appeals to you. How about posting a photo to Flickr or SnapFish? You can share your images with the world or just with family members without filling up your email. Don't worry about your photos for your scrap book. Simply, select print and you can pick them up at your local Target store. Blogs are also an excellent way to get involved and the best news is that they don't cost anything to get started. Blogger.com is an application that allows you to create a simple blog without the high cost of site administration. MySpace is another great example of a Web 2.0 communication medium that you can gain access free of charge. Like many of the free technologies, they are supported by the advertisement revenue. The key here is to create an account and get started now.

Slideshare is a social networking application that allows you to share information in the form of PowerPoint presentations or Open Office presentation files. Power Point documents (or any office documents) stored on the web with a permanent URL are a valuable resource. With Slideshare there is no need to email the file to recipients, or carry a copy around on a USB drive. The presentation can easily be shared (and with permission controls, kept relatively secure). The potential uses of online Power Point documents are numerous - from making sales pitches, lectures and conference presentations much easier, to having a permanent record of these and other presentations available on the Internet for easy access and reference (Arrington, 2006). Tags can be added which encourage the architecture of participation. You can post your thoughts where everyone in the world can review your ideas. This is a great example of how you can get your message out.

Education
We are still very early in the 2.0 phase but there are still a plethora of educational sources that you can review. Web 2.0 is one of the hottest subjects out there so you should be able to locate plenty of free resources but one of the better books on the subject is Wikinomics by Don Tapscott and Anthony Williams (2007). Wikinomics is mainly about innovation and how web-based collaboration is driving the transformation of the Web 1.0 environment. The book discusses the organizational dynamics and

how the web is destroying traditional hierarchies. The book provides some interesting insight into how organizations are looking at the value generation of this new technology. The underlying principles and strategies of Wikinomics include the openness, peering, sharing, and acting globally that is current underway.

Andrew P. McAfee (2006) published an excellent article entitled "Enterprise 2.0: The Dawn of Emergent Collaboration". MITSloan Review published the following overview: There is a new wave of business communication tools including blogs, wikis and group messaging software — which the author has dubbed, collectively, Enterprise 2.0 — that allow for more spontaneous, knowledge-based collaboration. These new tools, the author contends, may well supplant other communication and knowledge management systems with their superior ability to capture tacit knowledge, best practices and relevant experiences from throughout a company and make them readily available to more users. This article offers a paradigm that highlights the salient characteristics of these new technologies, which the author refers to as SLATES (search, links, authoring, tags, extensions, signals). The resulting organizational communication patterns can lead to highly productive and highly collaborative environments by making both the practices of knowledge work and its outputs more visible. Drawing on case studies and survey data, the article offers managers a set of ground rules for implementing the new technologies. First, it is necessary to create a receptive culture in order to prepare the way for new practices. Second, a common platform must be created to allow for a collaboration infrastructure. Third, an informal rollout of the technologies may be preferred to a more formal procedural change. And fourth, managerial support and leadership is crucial. Even when implanted and implemented well, these new technologies will certainly bring with them new challenges. These tools may well reduce management's ability to exert unilateral control and to express some level of negativity. Whether a company's leaders really want this to happen and will be able to resist the temptation to silence dissent is an open question. Leaders will have to play a delicate role if they want

Enterprise 2.0 technologies to succeed. This document is available with a little Google search ingenuity.

A quick search for Web 2.0, Enterprise 2.0 or Education 2.0 will result in a huge collection of articles and presentations that you can access. If your company subscribes to one of the research firms, like Gartner or Forrester, then you will be able to gain further insight into how 2.0 technologies will impact the organization. In the spirit of 2.0, be sure to share the information you have collected with co-workers and management.

Let Everyone Know
Be sure that everyone that you come into contact with knows that you are interested in 2.0 technologies and implementations. Do you have a company intranet where you can list information or research interests? IBM has refined its intranet with the employee directory; IBM's BluePages provides employees using the On Demand Workplace with the ability to locate information about IBM employees including professional skills, e-mail address, phone number, what geography they are from and what time it is there. The system even indicates whether people are currently online and available for an instant message. This integrated functionality makes it easier than ever for IBM employees to find and connect with the colleagues who have the knowledge and experience they need to help answer questions, build proposals, meet with clients and solve business problems. Insert your interests into conversations, emails, or at lunch. Get the word out that you want to be the person people want to go to in order to learn about your specialty.

Engage Correlated Areas
Another strategy is to get involved with Web 1.0 technology groups. Knowing that these groups will eventually integrate 2.0 technologies, you will already have your foot in the door. Examples of these groups might include Intranet client-support, architecture, search and development, web service delivery, SOA or registry teams. Each of these groups might be prime candidates for 2.0 transformations when the organization is ready. Every

organization needs knowledge and information experts so immerse yourself in the technology and see what you can contribute.

Go Mobile
Many of us go to the same location day after day because that's just what everyone else does. However, other people are going mobile which means getting a laptop and taking your business on the road. With the countless number of networks, including your local Starbucks, you should be able to connect in just about any city. Can you handle interfacing with management, customers, and co-workers without a physical presence? Humans are social by nature, so this new type of technology can take some time to get use to.

Another option is to get a Blackberry or Mobile 5.0 device so that you can stay in touch and access the intranet from a hand held device. Personally, I have had a hand held device for well over 10 years. To me, the key is that I am in constant communication and have access when ever it's needed at any time of the day. Recently on a trip to Orlando, Fl, we were looking for an Olive Garden to eat and couldn't locate the restaurant based on the directions of the hotel staff. No problem; take out the Blackberry and call up the Internet applications and within 5 minutes, we had easy directions. At the beginning, we talked about having all information freely available and constant communications and this can now be had for a few dollars a month and a hand held device.

Learn Excessively
Can you ever stop learning or innovating? The obvious answer is no. We are not in a protected economy where the events across the ocean have limited impact on us. Today, if the Asian stock market goes down, ours follows in short order. With increased globalization and offshore sourcing, global supply chain management is becoming an important issue for many businesses. The idea of lowering costs and decreasing risks is becoming the norm but this integrates suppliers from around the world. Suppliers include the labor and talent needed to manage and innovate in order to stay competitive. How are things changing?

Learning has begun to shift away from the predefined skills and competencies toward dynamically enabling knowledge workers to be more productive. In a world of active lifelong learning, an individual's skill portfolio will be built and documented based on a mix of real-life experiences, achievements, relationships and formal certifications (Straub, 2006). Certainly education will come from formal means such as higher education and online learning. As we have seen, organizations are placing less an emphasis on this type of education and more on the contextual learning of experience. Trilling (2005) defined seven basic skills that need to be mastered in the new world of work: critical thinking-doing, creativity, collaboration, cross-cultural understanding, communication, computing, and excessive learning. You must put yourself on a learning plan that includes various disciplines and technologies.

Becoming an Untouchable

In Thomas Friedman's book *"The World Is Flat: A Brief History of the Twenty-first Century"*, he discusses what it takes to be successful in a flat world. Specifically, he introduces a characterization of an untouchable. An untouchable is a position that cannot be outsourced either overseas or to another organization. The following section takes a look at Mr. Friedman's four classifications of workers and how this trademark program will impact that class of individual.

Special Workers

Special workers are individuals that attaché themselves to a specific category that makes them unique. It's not really associated with their skills but may be a result of timing, luck, and association. In other words, they may not be the best in the world but something makes them special. Take a look at the following examples:

- Business Owner – Steve Jobs
- Pop-Culture – Britney Spears
- Sports – Annika Sorenstam

- Patent Owners –Alexander Graham Bell
- Historical Influence – Gordon Bell
- High Profile or Organization Representative – Jared Fogle (Subway)
- Leadership – Michael Eisner (Disney)

Does the trademark framework impact this type of classification? Not really, sure we can classify the accomplishments of Gordon Bell, Steve Jobs and Michael Eisner. However, the truth is that their fame is more associated outside of a trademarked accomplishment. While Jared lost a ton of weight, he is by no means the most accomplished at this task nor is he an expert on healthy eating.

Specialized Workers
Clearly, this is where our program gets a direct hit. People who are at the top of their game fit into this classification.

- Brain Surgeons – Dr. Ben Carson
- Lawyers – Jonnie Cochran
- Web 2.0 – Tim O'Reilly or Don Tapscott
- Knowledge Management – Joseph Firestone
- Object Oriented Programming – Alan Kay
- Coaching – Lou Holtz
- Marketing – Sergio Zyman

These people are clearly the very best in their field and they have the trademarks to back it up. They have the real world experience and the winning record to support their claim as the world's best. There can only be a few people that can claim "specialized" under our definition. You must, must understand the criticality of the support information needed to reach this level. Looking at the list, I don't see anyone that didn't put in enormous amounts of time and commitment in developing their trademarks.

Anchored Workers

Anchored workers use the benefit of locality to hold down a job. Non information worker jobs like your barber, plumbers, nurses, doctors, and electricians provide excellent examples of careers that utilize the element of location to their benefit. These jobs have direct connection with the community. Clearly, small organizations have a direct dependency on local labor since these companies don't have the size to invest in large outsourcing projects. They may be able to utilize services but when labor is needed, the local community has the best pull. While larger organizations continue to lower costs by moving work to the lowest cost provider, there will always be some local jobs but the competition for these will increase. Most people prefer to work close to home or within their community. Salaries, availability, and growth will have a tremendous impact on the individual decision. Trademarks are still critical in an environment where demand is low and supply high; you must set yourself apart from the crowd.

Adaptable Workers
The term used by the research firms is "Versatilist" which is an individual that can adapt their skills to fit the demand of the role and responsibilities. These individuals are skilled at learning new skills and techniques very quickly. Specialists generally have deep skills and narrow scope, giving them expertise that is recognized by peers but seldom valued outside their immediate domain. Generalists have broad scope and shallow skills, enabling them to respond or act reasonably quickly but often without gaining or demonstrating the confidence of their partners or customers. Versatilists, in contrast, apply depth of skill to a progressively widening scope of situations and experiences, gaining new competencies, building relationships, and assuming new roles (Kerner, 2005).

One might see an issue with the Jack of all trades and master of none. While this sounds good and for most of us an easy answer to an obvious problem, we must be sure we completely understand the impact of this choice. If you take a look at the entire pool of information workers in your office, then how many of them would say they fall into this category? Would anyone actually say that they don't have this capability? I doubt you will ever hear, "No, I can't adapt to the new organization and learn new skills". The truth is you still need to be at the top of your game in this area. Some people learn faster than others; some people adapt faster than others. The one thing that you didn't really hear me say is that your trademarks must be focused in a single area, quite the opposite. I reiterate the point that you need to develop your trademarks in every area and try to map them to your brand. One can argue that metadata and Web 2.0 are miles apart but we have been able to combine these technologies in research papers, book chapters, as well as in our job.

Summary

Developing a personal brand supported with trademarks is nothing new. Brands are about perceptions that all of us carry with us as we progress in our careers. A couple of months ago, our organization was performing yearly reviews and I noticed an interesting thing about the employees. In the past, you could classify Information Workers as either "A", "B" or "C" players. Due to consolidation, outsourcing, and attrition, we have fewer and fewer C players. In some cases, even the "B" players are being reduced. What happens in a world where you have to compete with world class "A" players? How will compete when you are competing from "A" players around the world? The answer is simple; you build your trademarks in order to support your brand.

Branding isn't something that most of us are comfortable with. The good news is that personal branding is much easier than branding a product or company. You know who you are and what you stand for. Strong brands are consistent and supported by every aspect or representation. Although, I have a lot to say about politics, culture, and current events, I never blog about them. Giving my opinion in this area would be counter to my brand as a metadata or collaboration expert. The Web 2.0 opens up new world and new communication mediums for communicating your brand. Unfortunately, that door is open to every person in the world which makes for a very crowded space.

Final Thoughts

After reading this book, you may think that you don't have the skills, knowledge, or ability to actually be the best in the world. Fred Astaire's first screen test resulted in a memo that read "Can't act, slightly bald but can dance a little". An expert said of famous football coach Vince Lombardi: "He possesses minimal football knowledge and lacks motivation". No, the key isn't ability but perseverance. The trademark program isn't about developing the "big" hit; it's about hundreds of small ones that add up over time. The question isn't where you are today or where you have been. The real question is where do you want to be next year? How do you want to be remembered within your industry?

Will you make mistakes? Yes. Will you fail over and over again? Yes. Will the people around you try to hold you back or discourage you from trying? Yes. Will your employer tell you that you are wasting your time? Yes. As Will Rogers once said, "You've got to go out on a limb sometimes, because that's where the fruit is". Stay focused, and good luck.

References

Chapter 1: The World of the Information Worker
Anderian, R. Armstrong, D. & Yu, K. (1997). *The Persona Principle: How to Succeed in Business with Image-Marketing.* Simon & Schuster, Parsippany , NJ.

Colvin, G. (2006). *Catch a Rising Star.* Fortune Magazine, 153(02).

Gross, D. (2002). *Data Mine.* Stern Business.

Hopfinger, J. (2006). *Magazines Profile Top Business Talent.* Retrieved March 27, 2007 from
http://www.businessjournalism.org/pages/biz/2006/02/magazines_profile_top_business_1

Microsoft, (2006). *Digital Workstyle: The New World of Work.* Retrieved January 15, 2007 from
http://www.microsoft.com/presspass/events/ceosummit/docs/NewWorldofWork WP.doc

Peters, T. (2006). Reimagine!: *Business Excellence in a Disruptive Age.* DK Adult, London, England.

Wikipedia (2006). *Trademark Defined.* Retrieved March 2, 2007 from:
http://en.wikipedia.org/wiki/Trademark.

Chapter 2: The Imperative of High Performance
Bohn, R. & Jaikumar, R. (2000). *Firefighting by Knowledge Workers.* High Technology Manufacturing, 2000(03).

Bossidy, L., Burck, C. & Charan, R. (2005). *Execution: The Discipline of Getting Things Done.* Crown Business, New York, NY.

Collett, S. (2005). *Skills for the Vendor Management Office.* Retrieved January 12, 2007 from
http://www.computerworld.com/action/article.do?command=viewArticleTOC& specialReportId=761&articleId=99870

Deloitte (2004). *Enterprise Cost Reductions.* Retrieved October 15, 2006 from
http://www.deloitte.com/dtt/section_node/0,1042,sid%253D27761,00.html

Friedman, T. (2006). *The World Is Flat: A Brief History of the Twenty-first Century.* Farrar, Straus and Giroux, New York, NY.

Harris, D. (2003). *Today's Business Driven Information Technology: Answers to 100 Critical Questions for Every Manager.* Stanford University Press, Stanford, CA.

Hayes, R. (1981). *Why Japanese Factories Work.* Harvard Business Review. 6(81), pp. 57-65

Jones, W. (2004). *Relationship Management Gets Its Due.* Retrieved October 15, 2006 from http://www.cutter.com/research/2003/edge030902.html.

Lawler E. (2005) *Creating High Performance Organizations.* Asia Pacific Journal of Human Resources, 43, (1), pp. 10-17.

Levering, R. Katz, M. & Mosokowitz, M. (1985). *The Computer Entrepreneurs.* New American Library, New York, NY.

Kellaway, L. (2007). *Wanted: branding agent for self-googling job at Me, Inc.* Retrieved March 31, 2007 from http://www.ft.com/cms/s/945b2dca-db2d-11db-ba4d-000b5df10621.html

Microsoft, (2006). *Digital Workstyle: The New World of Work.* Retrieved January 15, 2007 from http://www.microsoft.com/presspass/events/ceosummit/docs/NewWorldofWorkWP.doc

Mindrum, C. (2007). *Learning and Innovation in a Flat World.* Retrieved March 8, 2007 from http://www.accenture.com/NR/rdonlyres/30B1C3F3-EC7E-4384-9DDA-EE261E2931C3/0/LearninginaFlatWorldFINAL.pdf

Tekiela, R. (2004). *How to get value from technology certifications.* Retrieved December 12, 2006 from http://www.computerworld.com/developmenttopics/development/story/0,10801,98449,00.html

Thompson, D. (2006). *Generating Revenue Through IT.* Retrieved January 5, 2007 from http://www.bitaplanet.com/business/article.php/3591251

Chapter 3: Everything 2.0
References
Abelson, J. (2006). Fast food drive-throughs go long distance. Boston Globe, 3(06).

Ahn, L., Davis, M., Fake, C., Fox, K., Furnas, G., Golder, S., Marlow, C., Naaman, M., & Schachter, J. (2006). Why do tagging systems work? *Proceedings of the SIGCHI conference on Human Factors in computing systems*. Montreal, Canada: The Association of Computing Machinery.

Baoill, A. (2004). Conceptualizing the weblog: Understanding what it is in order to imagine what it can be. *Interfacings: Journal of Contemporary Media Studies*, 5(2), 1-8.

Blood, R. (2004). How blogging software reshapes the online community. *Communications of the ACM*, 47(12), 53-55.

Boyd, D., Davis, M., Marlow, C., & Naaman, M. (2006). Social networks, networking & virtual communities: HT06, tagging paper, taxonomy, Flickr, academic article, to read. *Proceedings of the seventeenth conference on Hypertext and hypermedia*. Odense, Denmark: The Association of Computing Machinery.

Carr, N. (2003). *Does IT Matter? Information Technology and the Corrosion of Competitive Advantage*. Boston, MA. Harvard Business School Press.

Chellappa, R. & Gupta, A. (2002). Managing computing resources in active intranets. *International Journal of Network Management*, 12(2), 117-128.

Christodorescu, M., Ganapathy, V., Giffin, J., Kruger, L., Rubin, S., & Wang, H. (2005). An auctioning reputation system based on anomaly detection. *Proceedings of the 12th ACM conference on Computer and communications security*. Alexandria, VA: The Association of Computing Machinery.

Cold, S. (2006). Using Really Simple Syndication (RSS) to enhance student research. *ACM SIGITE Newsletter*, 3(1). 6-9

Davis, J., Farnham, S., and Jensen, C. (2002). Finding others online: Reputation systems for social online spaces. *Proceedings of the SIGCHI conference on Human factors in computing systems: Changing our world, changing ourselves*. Minneapolis, MN: The Association of Computing Machinery.

Gibson, F., Teasley, S., & Yew, J. (2006). Learning by tagging: group knowledge formation in a self-organizing learning community. *Proceedings of the 7th international conference on Learning sciences*. Bloomington, IA: The Association of Computing Machinery.

Godin, S. (1999). The Bootstrapper's Bible. Do You Zoom Inc. San Francisco, CA.

Greene, K.(2006). The $1 Million Netflix Challenge. Retrieved March 6, 2007 from
http://www.techreview.com/read_article.aspx?ch=specialsections&sc=briefcase&id=17587

Hof, R. (2005). Mix, Match, And Mutate. Business Week Online. Retrieved October 1, 2006 from
http://www.businessweek.com/@@76IH*ocQ34AvyQMA/magazine/content/05_30/b3944108_mz063.htm.

Hu, M, and Liu, B. (2004). Mining and Summarizing Customer Reviews. *Proceedings of the 10th Conference on Knowledge Discovery and Data Mining.* Seattle, WA: The Association of Computing Machinery.

Hu, N., Pavlou, P., and Zhang, J. (2006). Can online reviews reveal a product's true quality?: empirical findings and analytical modeling of Online word-of-mouth communication. *Proceedings of the 7th ACM conference on Electronic commerce.* Ann Arbor, MI: The Association of Computing Machinery.

Jhingran, A. (2006). Enterprise information mashups: Integrating information simply. *Proceedings of the 32nd international conference on Very large data bases.* Seoul, Korea: The Association of Computing Machinery.

Lerner, R. (2006). At the Forge: Creating Mashups. *Linux Journal,* 147, 10.

McNay, Heather E. (2000). Corporate Intranets: Building Communities with Data. *IEEE   Technology & Teamwork,* 197-201.

Millard, D. & Ross, M. (2006). Blogs, wikis & rss: Web 2.0: hypertext by any other name? *Proceedings of the seventeenth conference on Hypertext and hypermedia.* Odense, Denmark: The Association of Computing Machinery.

O'Neill, M. (2005). Automated use of a wiki for collaborative lecture notes. *Proceedings of the 36th SIGCSE technical symposium on Computer science education SIGCSE '05.* St. Louis, MO: The Association of Computing Machinery.

O'Reilly, T. (2005). *What Is Web 2.0: Design patterns and business models for the next generation of software.* Retrieved July 17, 2006 from
http://www.oreillynet.com/pub/a/oreilly/tim/news/2005/09/30/what-is-web-20.html.

Riehle, D. (2006). How and why wikipedia works: An interview with Angela Beesley, Elisabeth Bauer, and Kizu Naoko. *Proceedings of the 2006 international symposium on Wikis WikiSym '06*. Odense, Denmark: The Association of Computing Machinery.

Robb, D.(2006). GPS Repositions for Business. Retrieved November 10, 2006 from http://www.computerworld.com/printthis/2006/0,4814,108954,00.html

Smith, D. & Valdes, R. (2005). *Web 2.0: Get ready for the next old thing*. Gartner Research Paper. Stamford, CT.

Tapscott, D. & Williams, A. (2007). *Wikinomics: How Mass Collaboration Changes Everything*. Portfolio Hardcover, New York, NY.

Weiss, A. (2005). The power of collective intelligence. *netWorker*, 9(3), 16-23.

Wikipedia (2006). *Hierarchical Organization Defined*. Retrieved March 6, 2007 from: http://en.wikipedia.org/wiki/Hierarchical_organization.

Chapter 4: Maturity Model for High Performance
References
Allen, C. (2001). *Competencies: Measurable Characteristics*. Retrieved January 15, 2007 from http://xml.coverpages.org/HR-XML-Competencies-1_0.pdf.

Baskerville, R., & Pries-Heje, J. (1999). *Managing knowledge capability and maturity*. Information Systems: Current Issues and Future Changes, IFIP/Kluwer, Norwell, MA.

Bossidy, L., Burck, C. & Charan, R. (2005). *Execution: The Discipline of Getting Things   Done*. Crown Business, New York, NY.

Brown, J. (2005). *Performance Class Lecture*. Retrieved November 15, 2006 from http://pict.sdsu.edu/jsb_lecture18jan05.pdf

Carr, N. (2003). *Does IT Matter? Information Technology and the Corrosion of Competitive Advantage*. Boston, MA. Harvard Business School Press.

Curtis, B., Hefley, W. & Miller, S. (2001). *People Capability Maturity Model*. Addison-   Wesley Professional: Boston, MA.

Logan, R. & Stokes, L. (2004). *Collaborate to Compete: Driving Profitability in the Knowledge Economy*. Wiley: New York, NY.

Paulk, M., Curtis, B., Chrissis, M. & Weber, C. (1993), *Capability Maturity Model for Software, Version 1.1*, CMU-SEI-93-TR-24, Software Engineering Institute, Pittsburgh PA 15213.

Porter, M. (1998). *Competitive Advantage: Creating and Sustaining Superior Performance*. Free Press: New York, NY.

Chapter 5: Unique Value Opportunity
Bolton, P. & Olson, J. (2002). *Competencies*. Retrieved March 7, 2007 from http://www.wren-network.net/resources/benchmark/07-Competencies.pdf

Gladwell, M. (2006). *The Tipping Point: How Little Things Can Make a Big Difference*. Back Bay Books: Lebanon, IN.

IBM. (2005). *The Capability Within: The Global Human Capital Study 2005*. IBM Research.

Lazof, R. (2004). *Personal Passion: The Art of Business*. Retrieved January 22, 2007 from http://www.refresher.com/!rclpassion.html.

McCormack, J. (1990) *Self-Made in America: Plain Talk for Plain People About the Meaning of Success*. Perseus Books: New York, NY.

Microsoft, (2006). *Digital Workstyle: The New World of Work*. Retrieved January 15, 2007 from http://www.microsoft.com/presspass/events/ceosummit/docs/NewWorldofWork WP.doc

Moffat, A. (2002). *The Talent Myth*. Retrieved October 24, 2006 from www.zanthan.com/itymbi/archives/000590.html

Peters, T. & Waterman, R. (1988). *In Search of Excellence: Lessons from Americas Best Run Companies*. Warner Books: New York, NY.

Chapter 6: Networking Connections
Adamic, L. & Hogg, T. (2004). *Enhancing Reputation Mechanisms via Online Social Networks*. Proceedings from the 5th ACM Conference on Electronic Commerce: New York, NY.

Arceneaux, C. (1994). *Trust: an exploration of its nature and significance*. Journal of Invitational Theory and Practice, 3(1), 35-45

Cannon, J. & Doney, P. (1997). *An examination of the nature of trust in the buyer-seller relationship*. Journal of Marketing, 51, 35-51.

Gefen, D. & Straub, D. (2000). *Managing user trust in B2C e-services*. Retrieved August 21, 2001, from http://www.lebow.drexel.edu/gefen/eServiceJournal2001.pdf

Coyne, K., Nielsen, J., & Schwartz, M. (2006). *Intranet Design Annual 2007: The Year's 10 Best Intranets*. Nielsen Norman Group. Fremont, CA.

Rosen, C. (2000). *How to Do Just About Everything*. Free Press, New York, NY.

Seligman, A. (1997). *The Problem of Trust*. Princeton, NJ. Princeton University Press.

Chapter 7: Publishing Your Expertise
Bourne, P. (2005). *Ten Simple Rules for Getting Published*. PLoS Computational   Biology. 1(5).

Pine, J. & Gilmore, J. (1997). *The Experience Economy: Work Is Theater & Every Business a Stage*. Harvard Business School Press: Boston, MA.

Strickland, L. (2005). *Perfect Timing*. Retrieved March 5, 2007 from http://carolinanewswire.com/news/News.cgi?database=columns.db&command=viewone&id=185&op=t

Chapter 8: The Persona Principles
Andres, C. (1999). Great Web Architecture. Foster City, CA: IDG Books World Wide.

Arceneaux, C. (1994). Trust: an exploration of its nature and significance. Journal of Invitational Theory and Practice, 3(1), 35-45.

Becker, S. & Mottay, F. (2001, January). A global perspective on website usability. IEEE Software, 18(1), 61-54.

Bigley, G. & Pearce, J. (1998). Straining for shared meaning in organization science: Problems of trust and distrust. Academy of Management Review, 23(3), 405-421.

Burt, R., Camerer, C., Rousseau, D., & Sitkin, S. (1998). Not so different after all: A cross-discipline view of trust. Academy of Management Review, 23(3), 393-404.

Calongne, C. (2001, March). Designing for website usability. Journal of Computing in Small Colleges, 16(3), 39-45.

Cannon, J. & Doney, P. (1997). An examination of the nature of trust in the buyer-seller relationship. Journal of Marketing, 51, 35-51.

Christensen, C. & Tedlow, R. (2000, January). Patterns of disruption in retailing. Harvard Business Review, 42-45.

Eismann, K., McClelland, D., & Stone, T. (2000). Web Design: Studio Secrets. Foster City, CA: IDG Books World Wide.

Eliens, A., Veer, G., & Welie, M. (1999). Breaking down usability. Proceedings of Interact 99. Edinburgh, Scotland: British HCI Group.

Farkas, D. & Farkas, J. (2000). Guidelines for designing web navigation. Technical Communication, 47(3), 341-358.

Faulring, A., Morrison, J., Pirolli, P., & Woodruff, A. (2001). Using thumbnails to search the web. Proceedings of the SIGCHI on Human Factors in Computing Systems. Seattle, WA: The Association of Computing Machinery.

Fleming, J. (1998). Web Navigation Designing the User Experience. Sebastopol, CA: O'Reilly & Associates.

Flores, F. & Solomon, R. (1998). Creating trust. Business Ethics Quarterly, 8(2), 205- 232.

Forsythe, C., Grose, E., & Ratner, J. (1996). Characterization and assessment of HTML style guides. Proceedings of the SIGCHI on Human Factors in Computing Systems. Vancouver, Canada: The Association of Computing Machinery.

Frappaolo, D. (2003). Delphi Group report Information Intelligence: Content Classification and the Enterprise Taxonomy Practice. Retrieved October 25, 2006 from http://www.delphigroup.com/about/pressreleases/2004-PR/20040616-research.htm

Friedman, B., Howe, D., & Kahn, P. (2000, December). Trust online. Communications of the ACM, 43(12), 34-40.

Gale, S. (1996). A collaborative approach to developing style guides. Proceedings of the SIGCHI on Human Factors in Computing Systems. Vancouver, Canada: The Association of Computing Machinery.

Gefen, D. & Straub, D. (2000). Managing user trust in B2C e-services. Retrieved August 21, 2001, from http://www.lebow.drexel.edu/gefen/eServiceJournal2001.pdf.

Hodgson, J. (2001, January-February) Do HTML Tags Flag Semantic Content? IEEE Internet Computing, 20-25.

Horton, S. & Lynch, P. (1999). Web Style Guide. New Haven, CN: Yale University Press.

Karvonen, K. (2000). The beauty of simplicity. Proceedings of the ACM Conference on Universal Usability. Arlington, VA: The Association of Computing Machinery.

Keevil, B. (1998). Measuring the usability index of your website. Proceedings of the Special Interest Group for Documentation. Toronto, ON: The Association of Computing Machinery.

Krug, S. (2000). Don't Make Me Think. Indianapolis, IN: New Riders Publishing.

Kyrnin, J. (2006). GaGa for Google. Retrieved January 3, 2007 from http://webdesign.about.com/cs/promotion/a/aaaagoogle.htm

Lundgren, H., Seelen, J., & Walczuch, R. (2001). Psychological determinants for consumer trust in e-retailing. Proceedings of the 8th Research Symposium on Emerging Electronic Markets. Maastricht, The Netherlands: International Institute of Infonomics.

McClain, G. & Sachs, T. (2002). Back to the User: Creating User-focused Websites. Indianapolis, IN: New Riders Publishing.

Meehan, M. & Shubin, H. (1997, November). Navigation in web applications. Interactions, 4(6), 13-17.

Morkes, J. & Nielsen, J. (1997). Concise, scannable and objective: How to write for the web. Retrieved January 20, 2003, from http://www.useit.com/papers/webwriting/writing.html.

Morville, L. & Rosenfeld, P. (1998). Information Architecture for the World Wide Web. Cambridge, MA: O'Reilly & Associates.

Nielsen, J. (1998). Introduction to web design. Proceedings of the SIGCHI on Human Factors in Computing Systems. Los Angeles, CA: The Association of Computing Machinery.

Nielsen, J. (2000). Designing Web Usability. Indianapolis, IN: New Riders Publishing. Nielsen, J. & Tahir, M. (2002). Homepage Usability: 50 Websites Deconstructed. Indianapolis, IN: New Riders Publishing.

Ohnemus, K. (1997). Web style guides: Who, what where. Proceedings of the 15th Annual International Conference of Computer Documentation. Salt Lake City, UT: The Association of Computing Machinery.

Palmer, J. (2002, July). Designing for website usability. Computer, 35(7), 102-103.

Peattow, M. (2000). Web Site Usability Handbook. Charles River Media: Boston, MA.

Scanlon, T., Schroeder, W., Snyder, C., & Spool, J. (1998). Websites that work: Designing with your eyes open. Proceedings of the SIGCHI on Human Factors in Computing Systems. Los Angeles, CA: The Association of Computing Machinery.

Seligman, A. (1997). The Problem of Trust. Princeton, NJ. Princeton University Press.

Shneiderman, B. (1997). Designing information-abundant websites: Issues and recommendations. International Journal of Human-Computer Studies, 47(1), 5-29.

Shneiderman, B. (1998). Designing the User Interface (3rd ed.). Reading, MA: Addison- Wesley.

Siegel, D. (1997). Secrets of Successful Websites. Indianapolis, IN: New Riders Publishing.

Sullivan, D. (2002). Death of the MetaTag. Retrieved April 15, 2006 from http://searchenginewatch.com/showPage.html?page=2165061

Veen, J. (2001). The Art & Science of Web Design. Indianapolis, IN: New Riders Publishing.

Watchfire (2000) Metatags: They're not just for search engines anymore. Retrieved June 17, 2001. http://www.watchfire.com/resources/metatagswhite.pdf

Chapter 9: Portfolio Management
References
Beach, G. (2004). *Bricklayers or Architects?* Retrieved December 1, 2006 from http://www.cio.com/archive/080105/publisher.html.

Fahey, M. (2006). *How to Write Academic Articles for Publication.* Retrieved February 14, 2007 from http://www.marquette.edu/aegs/advice/publishing.htm.

The Sloan Consortium, (2004). *Entering the mainstream: The quality and extent of online education in the United States, 2003 and 2004.* Retrieved October 19, 2006 from http://www.sloan-c.org/resources/entering_mainstream.pdf.

Tittel, E. (2003). *Rating Certifications.* Retrieved March 1, 2007 from http://www.certmag.com/articles/templates/cmag_feature.asp?articleid=170&zoneid=9

Chapter 10: The Trademark Promise

Barber, L., Hirsh, W., & Tamkin, P. (2005). *Personal Development Plans: Case Studies of Practice*, IES Report 280, 8(74).

Beardsley, S., Johnson, B., & Manyika, J. (2006). *Competitive Advantage from Better Interactions.* McKinsey Quarterly: McKinsey & Company.

Becerra-Fernandez, I., & Sabherwal, R. (2001). *Organizational knowledge management: A contingency perspective.* Journal of Management Information Systems, 18(1), 23-56.

Bhattacharya, R., Devinney, T., & Pillutla, M. (1998). A formal model of trust based on outcomes. *Academy of Management Review*, 23(3), 459-472.

Gerber, M. (1995). *The E-Myth Revisited: Why Most Small Businesses Don't Work and What to Do About It.* HarperCollins Publishers, New York, NY.

Goldman, S. Nagel, R. and Preiss, N. (1996). *Agile Competitors and Virtual Organizations.* Van Nostrand Reinhold, New Yorl, NY.

Baltzan, P., Haag, S., & Phillips, A. (2006). *Business Driven Technology.* McGraw-Hill/Irwin: Columbus, OH.

Haag, S. Baltzan, P., & Phillips, A. (2006). *Business Driven Technology.* McGraw-Hill/Irwin: Columbus, OH.

Kerka, S. (2004). *Career Education for a Global Economy.* ERIC Digest.

Kerner, S. (2005). Gartner Predicts Key Tech Trends for 2006. Retrieved March 12, 2007 from http://www.internetnews.com/ent-news/article.php/3567251

Maslow, A. (1987). *Motivation and Personality.* HarperCollins Publishers, New York, NY.

Maznevski, M. L., & Chudoba, K. M. (2000). *Bridging space over time: Global virtual team dynamics and effectiveness.* Organization Science, 11(5), 473–492.

Simons, J., Irwin, D., & Drinnien, B. (1987). *The Search for Understanding.* Retrieved September 1, 2006 from http://chiron.valdosta.edu/whuitt/col/regsys/maslow.html

About the Author

Dr. Todd Stephens is the technical director of the Collaboration and Online Services for the AT&T. Todd has served as the director since 1999 and is responsible for setting the corporate strategy and architecture for the development and implementation of the Enterprise Collaborative Solutions, which includes metadata registries, information repositories, knowledge stores, and collaborative applications like SharePoint. For the past 20 years, Todd has worked in the Information Technology field including leadership positions at BellSouth, Coca-Cola, Georgia-Pacific and Cingular Wireless.

Todd writes a monthly online column in DMReview and has delivered keynotes, tutorials and educational sessions for a wide variety of technology conferences around the world. Todd holds degrees in Mathematics and Computer Science from Columbus State University, an MBA degree from Georgia State University., and a Ph.D. in Information Systems from Nova Southeastern University. The majority of his research is focused on Metadata Reuse, Semantic Zooming, Collaborative Workspaces, enabling Trust within the Internet, Usability and Repository Frameworks. On this, Todd has been awarded nine U.S. patented and pending patents in the field of Metadata as well as co-authored upcoming books on SOA, Open Source, Virtual Workspaces and integrating Web 2.0 technologies.